Richard P. Smiraglia, PhD
Editor

Metadata: A Cataloger's Primer

Metadata: A Cataloger's Primer has been co-published simultaneously as *Cataloging & Classification Quarterly*, Volume 40, Numbers 3/4 2005.

Pre-publication REVIEWS, COMMENTARIES, EVALUATIONS . . .

"A COMPREHENSIVE OVERVIEW OF METADATA written by experts in the field."

Michael Gorman
President-Elect
American Library Association

More pre-publication
REVIEWS, COMMENTARIES, EVALUATIONS . . .

"CATALOGERS WILL BE RIGHT AT HOME WITH THIS COLLECTION. . . . Presents the theoretical underpinnings behind cataloging and relates them to the digital world and metadata. The contributors are accomplished at presenting solid information to connect catalogers with the world of digital resource management."

Deborah J. Karpuk, PhD
Associate Professor
School of Library and Information Science
San Jose State University

"ENGAGING AND THOROUGH. . . . An excellent starting point for those familiar with bibliographic control but still curious about metadata. As an introductory text on metadata for catalogers, this book is instructive in its approach, coherent in its variety, and a welcome addition to the now-popular study of metadata's definition and its relationship to the functions and technologies of bibliographic control"

Joseph T. Tennis, PhD
Assistant Professor
The University of British Columbia

The Haworth Information Press®
An Imprint of The Haworth Press, Inc.

Metadata:
A Cataloger's Primer

Metadata: A Cataloger's Primer has been co-published simultaneously as *Cataloging & Classification Quarterly*, Volume 40, Numbers 3/4 2005.

Monographic Separates from *Cataloging & Classification Quarterly*™

For additional information on these and other Haworth Press titles, including descriptions, tables of contents, reviews, and prices, use the QuickSearch catalog at http://www.HaworthPress.com.

Metadata: A Cataloger's Primer, edited by Richard P. Smiraglia, PhD (Vol. 40, No. 3/4, 2005). *"A comprehensive overview of metadata written by experts in the field." (Michael Gorman, President-Elect, American Library Association)*

Functional Requirements for Bibliographic Records (FRBR): Hype or Cure-All? edited by Patrick LeBoeuf (Vol. 39, No. 3/4, 2005). *Examines the origin, and theoretical and practical aspects of IFLA's Functional Requirements for Bibliographic Records.*

Authority Control in Organizing and Accessing Information: Definition and International Experience, edited by Arlene G. Taylor, PhD, MSLS, BA, and Barbara B. Tillett, PhD, MLS, BA (Vol. 38, No. 3/4, 2004 and Vol. 39, No. 1/2, 2004). *Presents international perspectives on authority control for names, works, and subject terminology in library, archival, museum, and other systems that provide access to information.*

The Thesaurus: Review, Renaissance, and Revision, edited by Sandra K. Roe, MS, and Alan R. Thomas, MA, FLA (Vol. 37, No. 3/4, 2004). *Examines the historical development of the thesaurus, and the standards employed for thesaurus construction, use, and evaluation.*

Knowledge Organization and Classification in International Information Retrieval, edited by Nancy J. Williamson, PhD, and Clare Beghtol, PhD (Vol. 37, No. 1/2, 2003). *Examines the issues of information retrieval in relation to increased globalization of information and knowledge.*

Electronic Cataloging: AACR2 and Metadata for Serials and Monographs, edited by Sheila S. Intner, DLS, MLS, BA, Sally C. Tseng, MLS, BA, and Mary Lynette Larsgaard, MA, BA (Vol. 36, No. 3/4, 2003). *"The twelve contributing authors represent some of the most important thinkers and practitioners in cataloging." (Peggy Johnson, MBA, MA, Associate University Librarian, University of Minnesota Libraries)*

Historical Aspects of Cataloging and Classification, edited by Martin D. Joachim, MA (classical languages and literatures), MA (library science) (Vol. 35, No. 1/2, 2002 and Vol. 35, No. 3/4, 2003). *Traces the development of cataloging and classification in countries and institutions around the world.*

Education for Cataloging and the Organization of Information: Pitfalls and the Pendulum, edited by Janet Swan Hill, MA, BA, (Vol. 34, No. 1/2/3, 2002). *Examines the history, context, present, and future of education for cataloging and bibliographic control.*

Works as Entities for Information Retrieval, edited by Richard P. Smiraglia, PhD (Vol. 33, No. 3/4, 2002). *Examines domain-specific research about works and the problems inherent in their representation for information storage and retrieval.*

The Audiovisual Cataloging Current, edited by Sandra K. Roe, MS (Vol. 31, No. 2/3/4, 2001). *"All the great writers, teachers, and lecturers are here: Olson, Fox, Intner, Weihs, Weitz, and Yee. This eclectic collection is sure to find a permanent place on many catalogers' bookshelves. . . . Something for everyone. . . . Explicit cataloging guidelines and AACR2R interpretations galore." (Verna Urbanski, MA, MLS, Chief Media Cataloger, University of North Florida, Jacksonville)*

Managing Cataloging and the Organization of Information: Philosophies, Practices and Challenges at the Onset of the 21st Century, edited by Ruth C. Carter, PhD, MS, MA (Vol. 30, No. 1/2/3, 2000). *"A fascinating series of practical, forthright accounts of national, academic, and special library cataloging operations in action. . . . Yields an abundance of practical solutions for shared problems, now and for the future. Highly recommended." (Laurel Jizba, Head Cataloger, Portland State University Library, Oregon)*

The LCSH Century: One Hundred Years with the Library of Congress Subject Headings System, edited by Alva T. Stone, MLS (Vol. 29, No. 1/2, 2000). *Traces the 100-year history of the Library of Congress Subject Headings, from its beginning with the implementation of a dictionary catalog in 1898 to the present day, exploring the most significant changes in LCSH policies and practices, including a summary of other contributions celebrating the centennial of the world's most popular library subject heading language.*

Maps and Related Cartographic Materials: Cataloging, Classification, and Bibliographic Control, edited by Paige G. Andrew, MLS, and Mary Lynette Larsgaard, MA, BA (Vol. 27, No. 1/2/3/4, 1999). *Discover how to catalog the major formats of cartographic materials, including sheet maps, early and contemporary atlases, remote-sensed images (i.e., aerial photographs and satellite images), globes, geologic sections, digital material, and items on CD-ROM.*

Portraits in Cataloging and Classification: Theorists, Educators, and Practitioners of the Late Twentieth Century, edited by Carolynne Myall, MS, CAS, and Ruth C. Carter, PhD (Vol. 25, No. 2/3/4, 1998). *"This delightful tome introduces us to a side of our profession that we rarely see: the human beings behind the philosophy, rules, and interpretations that have guided our professional lives over the past half century. No collection on cataloging would be complete without a copy of this work." (Walter M. High, PhD, Automation Librarian, North Carolina Supreme Court Library; Assistant Law Librarian for Technical Services, North Carolina University, Chapel Hill)*

Cataloging and Classification: Trends, Transformations, Teaching, and Training, edited by James R. Shearer, MA, ALA, and Alan R. Thomas, MA, FLA (Vol. 24, No. 1/2, 1997). *"Offers a comprehensive retrospective and innovative projection for the future." (The Catholic Library Association)*

Electronic Resources: Selection and Bibliographic Control, edited by Ling-yuh W. (Miko) Pattie, MSLS, and Bonnie Jean Cox, MSLS (Vol. 22, No. 3/4, 1996). *"Recommended for any reader who is searching for a thorough, well-rounded, inclusive compendium on the subject." (The Journal of Academic Librarianship)*

Cataloging and Classification Standards and Rules, edited by John J. Riemer, MLS (Vol. 21, No. 3/4, 1996). *"Includes chapters by a number of experts on many of our best loved library standards. . . . Recommended to those who want to understand the history and development of our library standards and to understand the issues at play in the development of new standards." (LASIE)*

Classification: Options and Opportunities, edited by Alan R. Thomas, MA, FLA (Vol. 19, No. 3/4, 1995). *"There is much new and valuable insight to be found in all the chapters. . . . Timely in refreshing our confidence in the value of well-designed and applied classification in providing the best of service to the end-users." (Catalogue and Index)*

Cataloging Government Publications Online, edited by Carolyn C. Sherayko, MLS (Vol. 18, No. 3/4, 1994). *"Presents a wealth of detailed information in a clear and digestible form, and reveals many of the practicalities involved in getting government publications collections onto online cataloging systems." (The Law Librarian)*

Cooperative Cataloging: Past, Present and Future, edited by Barry B. Baker, MLS (Vol. 17, No. 3/4, 1994). *"The value of this collection lies in its historical perspective and analysis of past and present approaches to shared cataloging. . . . Recommended to library schools and large general collections needing materials on the history of library and information science." (Library Journal)*

Languages of the World: Cataloging Issues and Problems, edited by Martin D. Joachim (Vol. 17, No. 1/2, 1993). *"An excellent introduction to the problems libraries must face when cataloging materials not written in English. . . . should be read by every cataloger having to work with international materials, and it is recommended for all library schools. Nicely indexed." (Academic Library Book Review)*

ALL HAWORTH INFORMATION PRESS
BOOKS AND JOURNALS ARE PRINTED
ON CERTIFIED ACID-FREE PAPER

Metadata: A Cataloger's Primer

Richard P. Smiraglia, PhD
Editor

Metadata: A Cataloger's Primer has been co-published simultaneously as *Cataloging & Classification Quarterly*, Volume 40, Numbers 3/4 2005.

The Haworth Information Press®
An Imprint of The Haworth Press, Inc.

Published by

The Haworth Information Press®, 10 Alice Street, Binghamton, NY 13904-1580 USA

The Haworth Information Press® is an imprint of The Haworth Press, Inc., 10 Alice Street, Binghamton, NY 13904-1580 USA.

Metadata: A Cataloger's Primer has been co-published simultaneously as *Cataloging & Classification Quarterly*™, Volume 40, Numbers 3/4 2005.

Front cover credit: Metadata sample from "Metadata Standards for Archival Control: An Introduction to EAD and EAC" by Alexander C. Thurman.

Cover design by Lora Wiggins.

Library of Congress Cataloging-in-Publication Data

Metadata : a cataloger's primer / Richard P. Smiraglia, editor.
p. cm.
Published also as v. 40, no. 3/4, 2005 of Cataloging & classification quarterly.
Includes bibliographical references and index.
ISBN-13: 978-0-7890-2800-6 (hc : alk. paper)
ISBN-10: 0-7890-2800-X (hc : alk. paper)
ISBN-13: 978-0-7890-2801-3 (pbk. : alk. paper)
ISBN-10: 0-7890-2801-8 (pbk. : alk. paper)
1. Metadata. 2. Information organization. I. Smiraglia, Richard P., 1952- II. Cataloging & classification quarterly.

Z666.7 .M48 2005
025.3–dc22

2005009646

Indexing, Abstracting & Website/Internet Coverage

This section provides you with a list of major indexing & abstracting services and other tools for bibliographic access. That is to say, each service began covering this periodical during the year noted in the right column. Most Websites which are listed below have indicated that they will either post, disseminate, compile, archive, cite or alert their own Website users with research-based content from this work. (This list is as current as the copyright date of this publication.)

Abstracting, Website/Indexing Coverage . . . . Year When Coverage Began

- ***Computer and Information Systems Abstracts <http://www.csa.com>*** **2004**
- ***Current Cites [Digital Libraries] [Electronic Publishing] [Multimedia & Hypermedia] [Networks & Networking] [General] <http://sunsite.berkeley.edu/CurrentCites/>*** **2000**
- ***EBSCOhost Electronic Journals Service (EJS) <http://ejournals.ebsco.com>*** **2001**
- ***FRANCIS. INIST/CNRS <http://www.inist.fr>*** **1999**
- ***Google <http://www.google.com>*** **2004**
- ***Google Scholar <http://scholar.google.com>*** **2004**
- ***Haworth Document Delivery Center <http://www.HaworthPress.com/journals/dds.asp>*** **1980**
- ***IBZ International Bibliography of Periodical Literature <http://www.saur.de>*** **1995**
- ***Index Guide to College Journals (core list compiled by integrating 48 indexes frequently used to support undergraduate programs in small to medium sized libraries)*** **1999**
- ***Index to Periodical Articles Related to Law <http://www.law.utexas.edu>*** . . . **1989**
- ***Information Science & Technology Abstracts: indexes journal articles from more than 450 publications as well as books, research reports, and conference proceedings; EBSCO Publishing <http://www.epnet.com>*** **1980**
- ***Informed Librarian, The <http://www.informedlibrarian.com>*** **1993**

(continued)

- ***INSPEC is the leading English-language bibliographic information service providing access to the world's scientific & technical literature in physics, electrical engineering, electronics, communications, control engineering, computers & computing, and information technology <http://www.iee.org.uk/publish/>*** **1982**
- ***Internationale Bibliographie der geistes- und sozialwissenschaftlichen Zeitschriftenliteratur . . . See IBZ <http://www.saur.de>*** **1995**
- ***Journal of Academic Librarianship: Guide to Professional Literature, The*** **1997**
- ***Konyvtari Figyelo (Library Review)*** **1995**
- ***Library & Information Science Abstracts (LISA) <http://www.csa.com>*** **1989**
- ***Library & Information Science Annual (LISCA) <http://www.lu.com>*** **1998**
- ***Library Literature & Information Science <http://www.hwwilson.com>*** **1984**
- ***Links@Ovid (via CrossRef targeted DOI links) <http://www.ovid.com>*** **2005**
- ***Magazines for Libraries (Katz) . . . (see 2003 edition)*** **2003**
- ***OCLC ArticleFirst <http://www.oclc.org/services/databases/>*** **2002**
- ***OCLC ContentsFirst <http://www.oclc.org/services/databases/>*** **2002**
- ***Ovid Linksolver (Open URL link resolver via CrossRef targeted DOI links) <http://www.linksolver.com>*** **2005**
- ***PASCAL, c/o Institut de l'Information Scientifique et Technique. Cross-disciplinary electronic database covering the fields of science, technology, & medicine. Also available on CD-ROM, and can generate customized retrospective searches <http://www.inist.fr>*** **1999**
- ***Referativnyi Zhurnal (Abstracts Journal of the All-Russian Institute of Scientific and Technical Information– in Russian) <http://www.viniti.ru>*** **1992**
- ***SwetsWise <http://www.swets.com>*** **2001**

Special Bibliographic Notes related to special journal issues (separates) and indexing/abstracting:

- indexing/abstracting services in this list will also cover material in any "separate" that is co-published simultaneously with Haworth's special thematic journal issue or DocuSerial. Indexing/abstracting usually covers material at the article/chapter level.
- monographic co-editions are intended for either non-subscribers or libraries which intend to purchase a second copy for their circulating collections.
- monographic co-editions are reported to all jobbers/wholesalers/approval plans. The source journal is listed as the "series" to assist the prevention of duplicate purchasing in the same manner utilized for books-in-series.
- to facilitate user/access services all indexing/abstracting services are encouraged to utilize the co-indexing entry note indicated at the bottom of the first page of each article/chapter/contribution.
- this is intended to assist a library user of any reference tool (whether print, electronic, online, or CD-ROM) to locate the monographic version if the library has purchased this version but not a subscription to the source journal.
- individual articles/chapters in any Haworth publication are also available through the Haworth Document Delivery Service (HDDS).

Metadata: A Cataloger's Primer

CONTENTS

Introducing Metadata 1
Richard P. Smiraglia

PART I: INTELLECTUAL FOUNDATIONS

Understanding Metadata and Metadata Schemes 17
Jane Greenberg

Metadata and Bibliographic Control: Soul-Mates or Two Solitudes? 37
Lynne C. Howarth

Metadata, Metaphor, and Metonymy 57
D. Grant Campbell

An Exploratory Study of Metadata Creation in a Health Care Agency 75
Leatrice Ferraioli

The Defining Element–A Discussion of the Creator Element Within Metadata Schemas 103
Jennifer Cwiok

Content Metadata–An Analysis of Etruscan Artifacts in a Museum of Archeology 135
Richard P. Smiraglia

PART II: HOW TO CREATE, APPLY, AND USE METADATA

From Cataloging to Metadata: Dublin Core Records for the Library Catalog 153
Anita S. Coleman

Metadata Standards for Archival Control: An Introduction to EAD and EAC 183
Alexander C. Thurman

Introduction to XML 213
Patrick Yott

METS: The Metadata Encoding and Transmission Standard 237
Linda Cantara

Planning and Implementing a Metadata-Driven Digital Repository 255
Michael A. Chopey

Index 289

ABOUT THE EDITOR

Richard P. Smiraglia, PhD, is Professor at the Palmer School of Library and Information Science at Long Island University in Brookville, New York. He teaches courses in knowledge organization, broadly defined, and in research methods at the doctoral level. He has been with the Palmer School since 1992; prior to that, he was Assistant Professor at Columbia University's School of Library Service 1986-92, and Music Catalog Librarian at the University of Illinois at Urbana-Champaign 1974-86. He is the author of many books and monographs in the fields of knowledge organization, cataloging, and bibliography. He was editor of the journal *Library Resources & Technical Services* from 1990-96 and the Music Library Association's *Technical Reports* from 1988-94. He is currently a member of the editorial board of *Cataloging & Classification Quarterly* and is editor of the quarterly journal *Knowledge Organization*.

Dr. Smiraglia's 2001 monograph, *The Nature of 'A Work'* was the first monograph-length treatment of the topic of works and their role in knowledge organization. In 2002 he edited *Works as Entities for Information Retrieval*, in which an international panel of authors focused on domain-specific research about works and the problems inherent in their representation for information storage and retrieval. His most recent journal publications include "Authority Control of Works: Cataloging's Chimera?" (*Cataloging & Classification Quarterly* 38 n3/4 (2004)), "The History of 'The Work' in the Modern Catalog" (*Cataloging & Classification Quarterly* 35 n3/4 (2003)), "Works as Signs, Symbols, and Canons: The Epistemology of the Work" (*Knowledge Organization* 28 (2002)), and "Further Progress in Theory in Knowledge Organization" (*Canadian Journal of Information and Library Science* 26 n2/3 (2002)).

Introducing Metadata

Richard P. Smiraglia

The purpose of this volume is to provide a learning resource about metadata for catalog librarians and students. Part I of the volume contains introductory, theoretical material, and original research, and Part II contains instructive material.The point of view of the volume, overall, is that in library and information science there is an ongoing convergence of cataloging and metadata, such that the community will benefit from instructional material that demonstrates this convergence. Throughout the volume, readers will find metadata discussed alongside cataloging. The rationale for this is fundamental-resource description. Metadata, in one sense, are nothing new, and yet, in another sense, metadata schemes represent a very exciting forefront in resource description.

Some basic texts on metadata are already in wide circulation, and readers might want to have them handy for reference. These are, chronologically:

> Hillmann, Diane I. and Elaine L. Westbrooks, eds. 2004. *Metadata in Practice*. Chicago: American Library Association.
>
> Gorman, G. E. and Daniel G. Dorner, eds. 2004. *Metadata Applications and Management*. International yearbook of library in information management 2003/2004. Lanham, Md.: Scarecrow Press.

Richard P. Smiraglia is Professor, Palmer School Library and Information Science, Long Island University, 720 Northern Boulevard, Brookville, NY 11548 (E-mail: Richard.Smiraglia@liu.edu).

[Haworth co-indexing entry note]: "Introducing Metadata." Smiraglia, Richard P. Co-published simultaneously in *Cataloging & Classification Quarterly* (The Haworth Information Press, an imprint of The Haworth Press, Inc.) Vol. 40, No. 3/4, 2005, pp. 1-15; and: *Metadata: A Cataloger's Primer* (ed: Richard P. Smiraglia) The Haworth Information Press, an imprint of The Haworth Press, Inc., 2005, pp. 1-15. Single or multiple copies of this article are available for a fee from The Haworth Document Delivery Service [1-800-HAWORTH, 9:00 a.m. - 5:00 p.m. (EST). E-mail address: docdelivery@haworthpress.com].

Available online at http://www.haworthpress.com/web/CCQ

doi:10.1300/J104v40n03_01

Caplan, Priscilla. 2003. *Metadata Fundamentals for All Librarians*. Chicago: American Library Association.

Hudgins, Jean, Grace Agnew, Elizabeth Brown. 1999. *Getting Mileage Out of Metadata: Applications for the Library*. Chicago: ALA Books, 1999.

Baca, Murtha, ed. 1998. *Introduction to Metadata: Pathways to Digital Information*. Los Angeles: Getty Information Institute.

The essay that follows is introductory. I have subtitled the volume "a cataloger's primer." A primer is a kind of textbook used (back in the day) to teach reading, arithmetic, or other basic fundamentals. This essay, therefore, contains some elements necessary for understanding metadata in the bibliographic context. A set of basic operational definitions is expressed, the evolution of metadata in the cataloging community is outlined, and basic metadata techniques are described. The concluding section of this essay is a direct introduction to the content of this volume. Let us begin by defining metadata.

THREE DEFINITIONS

Part I of this volume is devoted to foundational issues in metadata, and the primary issue is the search for a definition. The authors whose papers follow have devoted careful thought to the issue, and very specific definitions emerge from their labor. But we must have a beginning point, so for now, let us define *metadata* as structured descriptors of information resources, designed to promote information retrieval. That is, at the most basic level, metadata describe information resources–such as websites, electronic texts, digital artifacts, etc.–through the compilation of descriptors that are structured according to a specific framework (called a *scheme*), and are placed together to serve an indexing function in information retrieval.

The Association for Library Collections & Technical Services (ALCTS, a division of the American Library Association (ALA)) has a committee known as the Committee on Cataloging: Description and Access (or CC:DA). CC:DA governs ALA's role in all standards for resource description, including the *Anglo-American Cataloguing Rules*. A 1999 report set out the parameters of library involvement in metadata (CCDA 1999, tf-meta3.html). The task force sought to understand and explicate the role of metadata in the realm of library cataloging by first and foremost casting the role of metadata under the aegis of resource description:

> Our RESOURCE DESCRIPTION NEEDS are grounded in the needs of our users to find, identify, select, and obtain some information thing (book, article, map, score, data set, etc.). We judge our tools–catalogs, indexes, search engines, etc.–primarily by how well they do these tasks. And not only must they perform the user tasks well, but they must make the management task or house keeping as simple, easy, flexible, and cheap as possible.

So we see here the primary purpose of metadata described in terms of the traditionally dual roles of retrieval and inventory. Retrieval must be user-centered, inventory is institution-centered, and both require a level of efficiency and standardization. The task force understood that a new age had arrived in the catalog department–one in which traditional cataloging had given way to a multiplicity of tools and techniques for providing access both in-house and via external resources, primarily those located on the World Wide Web. A central tenet of the new age is the search of *interoperability*–a way to move seamlessly from one tool to another. Interoperability must also demonstrate user-centeredness in retrieval, and institution-centeredness in inventory:

> Our catalogs have become one tool among many, but those many are not separate or isolated from one another. The catalog is one tool in a network of tools. THE BASIC OR NECESSARY PRINCIPLE OF TOOLS IN A NETWORK OF TOOLS IS INTEROPERABILITY. . . . Or if interoperability is too high a demand, each tool in a network of tools must be compatible with each other from the user's perspective. For example, a user employing an institution's catalog to find data sets relating to census and voting in Hartford, Connecticut may well need to analyze the data once [they have] been located, and then format the analysis into a presentation document dominated by images not numbers. While the catalog per se is only one tool in this scenario, it should be compatible with a wide range of other tools that may be used as functional extensions of the discovery and retrieval process. What is desirable is a network of tools that are portable, flexible, agile, mappable, extensible, adaptable, a coherent network of tools. The library catalog can be part of such a coherent environment, but

only if it is designed, maintained, and used as one tool in a network of tools.

The task force submitted three formal working definitions:

- METADATA are structured, encoded data that describe characteristics of information-bearing entities to aid in the identification, discovery, assessment, and management of the described entities.
- INTEROPERABILITY is the ability of two or more systems or components to exchange information and use the exchanged information without special effort on either system.
- A METADATA SCHEME provides a formal structure designed to identify the knowledge structure of a given discipline and to link that structure to the information of the discipline through the creation of an information system that will assist the identification, discovery, and use of information within that discipline.

METADATA CONCEPTS

The relationship between metadata and the knowledge artifacts these data represent (or, for which metadata serve as surrogates) is direct. In most cases, metadata are transcribed inherent data; that is, the data are taken directly from the resource and then reassembled according to the schema in such a way as to create a representation of the resource. Caplan (2003, 3) says metadata are "structured information about an information resource of any media type or format." Key terms here are "structured" and "information resource." There are many *kinds* of metadata at use in traditional library cataloging. In each instance, a structured description represents a resource–a journal article and its citation, a book and its catalog record, an electronic resource and its metadata. At the most elemental level, metadata provide structured terms that enable access to resources through information retrieval systems ranging from indexes, to catalogs, to search engines. For this purpose the metadata are intended to be user-centered, to provide the best possible access to specific resources. On another level, metadata vary by institutional purpose, and these go beyond the merely descriptive. Some are administrative, used by repositories to manage their resources, while others are structural, used for inventory control or to manipulate electronic information.

CONTENT DESIGNATION AND MARKUP LANGUAGES

Content designation is a term coined to describe the insertion of structural elements into plain text to facilitate computer manipulation. In library cataloging, content designation is used primarily to segment the components of a catalog record. In publishing, markup languages provide a form a content designation to drive the printing process. And, of course, in the World Wide Web markup languages are used to compel browsers to display content in a specific way. Markup languages provide vocabulary and syntax, which, when entered into a document, provide cues for computer manipulation of the text. It is markup language that turns normal text into a website.

International Standards for Bibliographic Description: Punctuation as Markup

The cataloging world met together in Paris in 1961 to create an international framework for the construction of bibliographic data. Even in those early days for library automation, there was great awareness that the ability to share data across linguistic and cultural boundaries would be vital for the control and dissemination of recorded knowledge. As a result of the Paris Conference, principles (known as the "Paris Principles") were formulated and agreed to. It is these principles that underlie the structure of *AACR2*, and most other catalog codes today (see ICCP 1971). One of the first implementations was a new, internationally agreed-upon framework for the descriptive portion of a bibliographic record (the title transcription, through the series transcription and annotations). Disseminated in 1974 in the first generic *ISBD* (*International Standard Bibliographic Description*), these conventions quickly became the norm worldwide.

A major aspect of *ISBD* description was the inclusion of "prescribed-punctuation." The purpose of prescribed-punctuation was to provide cues about the content of a bibliographic record, regardless of the user's ability to comprehend the language. Prescribed-punctuation, then, was an early form of markup, intended to cue users (and eventually, it was thought at the time, computers) about the contents of a record. For example, look at the following bibliographic record, which is in a made-up language:

Rhkjsow fjkslw bf ksjk jsiousol / w Hfuyse can Lqzx. -- 2c pj. -- Klana : Fry Psgh, 2001. -- 232 p.; 28 cm.

The punctuation, which always precedes an element, delineates the parts of this record. The title is followed by a statement of responsibility, which must be preceded by a space-slash-space, thus the title must be:

Rhkjsow fjkslw bf ksjk jsiousol

because the statement of responsibility is:

w Hfuyse can Lqzx.

The conventions of *ISBD* punctuation can be found in *AACR2*. A summary:

. -- (full-stop, space, dash, space) precedes a new area of description

/ (space, slash, space) precedes a statement of responsibility

: (space, colon, space) precedes the second element of an area (the publisher in area 4, the illustrations in area 5)

; (space, semi-colon, space) precedes the third element of an area (a second author in area 1, a second city or publisher in area 4, the dimensions in area 5)

Machine-Readable Cataloging (MARC) as Markup

No discussion of "markup" would be complete without a nod to the MARC coding language, which has fueled the great international effort to make catalogs electronic and to share catalog data worldwide via computer transmission. Essentially, catalog data are compiled according to standards (mostly *AACR2*) then marked up with MARC. The MARC tags, which one can view on OCLC or in "full" displays in online catalogs, but which are not visible to the searching public, designate for the computer the contents of fields and sub-fields. Their function is similar to that of the *ISBD* punctuation, but the language of MARC is much more complex. Here is a MARC markup of the bibliographic record from the preceding example:

245 10 Rhkjsow fjkslw bf ksjk jsiousol / $c w Hfuyse can Lqzx.

250 2c pj.

260 0 Klana : $b Fry Psgh, $c 2001.

300 232 p. ; $c 28 cm.

MARKUP LANGUAGES IN PUBLISHING

In the early automation of publishing, markup was used to set cues within an author's text, which would tell a typesetting program how to set the type when it printed out the book (article, etc.). A simple version might look like this:

<b><t>Introduction to Markup Languages</t></b><a>by Jon Smith</a><pl>Chicago</pl><pu>Silly Press</pu><b><d>2001</d></b>

This markup (which I also invented) might turn that text into a title page something like this:

Introduction to Markup Languages

by Jon Smith

Chicago
Silly Press
2001

Note that each element is marked on both ends; that is, text is enclosed between a start tag "<a>" and an end tag "</a>."

STANDARD GENERALIZED MARKUP LANGUAGE (SGML)

SGML was the first "meta" markup language. Developed to serve as a standard platform for the development of other languages, SGML provides conventions for naming the logical elements of documents, and syntax for expressing the logical relations among document components. SGML was intended to be used by specific communities to develop specific markup languages, known as Document Type Definitions or DTDs. Many of the metadata schemes described in this volume, are in fact, SGML-derived DTDs.

HYPERTEXT MARKUP LANGUAGE (HTML)

HTML is an SGML DTD that underlies the World Wide Web. HTML is the source code that resides behind the displayed website, telling browsers how to display the text to the viewer, and serving as source data for search engines. According to Graham (1995), HTML requires a document to be constructed with sections of text marked as logical units, such as titles, paragraphs, or lists, and leaves the interpretation of these marked elements up to the browser displaying the document.

An HTML document is composed of elements, which are marked by tags. Some elements do not affect a block of text (such as a paragraph command); these are called empty elements, and do not require end tags. Element names and attributes (which instruct the browser but do not display) are case-insensitive. But the attribute value (the text that will display) is case-sensitive.

An HTML document has two main elements: HEAD and BODY. Each main element has sub-elements. The TITLE sub-element is the only required element of HEAD. The BODY has many sub-elements, such as:

Headings, which come in six levels:

<H1> ... words ... </H1>
<H2> ... words ... </H2>
<H3> ... words ... </H3>
<H4> ... words ... </H4>
<H5> ... words ... </H5>
<H6> ... words ... </H6>

These tags cause headings to display in different sizes of type, from large, bold-face (h1) to small type (h6).

Highlighting, which gives special emphasis:

<EM></EM> will render the phrase in *italics*
<STRONG></STRONG> will render the phrase in bold.

Paragraphs, an empty element, causes the text to break into paragraphs <P>.

Break is similar <BR>.

Lists cause a list to appear indented and bulleted. Lists may be unordered (ul) or ordered (ol):

```
<UL>
List items, each tagged with <LI>
</UL>
```

Horizontal Rule draws a horizontal line across the page <HR>.

Hypertext Links can be used to move between documents:

```
<A HREF="http://smiraglia.org">Click here for my Vita</A>
```

Images can be embedded in a webpage. For instance, a still image in the form of a graphical interface file (gif) can appear to be embedded in the website by using a hyperlink:

```
<IMG SRC="portrait.gif">
```

Tables format text into tabular form. The following code creates a table with three columns and two rows:

```
<TABLE>
<TR><TD> first data</TD><TD>second data</TD><TD>third data</TD></TR>
<TR><TD>fourth data</TD><TD>fifth data</TD><TD>sixth data</TD></TR>
</TABLE>
```

Here is a little exercise. Open *Notepad* and type the following:

```
<html>
<head>
<title>A Sample HTML Document</title>
</head>
<body>
<h1>A Sample HTML Document</h1>
</body>
</html>
```

Save the file as "all files" and give it the file extension ".html" then open the file using *Netscape* or *Internet Explorer*. You should see the line of text in large bold characters. Notice that your "title" appears in the blue bar at the top of your screen. Using the "view" menu click on "Page source" and you will see your original html file. Now go back to *Notepad* and add another line of text, thus:

```
<html>
<head>
<title>A Sample HTML Document</title>
</head>
<body>
<h1>A Sample HTML Document</h1>
<h2>This is how to vary the typesize in an html file</h2>
</body>
</html>
```

Save the file again and reopen it in *Netscape*. Notice that "markup" per se is structural metadata that tell the browser how to display otherwise normal text. In metadata, the distinction between content and structure is essential.

METADATA FOR RESOURCE DESCRIPTION

Metadata such as catalog records and index citations have been used now for thousands of years (literally since antiquity). Always there has been a yearning among knowledge organization professionals to find more efficient and accurate means for providing resource description. Yet, even now, metadata mostly are compiled by individuals working with loosely-defined standards. Here we introduce several metadata projects and schemes in simple terms and in chronological order, to set the stage for the remainder of the volume.

Cataloging in Publication

In the early twentieth century (1901 in fact) the Library of Congress began to make copies of its catalog cards available for purchase by librarians. This was the real beginning of cooperative cataloging. For any book for which the Library of Congress had prepared cataloging, you (the local librarian) were freed from that effort. All you had to do was buy the cards, type added entries on top of them and call numbers in the upper left corner, and then file the cards. Savings were dramatic. As a result, standardization of cataloging spread across the United States, then North America, then throughout the English-speaking world, as cooperation grew among the Library of Congress, the British Library (then the library of the British Museum), and the National Library of Canada.

In the 1950s, there were many projects undertaken to provide copies of proof sheets for LC cards in the books libraries were buying as new acquisitions. This meant that, if your jobber participated in the program, the mere act of buying the book also brought with it the professional and standardized cataloging. This was pretty close to in-source metadata for the time. Beginning in 1961, publishers and librarians in the U.S. (and later worldwide) began to cooperate on a larger scale, implementing a project known as Cataloging in Publication, or CIP. CIP is a form of metadata literally in the resource, printed always on the verso of a book's title page. If we extend this notion to the arena of markup languages, we arrive at the promise of self-describing resources.

Text Encoding Initiative (TEI)

The Text Encoding Initiative (TEI) is an international project to develop guidelines for the preparation and interchange of electronic texts for scholarly research, and to satisfy a broad range of uses by the language industries more generally. The TEI is sponsored by the Association for Computers and the Humanities (ACH), the Association for Computational Linguistics (ACL), and the Association for Literary and Linguistic Computing (ALLC). Major support for the project has come from the U.S. National Endowment for the Humanities (NEH), Directorate XIII of the Commission of the European Communities (CEC/DG-XIII), the Andrew W. Mellon Foundation, and the Social Science and Humanities Research Council of Canada. There is a pressing need for a common text encoding scheme researchers can use in creating electronic texts. Three organizations sponsor TEI: the Association for Computers and the Humanities (ACH), the Association for Computational Linguistics (ACL), and the Association for Literary and Linguistic Computing (ALLC). (See the TEI Homepage http://www.tei-c.org/, and Text Encoding in Libraries http://www.indiana.edu/~letrs/tei/.)

The Dublin Core Metadata Set

One prominent metadata scheme is known as the Dublin Core. It was developed using large government-funded grants that brought together teams of librarians and software and Internet experts to create a "core" set of metadata elements and coding conventions. The intent of this program was (a) to share the expertise of both communities; and (b) to prevent either community from creating a standard that would be unusable by the other.

Using Dublin Core is a usage guide by Diane Hillmann, which can be found at http://dublincore.org/documents/2001/04/12/usageguide/. Dublin Core metadata sets reside in the header of web-resources, fueling search engines. With a metadata set a web-resource becomes, essentially, self-describing. Core elements are described at http://purl.org/metadata/dublin_core_elements and http://dublincore.org/documents/dces/. Other instructional material can be found at http://dublincore.org. The Dublin Core set is very much a work in progress, as you can see at the homepage. That is, it is a dynamic standard, being updated and revised more or less constantly. This means that keeping an eye on changes will be critical for staying up to date with the DCMI. Syntax is described in the usage guide. A basic Dublin Core set looks like this:

```
<dc:creator>Rose Bush</dc:creator>
<dc:title>A Guide to Growing Roses</dc:title>
<dc:description>Describes process for planting and nurturing different kinds
of rose bushes.</dc:description>
<dc:date>2001-01-20</dc:date>
```

Encoded Archival Description (EAD)

The growth of the Web created demand for publishing of archival repositories' finding aids on websites. To accommodate this activity, EAD was created. The EAD Document Type Definition (DTD) is a standard for encoding archival finding aids using the Standard Generalized Markup Language (SGML). The standard is maintained in the Network Development and MARC Standards Office of the Library of Congress (LC) in partnership with the Society of American Archivists. Development of the EAD DTD began with a project initiated by the University of California, Berkeley, Library in 1993. The goal of the Berkeley project was to investigate the desirability and feasibility of developing a nonproprietary encoding standard for machine-readable finding aids such as inventories, registers, indexes, and other documents created by archives, libraries, museums, and manuscript repositories to support the use of their holdings. The project directors recognized the growing role of networks in accessing information about holdings, and they were keen to include information beyond that which was provided by traditional machine-readable cataloging (MARC) records. (See the official EAD homepage at http://www.loc.gov/ead/ and an overview at http://sunsite.berkeley.edu/FindingAids/EAD/eadmodel.html.)

*Descriptive Cataloging–*AACR2 *and* MARC 21 *as Metadata*

The *Anglo-American Cataloguing Rules*, now in advanced permutations of the second edition, provide the primary means for resource description in libraries. *AACR2* is an internationally managed standard, based on the provisions of the *International Standard Bibliographic Description* (*ISBD*), and carefully extended to provide description of and access to resources in all media collected by libraries. As such, bibliographic descriptions constructed using *AACR2* constitute descriptive metadata. We already looked briefly at MARC and its role as a kind of markup, and Jul (2003) describes *MARC 21* alongside other markup languages. In fact, most *AACR2* bibliographic records are constructed within the framework of the *MARC 21* format, which facilitates their exchange between and among online systems. Several authors have described *AACR2* and *MARC 21*, therefore, as a metadata-suite, though it is a stretch to consider them as a metadata scheme. In particular, Tillett (2003) describes ways in which *AACR2* has evolved to provide metadata-like descriptions of electronic resources.

Essentially, *AACR2* describes the content of a resource and *MARC 21* provides the markup to facilitate record manipulation. Both *AACR2* and *MARC 21* make use of syntax, and the interplay of the two can be somewhat confusing. I will not describe *AACR2* or *MARC 21* in detail in this volume: instead readers are referred to general cataloging texts (see Wynar 1992, for example), and those interested in cataloging for the Web should refer to the recent volume by Jones, Ahronheim, and Crawford (2002). However, it is useful to understand the framework that undergirds bibliographic description in the context of the creation of metadata. Basic elements are *transcription* from *prescribed sources*. That is, catalogers do not generate free-text descriptions for the most part. Rather, the content of a catalog record is intended to provide a photo-like image of the actual item by literally copying (transcribing) inherent elements such as titles, names, etc., from specific parts of the resource. In bibliographic terms we say that cataloger transcribes descriptive detail from sources such as title pages and their versos, and then makes reference to other parts of the resource as well. For instance, the table of contents will be consulted in the analysis of subject content, and it might be partially transcribed to enhance retrieval. These data, then, are arrayed according to *ISBD*-proscribed syntax within eight areas of description:

Area 1: Title and statement of responsibility
Area 2: Edition
Area 3: Material-specific details
Area 4: Details of publication, distribution, etc.
Area 5: Physical description
Area 6: Series
Area 7: Notes
Area 8: Standard numbering and terms of availability.

Once the description is complete, access points are selected and formulated. Subject headings and classification are provided from additional tools (usually *Library of Congress Subject Headings* and *Library of Congress Classification* or *Dewey Decimal Classification*). These, together with the bibliographic description, constitute the descriptive metadata. Then the entire package is encoded using *MARC 21* field tags and subfield indicators, and the complete record is integrated into the catalog. Unlike most of the metadata schemes, bibliographic metadata constructed in this manner reside in the catalog as parallel surrogates for the resources, rather than residing within the resource (although, as I noted above, CIP serves that role to some extent).

PAPERS IN THIS VOLUME

Part I includes papers that are intended to introduce readers to concepts of metadata in the bibliographic sphere. The volume opens with two papers that present essential metadata concepts and trace their history within the context of the bibliographic resource description community. Jane Greenberg opens the volume with "Understanding Metadata and Metadata Schemes." She provides a basic framework for the study of metadata schemes, while thoroughly analyzing the definitions and attributes of metadata of all types. Next, Lynne Howarth provides a historical evaluation of the evolution of metadata and bibliographic control. Then follow four papers that present original research, to demonstrate ways in which we have only begun to attempt to exploit the potential of metadata for resource description. D. Grant Campbell uses literary concepts of metaphor and metonymy to demonstrate how metadata function as a sort of language. Leatrice Ferraioli explores the creation and use of personal metadata in a business environment. Jennifer Cwiok surveys various metadata approaches to the identification of creators of resources. And Richard Smiraglia describes the evolution and use of content metadata for museum artifacts.

Part II of the volume is intentionally instructive, and comprises papers that introduce metadata schemes and demonstrate their use. Anita S. Coleman describes the Dublin Core, Alexander Thurman demonstrates the use of Encoded Archival Description (EAD), and Patrick Yott explains Extensible Markup Language (XML). Linda Cantara describes the Metadata Encoding and Transmission Standard (METS) designed for exchange and preservation of information packages in the digital library environment. And Michael Chopey contributes a discussion of how to plan and implement a metadata-driven digital repository. In the end the contents go beyond the definition of primer as "introductory textbook." But the authors have collectively compiled a thought-provoking volume about the uses of metadata.

WORKS CITED

Caplan, Priscilla. 2003. *Metadata Fundamentals for All Libraries*. Chicago: American Library Association.

Committee on Cataloging: Description and Access. 1999. Task Force on Metadata Report. http://www.ala.org/cfapps/archive.cfm?path=alcts/organization/ccs/ccda/tf-meta3.html.

Graham, Ian S. 1995. *HTML Sourcebook*. New York: Wiley.

International Conference on Cataloguing Principles. 1971. *Statement of Principles*. Adopted at the International Conference on Cataloguing Principles, Paris, October 1961. Annotated ed., with commentary and examples by Eva Verona, assisted by Franz Georg Kaltwasser, P. R. Lewis, and Roger Pierrot. London: IFLA Committee on Cataloguing.

Jones, Wayne, Judith R. Ahronheim, and Josephine Crawford, eds. 2002. *Cataloging the Web: Metadata,* AACR, *and* MARC 21. ALCTS papers on library technical services and collections no. 10. Lanham, Md.: Scarecrow Press.

Jul, Erik. 2003. MARC and Markup. *Cataloging & Classification Quarterly* 36n3/4: 141-53.

Tillett, Barbara B. 2003. *AACR2* and Metadata: Library Opportunities in the Global Semantic Web. *Cataloging & Classification Quarterly* 36n3/4: 101-19.

Wynar, Bohdan. 1992. *Introduction to Cataloging and Classification*. 8th ed. by Arlene G. Taylor. Englewood, Colo.: Libraries Unlimited.

PART I: INTELLECTUAL FOUNDATIONS

Understanding Metadata and Metadata Schemes

Jane Greenberg

SUMMARY. Although the development and implementation of metadata schemes over the last decade has been extensive, research examining the sum of these activities is limited. This limitation is likely due to the massive scope of the topic. A framework is needed to study the full extent of, and functionalities supported by, metadata schemes. Metadata schemes developed for information resources are analyzed. To begin, the author presents a review of the definition of metadata, metadata functions, and several metadata typologies. Next, a conceptualization for metadata schemes is presented. The emphasis is on semantic container-like metadata schemes (data structures). The last part of this paper introduces the MODAL (Metadata Objectives and principles, Domains, and Architectural

Jane Greenberg is Associate Professor, School of Information and Library Science, University of North Carolina at Chapel Hill, 205 Manning Hall, CB #3360, Chapel Hill, NC (E-mail: janeg@ils.unc.edu).

[Haworth co-indexing entry note]: "Understanding Metadata and Metadata Schemes." Greenberg, Jane. Co-published simultaneously in *Cataloging & Classification Quarterly* (The Haworth Information Press, an imprint of The Haworth Press, Inc.) Vol. 40, No. 3/4, 2005, pp. 17-36; and: *Metadata: A Cataloger's Primer* (ed: Richard P. Smiraglia) The Haworth Information Press, an imprint of The Haworth Press, Inc., 2005, pp. 17-36. Single or multiple copies of this article are available for a fee from The Haworth Document Delivery Service [1-800-HAWORTH, 9:00 a.m. - 5:00 p.m. (EST). E-mail address: docdelivery@haworthpress.com].

Available online at http://www.haworthpress.com/web/CCQ

doi:10.1300/J104v40n03_02

Layout) framework as an approach for studying metadata schemes. The paper concludes with a brief discussion on the value of frameworks for examining metadata schemes, including different types of metadata schemes.

KEYWORDS. Information resources, metadata, metadata schemes, data structures, MODAL (Metadata Objectives and principles, Domains, and Architectural Layout) framework

INTRODUCTION

Digital repositories have grown at an explosive rate over the last decade due to new information technologies, particularly those supporting World Wide Web (Web) applications. This growth has led to a tremendous increase in the need for data management, an intense interest in metadata in a wide range of communities (e.g., education, government, scientific, business, etc.), and extensive development of metadata schemes. There are hundreds of metadata schemes being used, many of which are in their second, third, or *n*th iteration. Many specifications developed for information resources have been endorsed by standards bodies. For example, the Dublin Core Metadata Element Set, Version 1.1 (2003) (hereafter referred to as the Dublin Core) has been formally endorsed as a standard by Comité Européen de Normalisation (CEN) as CEN Workshop Agreement (CWA) 13874 (http://www.cenorm.be/cenorm/businessdomains/businessdomains/informationsocietystandardizationsystem/published+cwas/13874.pdf), the National Information Standards Organization (NISO) as NISO Z39.85-2001 (http://www.niso.org/standards/resources/Z39-85.pdf), and most recently the International Standards Organization (ISO) as ISO 15836-2003 (http://www.niso.org/international/SC4/n515.pdf).

An official list of all available metadata schemes does not exist, not even one specific to information resources, although a number of metadata registries are becoming fairly extensive. The CORES registry (http://www.cores-eu.net/registry/) is a good example, currently listing 40 metadata schemes, and supporting searching and browsing by metadata scheme developer, maintenance agency, element sets, elements, encoding schemes, application profiles, and element usages. Additionally, Web resources, such as the IFLA DIGITAL LIBRARIES: Metadata Resources Web page (http://www.ifla.org/II/metadata.htm) and the UKOLN Metadata Web site (http://www.ukoln.ac.uk/metadata/), provide ample information about metadata schemes by referencing and linking to papers, presentations, electronic listservs and newsgroups, and metadata specifications. These resources are useful for studying the population of metadata schemes, although it is difficult to study this topic in its entirety, given the multiplicity of schemes, their evolutionary nature (different versions or releases produced over time), their different constituencies, and their varied functional emphases.

Despite these challenges, it is important to conceptualize the nature of metadata schemes. We need to study schemes in order to understand their place in the larger context of information organization, management, and access. The intense interest in, and extensive development of, metadata schemes over the last decade brings this need to the forefront and calls for an examination of the population of these semantic container-like systems. A framework is needed to study the full extent of and functionalities supported by metadata schemes. In this paper I consider this need by examining schemes developed for information resources. The first part is a review of the definition of metadata, metadata functions, and several metadata typologies. Next, I present conceptualization for metadata schemes. The emphasis is on semantic container-like metadata schemes (data structures). The last part of this paper introduces the MODAL (**M**etadata **O**bjectives and principles, **D**omain, and **A**rchitectural **L**ayout) framework as an approach for studying metadata schemes. The paper concludes with a brief discussion on value of frameworks for examining metadata schemes, including different types of metadata schemes.

METADATA AND METADATA SUPPORTED FUNCTIONS

Defining Metadata

It is well documented that Jack E. Myers coined the term "metadata" in 1969, and it was first printed in a product brochure in 1973. Meyers used the term to represent current and future products associated with his MetaModel and to designate a company that would develop and market those products. METADATA® was registered in 1986 as a U.S.

Trademark for The Metadata Company, where Meyers is a principle (The Metadata Company: http://www.metadata.com/).

Building upon Meyer's usage, the terms *metadata*, *meta data* and *meta-data* (all in lower case) have been adopted by the computer science, statistical, database, and library and information science communities to mean "data about data." The term *metadata*, in these realms, addresses data attributes that describe, provide context, indicate the quality, or document other object (or data) characteristics.

Information and library scientists both equate (e.g., Milstead & Feldman, 1999; Caplan, 1995) and distinguish (e.g., Heery, 1996) creating metadata from cataloging. The main distinction is that metadata is exclusive to electronic information. This interpretation is, however, not hard-and-fast, as librarians have been cataloging electronic resources for decades prior to the Web, and many metadata schemes are applicable to physical as well as digital resources. Definitions of metadata specific to information resources (the types of materials found in both physical and digital libraries, archives, museums, and other information agencies) are consistent in that they emphasize the functional aspect of metadata, with the common definition of "structured data about data" (e.g., Duval et al. 2002; Woodley et al. 2003). Metadata can be viewed as "structured data about an object that supports functions associated with the designated object"–with an object being "any entity, form, or mode for which contextual data can be recorded" (Greenberg, 2003).

Metadata Functions

Many discussions, particularly those exploring metadata in the information resource community (libraries, archives, museums, and other information centers), tend to group metadata elements by the various functions they support. The result is the identification of different types of metadata (or metadata classes), each of which comprises multiple metadata elements. Table 1 provides typologies of different types of metadata identified by Lagoze et al. (1996), Gilliland-Swetland (2000), Greenberg (2001), and Caplan (2003).

Lagoze et al. have developed one of the most extensive typologies, presented in Table 1, columns one through three. Column one summarizes the Lagoze et al. typology, column 2 describes the metadata functions corresponding to the typology, and column three lists examples of metadata elements that facilitate the functions in column 2.

Gilliland-Swetland's (2000), Greenberg's (2001), and Caplan's (2003) typologies are presented in Table 1, columns four, five, and six respec-

TABLE 1. Metadata Typologies and Functionalities

Lagoze et al. (1996):			**Gilliland-Swetland (2000): Typology of 5 types of metadata**	**Greenberg (2001): Typology of 4 types of metadata (2 sub-types of Use metadata)**	**Caplan (2001): Typology of 4 types of metadata**
Typology of 7 types of metadata	**Metadata Functions "This type of metadata *facilitates*":**	**Element examples***			
Identification/ description metadata	***RESOURCE DISCOVERY/ INFORMATION RETRIEVAL***	Creator (Author), Title, Subject	Descriptive metadata	Discovery metadata	Descriptive metadata
Administrative metadata	***RESOURCE MANAGEMENT***	Price, Condition	Administrative and Preservation metadata	Administrative metadata	Administrative metadata
Terms and conditions metadata	***RESOURCE USAGE***	Rights, Reproduction restrictions	Administrative, Preservation, and Use metadata	Technical Use, Intellectual Use, and Administrative metadata	Administrative and linking metadata
Content ratings metadata	***RESOURCE USE BY APPROPRIATE AUDIENCES***	Audience	Use metadata	Technical Use and Intellectual Use metadata	Administrative and linking metadata
Provenance metadata	***RESOURCE AUTHENTICATION AND OTHER PROVENANCE-RELATED ACTIVITIES***	Creator, Source	Administrative and Use metadata	Authenticity and Administrative metadata	Administrative metadata
Linkage/ relationship metadata	***RESOURCE LINKING WITH RELATED RESOURCES***	Relation, Source	Administrative metadata	Authenticity and Administrative metadata	Linking metadata
Structural metadata	***RESOURCE HARDWARE AND SOFTWARE NEEDS***	Compression ratio	Technical and Use metadata	Technical Use metadata	Structural metadata

*Individual metadata elements can be multi-functional. For example, "source" metadata facilitates resource authentication and resource linking, and can be classed as both "Provenance metadata" and "Linkage/relationship metadata" following Lagoze et al.'s typology (for a discussion on metadata element multifunctionality see Greenberg, J. (2001)).

tively; and these typologies are mapped to the functions identified by Lagoze et al. (column 2). The typologies developed by these three authors (Gilliland-Swetland, Greenberg, and Caplan) are not as extensive as the Lagoze et al. typology and definitions vary among authors. As a result, metadata types are repeated in the mapping, and often more than one type is listed to match the Lagoze et al. metadata functions.

Table 1 illustrates similarities among metadata typologies, yet it also makes evident the challenge in establishing one universal metadata classification. Most important is that the naming of different types of metadata, with labels such as "resource discovery" and "use," demonstrates that *functionality* is the principal reason for metadata.

A CONCEPTUALIZATION FOR METADATA SCHEMES

A Context for Metadata Schemes

While literature includes analyses on the different types of metadata, discussions on the meaning of *scheme* (or *schema*), in the metadata context, are scarce. It may simply be that "scheme" is generally understood to be "a structured framework or plan" (*Miriam-Webster Online*: http://www.m-w.com/cgi-bin/dictionary?va=schema), and adopting this concept for representation systems used in information databases seems very reasonable. The term *scheme* has historically been applied to classificatory and terminological systems used in library catalogs and other information databases, such as the *Dewey Decimal Classification* (*DDC*) system and *Library of Congress Subject Headings* (*LCSH*); this practice continues with little debate–if any. Here I focus on the semantic container-like schemes, also referred to as data structures. These are the higher-level structured schemes that may require or recommend the use of schemes containing acceptable data values (e.g., *DDC* or *LCSH*).

The philosopher Kant provides insight into the meaning of *scheme* in his 1785 treatise *Critique of Pure Reason* (1998). Kant reasons that a *schema* is a system based on experience and the gathering of empirical data. Kant's model, emphasizing experience and empirical analysis, is applicable to developments underlying metadata schemes today. The experience aspect is evident via expert collaboration during scheme design activities. Subject discipline experts and technical experts, in areas such as electronic markup, thesaurus development, representation, and data processing, frequently join forces through committees or designated initiatives to design a metadata scheme. These committees and initiatives can be locally, nationally, or internationally positioned. For example, the Dublin Core Metadata Initiative is an international and interdisciplinary group that has developed and maintains the Dublin Core through committee consensus. Metadata scheme designers, working together, draw upon experience gained in their areas of expertise.

Referring back to Kant's model, the empirical aspect of scheme design is evident mainly through the counting of metadata elements, sub-elements, qualifiers, and other components. Nascent metadata scheme design can be guided by a pre-determined number of elements, dictating the scheme's extent and often granularity (refinement). This restriction requires element counting during the design process. The empirical aspect of metadata scheme design is also evident in analyses of pre-existing metadata schemes–even those developed during the pre-digital era. The crosswalk analysis, a common analytical method, often employed as a first step to scheme design, is heavily empirical (e.g., Woodley, 2000; Zeng, 1997). Equivalent or similarly functioning metadata elements from two or more metadata schemes are mapped to one another via a table that allows for an element-level detailed comparison among schemes. Other empirical methods include counting how many institutions or initiatives have adopted a scheme; counting the number of metadata elements being used (or not used) in a particular scheme; and analyzing the strength of the relationship among metadata elements (e.g., Moen and Benardino, 2003).

The "conceptualization" of a metadata scheme is generally "formalized in a specification" (Greenberg, 2003), and there are standards to guide this process. Arguably, the most important standard guiding this process is ISO/IEC (International Standards Organization/International Electrotechnical Commission) 11179, Metadata Registries Standard, developed by ISO/IEC JTC1 SC32 WG2 Development/Maintenance (http://metadata-stds.org/11179/). The standard has six parts: (1) Framework, (2) Classification, (3) Registry Metamodel and Basic Attributes, (4) Formulation of Data Definitions, (5) Naming and Identification Principles, and (6) Registration. The standard includes extensive instructions on how to identify data elements and register a scheme with a registration authority. ISO/IEC 11179 is essential for the database community, and has been a vital resource for the development of metadata schemes for digital resources. Part 1 and Part 4 of ISO/IEC 1179 appear to be the most important sections for metadata scheme development. Part 1 "introduces and discusses fundamental ideas of data elements, value domains, data element concepts, conceptual domains, and classification schemes," and Part 4 "provides guidance on how to develop unambiguous data definitions." Additional standards guiding metadata scheme development include ISO/IEC 20943, Procedures for Achieving Metadata Registry Content Consistency; ISO/IEC 20944, Metadata Registry Interoperability and Bindings; and ISO/IEC 18038, Identification and Mapping of Various Categories of Jurisdictional Domains (see http://metadata-stds.org/).

Metadata Scheme Conceptualized

Exploring the meaning of "scheme," including referencing ISO/IEC 11179, and reviewing metadata functionalities aid in conceptualizing what a metadata scheme is. Described as "a systematic, orderly combination of elements or terms" (Woodley et al., 2003) and "a set of metadata elements and rules for their uses that has been defined for a particular purpose" (Caplan, 2003), literature does not reveal a universally accepted definition for metadata scheme–unlike the standard definition of "data about data" for metadata. A metadata scheme can, however, be identified by three main features. A metadata scheme is:

1. A collection of metadata elements gathered to support a function, or a series of functions (e.g., resource discovery, administration, use, etc.), for an information object.
2. A collection of metadata elements, forming a structured container, to which data values are added. Data values may be uncontrolled or controlled (e.g., taken from a source such as *LCSH* or a standardized list of values).
3. A collection of data elements, with their attributes formalized in a specification (or a data dictionary). Examples of element attributes include the metadata element's "name," "identifier," "label," "definition," and the "date the element was declared."

Specifications vary tremendously from fairly flexible guidelines, such as the Dublin Core, to detailed and complex rules, such as Federal Geographic Documentation Committee (FGDC) Content Standard for Digital Geospatial Metadata (CSDGM) (1998), or the CSDGM's extension for biological data (Content Standard for Digital Geospatial Metadata Part 1: Biological Data Profile, 1999). Specifications almost always provide element definitions–first and foremost. In reference to other element attributes, specifications might or might not:

- Define relationships among metadata elements.
- Identify specific acceptable content values or content value systems (e.g., *LCSH*) to be used with the scheme.
- Provide syntactical guidelines. Content syntax guidelines, such as "surname" before "forename" or "year" "month" "day" [YYYY-MM-DD], or encoding and markup syntax guidelines for XML or HTML languages.
- Declare metadata element *cardinality*. That is, how many times a metadata element can or must appear in a metadata description.
- Further refine metadata elements definitions through qualification. For example, the metadata element "creator" can be further refined by "person" or "corporate body."

ANALYZING METADATA SCHEMES

A comprehensive study of metadata schemes seems daunting when considering the wide range of metadata schemes, their evolutionary nature (different versions or releases produced over time), their different constituencies, and their varied functional emphases. Despite this challenge, research is needed to better understand the range of metadata schemes and how they fit into the information context. The MODAL framework, defined by *objectives and principles*, *domains*, and *architectural layout*, provides a way to examine the population of metadata schemes. Figure 1 illustrates the MODAL framework, which is discussed in more detail in this section.

Objectives and Principles

One way to further understand a metadata scheme is to study its underlying objectives and principles. Objectives identify the overall aims and goals of the scheme, while principles are rules or means for accomplishing tasks to meet an objective. Objectives and principles are often published as a series of statements, and frequently appear as metadata specification introductions. These underlying features of metadata schemes are often inter-woven, making it difficult to distinguish the objectives from the principles.

Among the most influential historical statements of bibliographic control objectives, are Charles A. Cutter's (1904) objectives for a library catalog, printed in the 4th edition of his *Rules for a Dictionary Catalog*. Emphasizing resource discovery, almost one hundred years

FIGURE 1. The MODAL Framework for Metadata Objectives and Principles, Domains, and Architectural Layout

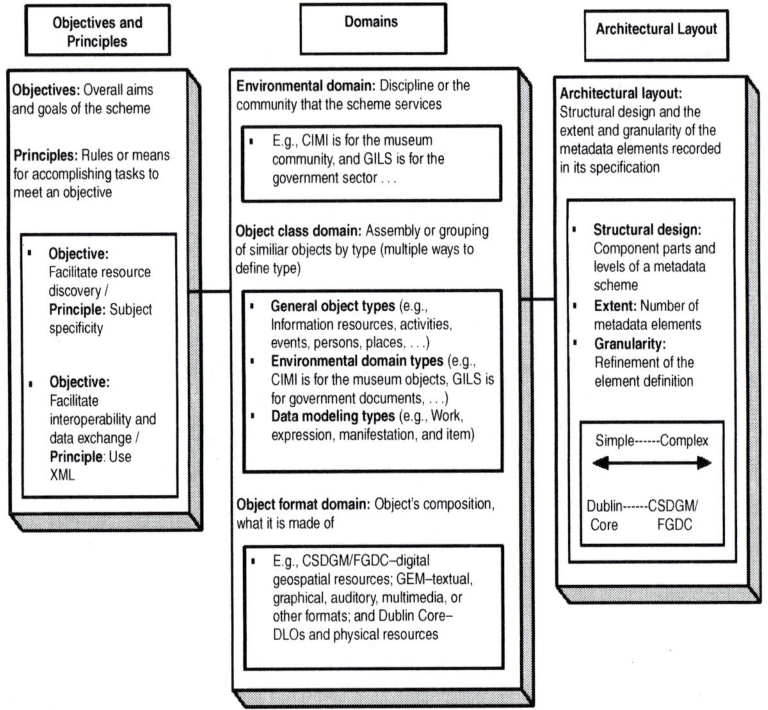

prior to the development of the World Wide Web and digital technologies, Cutter's objectives state that a library catalog is to:

1. Enable a person to find a book when the author, title, or subject is known;
2. Show what the library has by author, subject, and literature genre; and
3. Assist in the selection of a book by its edition and literary or topical composition. These objectives have a functional end: they exemplify resource discovery, and with a little tweaking of terminology (e.g., changing book to digital resource), they represent the objectives of many current metadata schemes developed for digital resources.

Cutter's *Rules for a Dictionary Catalog* (1904) also includes principles to meet the stated objectives. An example of the subject specificity principle, which aids Cutter's first two objectives, is: "Enter a work under its subject-heading, not under the heading of a class which includes that subject. Example: Put Lady Cust's book on *The cat* under **Cat**, not under **Zoology** or **Mammals**, or **Domestic animals**; and put Garnier's *Le fer* under **Iron**, not under **Metals** or **Metallurgy**" (1904, p. 66).

Among one of the best known historical examples of principles of bibliographic control is the "Statement of Principles," commonly known as the "Paris Principles," resulting from the International Conference on Cataloguing that took place in Paris in 1961 (International Federation . . . , 1963). Adopted by delegates from 53 different countries, the Paris Principles were established to guide the selection and form of access points for library materials and to harmonize and direct future cataloging on an international level (Carpenter, 1985). It is interesting to note that the second statement in the Paris Principles is a rendition of Cutter's objectives.

The synthesis of objectives, principles, and functional requirements continues to be a fundamental component of metadata schemes that guide online cataloging. Exploring these underlying components was a major theme in the 1996 International Conference on the Principles and Future Development of *AACR* (Weihs, 1998), which explored the adaptation of *AACR2* for cataloging electronic resources. The *Functional Requirements for Bibliographic Records* (*FRBR*) (1997), an International Federation of Library Associations and Institutions' (IFLA) model for bibliographic control, provides another recent example of a synthesis of these fundamental components.

Historical and contemporary cataloging developments are indicative of the objectives and principles stated in metadata schemes developed for digital resources. A key objective of many metadata schemes is to facilitate resource discovery, and, thus many specifications indicate this. The first item listed in the Dublin Core Metadata Initiative's mission statement Web page (http://www.dublincore.org/about/) is to improve means for finding resources on the Internet by "developing metadata standards for discovery across domains." Another objective, found in a number of fairly recent metadata schemes, is to document preservation and reformatting. The final report of RLG's Working Group on Preservation Issues of Metadata (1998) states that the scheme's 16 elements are deemed "crucial to the continued viability of a digital master file." This objective, or variations of it, is found in the introductions of many other preservation metadata schemes (for links to preservation metadata see: http://www.dublincore.org/groups/preservation/).

A number of metadata schemes have formal statements of principles to help accomplish objectives and to guide scheme design. A case in point is the Poughkeepsie Principles, an outcome of the Vassar Planning Conference that led to the Text Encoding Initiative (TEI) guidelines (Design Principles . . . , 1988). These Principles consist of nine statements that highlight the need to establish a set of guidelines for data interchange, define a meta-language, recommend encoding principles, support compatibility with existing standards, and permit the conversion of resources to newer communication formats, among other goals–all for electronic text in the humanities. Many of these statements appear more like objectives and weave in the principles. The TEI standard includes a series of metadata schemes for different types of text in the humanities, such as novels, plays, lexicons, and bibliographic information–to name a few components. The most current version is TEI P4 (Sperberg-McQueen and Burnard, 2002).

Another set of metadata scheme principles is the Ann Arbor Accords (1996) (hereafter referred to as the Accords), developed for metadata about electronic archival finding aids. The Accords were influenced by the Poughkeepsie Principles, and appear to also interweave objectives and principles. The Accords "defines principles and criteria for designing, developing, and maintaining SGML-based encoding schemes for archive and library finding aids," and have guided the development of the SGML (now XML) document type definition (DTD) for the Encoded Archival Description (EAD) (2002). The "General Principles" section of the Accords (principles 4 through 8) defines the chief aim of archival finding aids, and emphasizes goals of the EAD, such as facilitating interchange and portability, increasing the intelligibility of finding aids within and across institutions, and fostering data sharing. The "Structural Features" section of the Accords (principles 9 through 12) includes EAD design principles. This section explains that the EAD encoding scheme is based on SGML with a formal DTD, that the scheme consists of two parts (an SGML-compliant DTD and detailed application guidelines), and that more generic terms, such as "unit" and "component," were used to ensure broad application of the scheme.

A final example of principles with a slightly different tenor than the Poughkeepsie Principles and the Ann Arbor Accords are the Dublin Core's principles of simplicity, semantic interoperability, international consensus, and flexibility for Web resource description (e.g., Dublin

Core Metadata, 1997). These principles define general modes of operation and are the tenets upon which the Dublin Core has developed.

Objectives and principles, as reviewed here, highlight one way in which the population of metadata schemes may be examined and further understood. In the next section, I will focus on metadata scheme domains.

Domains

Additional insight into the population of metadata schemes can be gained by examining a scheme's application domains–that is, the realms in which the scheme operates. This discussion presents three domains for studying metadata schemes. They are the environmental domain, object class domain, and object format domain. The distinctions between these domains are not absolute, but they are discussed separately for the sake of clarity.

Environmental Domain

The environmental domain is the discipline or the community that the scheme serves. The majority of schemes in the Web environment have been developed to meet the needs of a specified community. Examples include Consortium for the Computer Interchange of Museum Information (CIMI) (2000), developed primarily for the museum community and art world; Government Information Locator Service (GILS) (1997), developed for the government sector; Rich Site Summary (RSS) (2000), developed for the news community; and Data Documentation Initiative (DDI) (2000), developed for the social science research community. The Dublin Core is a multidisciplinary schema developed to facilitate resource discovery and support interoperability and data exchange among communities. As a result, the Dublin Core's environmental domain includes the larger information resource description community (Weibel, 1995), which may be thought of as a community uniting smaller communities or disciplines.

Object Class Domain

Object class domain is the assembly or grouping of similar objects by "type." There are a variety of ways that type can be defined for the object class domain. A majority of the schemes identified in this article (e.g., Dublin Core, TEI, and EAD) have been designed for information resources–the class of objects commonly found in libraries, museums, archives, or other information agencies. Other types of objects include activities, events, persons, places, structures, relationships, transactions, execution directions, and programmatic applications. Each of these object types can have sub-domains, which can be further divided by genre. For example, information resources can be further refined by format (e.g., textual, graphical, auditory, and multi-media, among other formats), a topic that is covered below under *object format domain.*

The environmental domains identified above each cater to a specific type of resource, and illustrate another way to look at the object class. For example, CIMI is for art objects, GILS is for government documents, RSS is for channel information, and DDI is for social science statistical data.

Data modeling activities lend to another way of typing objects. For example, the *FRBR* model supports representation of works, expressions, manifestations, and items, which may be viewed as different classes or objects. Traditionally, metadata schemes have combined these representations. The *Machine Readable Cataloging* (*MARC*) bibliographic format illustrates this point and is considered a flat data structure. Research on the nature of a work and multiple derivations (e.g., Smiraglia, 2001) is important for forwarding information object representation, particularly in the digital environment where derivations are likely to be even more significant compared to the high numbers already found in catalogs representing more traditional bibliographic resources (e.g., monographs, videos, musical works, and so forth) (Smiraglia and Leazer, 1999).

Object Format Domain

Object format domain is the object's composition–what it is made of. FGDC/CSDGM was designed for digital geospatial materials and is an example of a format-specific scheme. The majority of information resource-oriented metadata schemas are applicable to multiple formats. For example, the Gateway to Educational Material (GEM) Element Set (1999) is a metadata schema for educational resources, available in textual, graphical, auditory, multimedia, or other formats. The Dublin Core, designed initially for digital like objects (DLOs), which are defined as textual objects, is also applicable to physical objects in many different formats (Weibel and Hakala, 1998). Extending beyond information resources, object format is a likely factor in other schemas as well. Consider the ontology developments in the field of genomics, where metadata schemes designed for human beings or animals document different blood types, e.g., the DNA (deoxyribonucleic acid) gene sequence. This example is beyond the scope of this article, but it demonstrates another view of domain format.

Architectural Layout

Architectural layout involves the structural design of a scheme, and the extent and granularity of the metadata elements. (Scheme architecture is not to be confused with information architecture, which applies to design framework for entire information systems or environments.) Scheme structures range from fairly simple flat designs–that generally have a limited number of general metadata elements–to complex modular structures with a higher number and usually more granular metadata elements.

At the simple end of the spectrum is the Dublin Core, which comprises 15 basic metadata elements that are deemed essential for resource discovery. The simplicity of the Dublin Core is predicated on its existence as a low-level common denominator that aims to support interoperability among resource description environments using more complex schemas. This activity is facilitated by crosswalk analyses that map metadata elements to achieve semantic interoperability. Another factor underlying the Dublin Core's simplicity is connected to its goal to serve as the core or base for the development of more elaborate or domain specific schemas. An example is found with GEM, which incorporates all 15 Dublin Core metadata elements and their exact definitions, but includes a set of specialized metadata elements (e.g., "pedagogy," "grade level," "audience," to name a few) that are important for organizing and accessing Web-based educational resources. Resources containing GEM metadata can easily be transferred to any database that uses equivalent Dublin Core elements.

Slightly more complex than the Dublin Core's architecture, but still relatively simple, is Metadata Object Description Schema (MODS) (2003). This scheme has 19 top level elements and two root elements, each with sub-elements and most with attributes to describe the element. Another slightly more complex metadata scheme is the Visual Resource Association's Core Categories (VRA Core, 3.0) (2000) for visual objects (e.g., paintings, antiques, other cultural objects) and images that document them (e.g., slides, photographs, digital images used for studying these objects). Initially modular, with one component for the work (the visual object) and one component for the image of the work (see Core Categories for Visual Resources, 1997), this schema now conflates these two parts into a single arrangement. VRA, version 3.0, has 17 metadata elements and recommends one metadata record per object, whether the work itself or an image of the work is being represented. The VRA is more granular than the Dublin Core in that the elements are specifically defined for the visual resource domain.

Compared to the VRA Core, the DIG35 Specification: Metadata for Digital Images (2000) has a fairly complex architectural layout. This scheme includes five top-level structural components: basic image, image creation, content description, history, and intellectual property rights, and over 150 metadata elements for documenting images. The "image creation" section includes sub-sections labeled general information, camera capture metadata, device characterization, camera settings, scanner capture metadata, and captured item metadata, each of which are further defined by a collection of metadata and meta-metadata elements, the majority of which are not prescribed in the VRA Core.

A final example of a scheme with a complex architectural layout is the FGDC/CSDGM developed for digital geospatial resources. The structural design consists of ten top-level sections; this schema has over 320 compound metadata elements. FGDC/CSDGM, Section 4, Spatial Reference Information, provides a good example of this scheme's granularity with over 40 metadata elements–all of which map to the Dublin Core "coverage" metadata element to achieve semantic interoperability. For example, a data exchange sequence between the two schemes would require that FGDC/CSDGM "Map_Projection_Parameters," "Grid_Coordinate_System," "Universal_Transverse_Mercator," "State_Plane_Coordinate_System," "ARC_Coordinate_System," "Planar_Coordinate_Information," "Distance_and_Bearing_Representation," and "Geodetic_Model" metadata elements (a few element examples) be mapped to the Dublin Core's "coverage" metadata element.

In observing schema architectures, particularly the extent of and granularity of metadata elements, factors such as metadata element cardinality and qualification must also be taken into account. This is because element repeatability in one specification might be able to achieve the extensity and granularity documented in another specification. This point is illustrated with the example above where FGDC/CSDGM, Section 4, metadata elements, which are quite as granular and have obligation and occurrence restrictions, were mapped to the Dublin Core "coverage" metadata element, which is optional and repeatable.

Although the architectural layout examples provided here are fairly representative of scheme architectural compositions, it is important to point out that greater complexity in structural design is not always correlated with a higher number of and more granular metadata elements. For example, RSS has a slightly complex structural design with four main components (channel, item, text input, and image), but only 16 metadata elements that, with the exception of the granular descriptions given for the "channel," are applicable to a wide range of information resources. The EAD scheme for archival finding aids deviates from the norm as well, albeit in the other direction. EAD has a simple structure comprising two main components (header and archival description), but is extensive in that it contains over 143 metadata elements with descriptions that range from general to quite granular.

CONCLUSIONS: FRAMEWORKS AS AN APPROACH OF STUDY

Metadata is generally defined as structured data about data, and information and library scientists emphasize the functional goals in their discussions. The functional aspect is evident when reviewing metadata typologies. Defining what specifically a metadata scheme is presents a greater challenge, given the multiplicity of schemes, their evolutionary nature, their different constituencies, and their varied functional emphases. The MODAL framework presents a way to study this complex topic.

Frameworks are useful for understanding complex topics: they help divide, categorize, and analyze concepts. Although metadata schemes vary tremendously, they are shown to be similar when examining their objectives and principles, domain foci, and architectural layout. The MODAL framework focuses on these features and provides a structure for examining and interpreting metadata schemes. The MODAL framework can also aid with metadata scheme design.

Although frameworks facilitate study, it is important to note that they are artificial creations, with accompanying shortcomings. The MODAL framework will likely not support every analysis of metadata schemes, and it might require enhancement and modification over time. It is also likely that researchers will develop new frameworks supporting analyses of different types of metadata schemes. This point becomes evident when considering the different uses of the term metadata scheme: "metadata scheme" connotes not only the semantic container-like structures focused on in this article, but also topics we commonly refer to as content standards (e.g., *AACR*), controlled vocabularies (e.g.,

LCSH), taxonomies and ontologies (e.g., Yahoos! main classification), and full markup language, such as Mathematical Markup Language (MathML™) (1999). These different types of metadata schemes require further investigation, and point to an exciting research agenda.

Studying more semantic container-like metadata schemes, as emphasized in this paper, and the different types of metadata schemes noted above will help improve the MODAL framework approach. The MODAL framework can be used to study different types of metadata schemes, and testing of its applicability is warranted. Together these approaches will contribute to a body of knowledge about the population of metadata schemes and help us understand the role of metadata schemes in the larger context of information organization, management, and access.

WORKS CITED

Ann Arbor Accords: Principles and Criteria for an SGML Document Type Definition (DTD) for Finding Aids. (1996). http://sunsite.berkeley.edu/FindingAids/EAD/accords.html.

Caplan, P. 1995. You call it corn, we call it syntax–Independent metadata for document-like-objects. *The Public-Access Computer Systems Review*, 6 (94): http://info.lib.uh.edu/pr/v6/n4/capl6n4.html/.

Caplan, P. 2003. *Metadata Fundamentals for All Libraries*. Chicago: American Library Association.

Carpenter, M. 1985. Statement of the Principles: International Conference on Cataloguing Principles, Paris, October, 1961, Editor's Introduction. In Svenonius, E. and Carpenter, M. (Eds), *Foundations of Cataloging: A Source Book*. Littleton, CO: Libraries Unlimited, p. 176-178.

CIMI Consortium. 2001. CIMI Consortium for the Computer Interchange of Museum Information. Guide to Best Practice: Dublin Core, Version 1.1. http://www.cimi.org/old_site/documents/meta_bestprac_v1_1_210400.pdf.

Content Standard for Digital Geospatial Metadata, Part 1: Biological Data Profile. 1999. Biological Data Working Group Federal Geographic Data Committee and USGS Biological Resources Division. http://www.fgdc.gov/standards/documents/standards/biodata/biodatap.html.

Cutter, C. A. 1904. *Rules for a Dictionary Catalog*, 4th ed., (rewritten). Washington, DC: Government Printing Office.

Data Documentation Initiative (DDI) Codebook DTD. 2000. http://www.icpsr.umich.edu/DDI/CODEBOOK.TXT.

Design Principles for Text Encoding Guidelines: TEI ED P1. 1988 [rev. January 1990]. (The Poughkeepsie Principles were original published November, 13, 1987. The original publication is not accessible on the Web.)

DIG35 Specification: Metadata for Digital Images, Version 1.0. 2000. Digital Imaging Group, Inc. http://www.bgbm.fu-berlin.de/TDWG/acc/Documents/DIG35-v1.0-Sept00.pdf.

Dublin Core Metadata Element Set, Version 1.1: Reference Description. 2003. http://www.dublincore.org/documents/2003/06/02/dces/.

Duval, E., Hodgins, W., Sutton, S., and Weibel, S. 2002. Metadata Principles and Practicalities. *D-Lib Magazine* http://www.dlib.org/dlib/april02/weibel/04weibel.html.

Encoded Archival Description Tag Library, Version 2002. 2002. Prepared and Maintained by the Encoded Archival Description Working Group of the Society of American Archivists and the Network Development and MARC Standards Office of the Library of Congress.

Federal Geographic Metadata Committee. 1998. *Content Standard for Digital Geospatial Metadata (CSDGM).* http://fgdc.er.usgs.gov/metadata/csdgm/.

Functional Requirements for Bibliographic Records [final report]. 1997. Recommended by the IFLA Study Group on the Functional Requirements for Bibliographic Records; International Federation of Library Associations and Institutions, IFLA Universal Bibliographic Control and International MARC Programme. Frankfurt Am Main: IFLA UBCIM. http://www.ifla.org/VII/s13/frbr/frbr.htm.

Gateway to Educational Materials (GEM) Element Set. 1999. http://www.geminfo.org/Workbench/Metadata/GEM_Element_List.html [last modified 2001].

Gilliland-Swetland, A. 2000. Defining metadata, in M. Baca (ed.), *Introduction to Metadata: Pathways to Digital Information.* Los Angles, CA: Getty Information Institute. http://www.getty.edu/research/conducting_research/standards/intrometadata/2_articles/index.html.

Government Information Locator Service (GILS). 1997. http://www.gils.net/prof_v2.html.

Greenberg, J. 2001. A quantitative categorical analysis of metadata elements in image applicable metadata schemas. *Journal of the American Society for Information Science and Technology* 52: 917-914.

Greenberg, J. 2003. Metadata and the World Wide Web. *Encyclopedia of Library and Information Science*, pp. 1876-1888. New York: Marcel Dekker, Inc.

Heery, R. 1996. Review of metadata formats. *Program*, 30: 345-373.

International Federation of Library Associations and Institutions. 1963. *Report: International Conference on Cataloguing Principles, Paris, 9th-18th October, 1961.* London: Organizing Committee of the International Conference on Cataloguing Principles, p. 91-96.

Kant, Immanuel. 1998. *Critique of Pure Reason.* Paul Guyer and Allen W. Wood, eds., and translators. Cambridge: Cambridge University Press.

Lagoze, C., Lynch, C. A., and Daniel, R. 1996. The Warwick Framework: A container architecture for aggregating sets of metadata. Available at: http://cs-tr.cs.cornell.edu:80/Dients/Repository/2.0/Body/ncstrl.cornell%2fTR96-1593/html.

Mathematical Markup Language (MathML™) 1.01 Specification W3C Recommendation. 1999. Available at: http://www.w3.org/TR/REC-MathML/.

Milstead, J. and Feldman, S. 1999. Metadata: Cataloging by any other name. *Online* 25-31. Also available at: http://www.onlineinc.com/onlinemag/OL1999/milstead1.html.

MODS Version 3.0. 2003. http://www.loc.gov/standards/mods/v3/mods-3-0.xsd.

Moen, W. E., and Benardino, P. 2003. Assessing metadata utilization: An analysis of *MARC* content designation use. In Sutton, S., Greenberg, J., and Tennis, J. eds. *2003 Dublin Core Conference: Supporting Communities of Discourse and Practice–Metadata Research and Applications. DC-2003: Proceedings of the International DCMI Conference and Workshop. September 28-October 2, 2003, Seattle, Washington.* Syracuse, NY: Information Institute of Syracuse.

RDF Site Summary 1.0 Specification (RSS). 2000. http://www.egroups.com/files/rss-dev/specification.html#.

RLG and Preservation. 1998. Working Group on Preservation Issues of Metadata Final Report. http://www.rlg.org./preserv/presmeta.html.

Smiraglia, R. P. 2001. *The Nature of 'A Work': Implications for the Organization of Knowledge.* Lanham, MD: Scarecrow.

Smiraglia, R. P. and Leazer, G. H. 1999. Derivative bibliographic relationships: the work relationship in a global bibliographic database. *Journal of the American Society for Information Science* 50: 493-504.

Sperberg-McQueen, C. M. and Burnard, L. eds. 2002. *TEI P4: Guidelines for Electronic Text Encoding and Interchange.* Text Encoding Initiative Consortium. XML Version: Oxford, Providence, Charlottesville, Bergen.

Visual Resource Association Core Categories for Visual Resources (VRA CORE), version 2.0 1997. http://www.oberlin.edu/~art/vra/wc1.html.

VRA Core Categories, Version 3.0. 2000. Visual Resources Association Data Standard Committee. http://www.vraweb.org/vracore3.htm [last modified 2002].

Weibel, S. and Hakala, J. 1998. A report on the workshop and subsequent developments. *D-Lib Magazine*: http://www.dlib.org/dlib/february98/02weibel.html.

Weibel, Stuart. 1995. Metadata: The foundations of resource description. *D-Lib Magazine.* http://www.dlib.org/dlib/July95/07weibel.html.

Weihs, J. ed. 1998. *The Principles and Future of* AACR2*: Proceedings of the International Conference on the Principles and Future Development of* AACR2. Chicago: American Library Association.

Woodley, M. 2000. Metadata standards crosswalks. In Baca, M. ed., *Introduction to Metadata: Pathways to Digital Information.* Los Angeles, CA: Getty Information Institute. http://www.getty.edu/research/conducting_research/standards/intrometadata/3_crosswalks/index.html.

Woodley, M. S., Clement, G. and Winn, P. 2003. *DCMI Glossary.* http://dublincore.org/documents/2003/08/26/usageguide/glossary.shtml [last update, April 2004].

Zeng, M. L. 1999. Metadata elements for object description and representation: A case report from a digitized historical fashion collection project. *Journal of the American Society for Information Science* 50: 1193-1208.

Metadata and Bibliographic Control: Soul-Mates or Two Solitudes?

Lynne C. Howarth

SUMMARY. The historical interweaving of evolving trends and applications in metadata and bibliographic control seems largely absent from the literature. To address this apparent gap in perspective, some historic and more recent developments related to each are traced, along with some speculation about future directions. Cataloguing rules are ancestors to the current lineage of bibliographic standards. Metadata schemas have been developed to meet the needs of particular fields or domains and to support a variety of functions related to resource discovery. While differences between the tools of bibliographic control and of metadata application still remain, the similarities have become sufficient to warrant a confluence in terminology and definition. While internationally determined codes and standards have fostered the goal of universal bibliographic control, syntactic structures, semantic element sets, transmission protocols, cross-schema mappings, and metadata harvesting tools have been instrumental to realizing the concept of interoperability.

KEYWORDS. Metadata schemas, bibliographic control, cataloguing rules, bibliographic standards, interoperability

---

Lynne C. Howarth is Professor, Faculty of Information Studies, University of Toronto, 140 St. George Street, Toronto, Ontario M5S 3G6 Canada (E-mail: howarth@fis.utoronto.ca).

[Haworth co-indexing entry note]: "Metadata and Bibliographic Control: Soul-Mates or Two Solitudes?" Howarth, Lynne C. Co-published simultaneously in *Cataloging & Classification Quarterly* (The Haworth Information Press, an imprint of The Haworth Press, Inc.) Vol. 40, No. 3/4, 2005, pp. 37-56; and: *Metadata: A Cataloger's Primer* (ed: Richard P. Smiraglia) The Haworth Information Press, an imprint of The Haworth Press, Inc., 2005, pp. 37-56. Single or multiple copies of this article are available for a fee from The Haworth Document Delivery Service [1-800-HAWORTH, 9:00 a.m. - 5:00 p.m. (EST). E-mail address: docdelivery@haworthpress.com].

Available online at http://www.haworthpress.com/web/CCQ

doi:10.1300/J104v40n03_03

INTRODUCTION

The proliferation and increasing pervasiveness of the Internet with its plethora of Web-enabled digital resources, is no longer the domain of futurists, but rather, the stuff of everyday organizational and individual life. According to figures compiled by *Global Reach,*[1] to 30 March, 2004, nearly 730 million of the world's 6.33 billion inhabitants had Internet access.[2] Likewise, the number of Websites registered with domain names has jumped from 20,000 in 1995, to just under 10 million in 2002, to over 36 million in 2004.[3] While the novelty of accessing electronic information through relatively sophisticated Web search engines anywhere, anytime, has perhaps worn off and become almost commonplace, the pressing need to organize and manage bourgeoning types and formats of digital content effectively has not.

That this same requirement could be said to apply equally to the domain of library collections, and its related realm of bibliographic control, provides a logical connector to the thrust of this paper. While Burnett, Kwong, and Park (1999, 1) have compared the conceptual foundations and orientations of two metadata "traditions," namely, (1) the bibliographic control approach with its roots in library science, and (2) the data management approach, with its origins in computer science, others, such as Tillett (2003) and Huthwaite (2003) have compared specific metadata schemas, such as the *Anglo-American Cataloguing Rules* and the Dublin Core. Nonetheless, the historical interweaving of evolving trends and applications relative to the areas of metadata and bibliographic control, respectively, seems largely absent from the literature. To address this apparent gap in perspective, the paper will trace some historic and more recent developments related to each area, will discuss how early parallel tracks have shifted towards greater convergence, and will speculate on future directions and their implications for libraries and other information-intensive institutions.

SETTING THE STAGE: BACKGROUND AND OPERATIONAL DEFINITIONS

Bibliographic Control

Situating metadata in relation to bibliographic control first requires a definition of each. Described by Chan (1994, 3) as, "the operations by which recorded information is organized or arranged according to established standards and thereby made readily identifiable and retrievable," the theory and practice of bibliographic control have evolved for over a century and a half since Sir Alfred Panizzi devised his ninety-one rules for compiling a new printed catalogue for the British Museum (1841), and Charles Cutter (1904) articulated his three "objects" for library catalogues, and a code of rules for realizing each. Dedicated to the creation of surrogates–or bibliographic records–to represent actual physical–and more recently, virtual–items or objects, the theory and practice of bibliographic control has focused on systematic, uniform, and consistent approaches to describing intellectual or artistic content and physical characteristics. As the type and numbers of textual and media formats have expanded, so too has the codification of common approaches to describing, organizing, and providing access to bibliographic entities through surrogate representations. Cataloguing rules, such as those of Cutter (1904), the American Library Association (1908), the Library of Congress (1949), and The Vatican Code (1931), are ancestors to the current lineage of bibliographic standards, such as the International Standard Bibliographic Descriptions (*ISBD*s), and the *Anglo-American Cataloguing Rules*, which, themselves, derive from internationally determined principles–the Paris Principles of 1961.

Provisions for identifying and locating materials based on their subject content have been realized through the development of standardized lists of subject headings and structured subject thesauri, and through the application of classification systems such as the *Dewey Decimal Classification*, the *Universal Decimal Classification*, and the enumerative *Library of Congress Classification*, to name only a few. Addressing the vagaries of nomenclature and terminology, authority control, or procedures for linking variations with one designated and representative uniform term (personal or corporate name; subject; title; series; class notation) has been added to the staples inherent to bibliographic control. With the development of communications formats (such as Machine-Readable Cataloging [MARC] and UNIMARC) and protocols (such as the open systems interchange or Z39.50 protocol), the exchange of bibliographic surrogates has been greatly facilitated and eagerly embraced within an international context. The landscape of bibliographic control can thus be characterized as one that attempts to facilitate access to a variety of information types and formats based on internationally determined and universally applied codes and standards.

Metadata

Definitions of "metadata" abound, with "data about data" (Miller 1996) being one of the more frequently cited. Somewhat more precise definitions speak to "*structured* data about data" (EU-NSF Working Group on Metadata 1999), while Gilliland-Swetland's "big picture" summary (2000, 1) offers, "the sum total of what one can say about any information object at any level of aggregation." The ubiquitous "data about data," while inherently imprecise, is also misleading, and belies the term's richer inheritance from the information systems domain. As Gilliland-Swetland (2000, 1) reminds us:

> Until the mid-1990s, '*metadata*' was a term most prevalently used by communities involved with the management and interoperability of geospatial data, and with data management and systems design and maintenance in general. For these communities, 'metadata' referred to a suite of industry or disciplinary standards as well as additional internal and external documentation and other data necessary for the identification, representation, interoperability, technical management, performance, and use of data contained in an information system.

Gill (2000, 1) elaborates further on the definition of metadata deriving from its roots in computer science, explaining that, in addition to their facility with storing and manipulating large collections of structured data:

> Computers have always employed catalogs internally . . . to keep track of different discrete data objects. In order to function correctly, they must keep an accurate record of the identity and location of every item of data stored in the various memories. For example, the operating system of a computer uses a catalog called the File Allocation Table to store the names of files and their physical position on a disk. This type of data catalog is itself stored by the computer as data, a recursive relationship that has resulted in it being referred to as 'metadata.'

Confining his definition to the context of the World Wide Web, Gill (2000, 2) describes metadata as, "structured descriptions, stored as computer data, that attempt to describe the essential properties of other discrete computer data objects. . . . "

For their parts, Burnett, Ng, and Park (1999, 1212) marry definitions of metadata from bibliographic control and data management approaches, respectively, to propose the following "expedient compromise": ". . . metadata is [sic] data that characterizes source data, describes their relationships, and supports the discovery and effective use of source data."

Metadata schemas have been developed to meet the needs of particular fields or domains (publishing, rights management, museums, education, pure and applied science, clinical trials management, etc.), and to support a variety of functions. In general, metadata can be categorized according to one or more of the following types (IFLA 2005 in preparation):

- *Administrative metadata*: information about the record itself–its creation, modification, relationship to other records, location, etc.;
- *Descriptive metadata*: information describing the physical and intellectual properties or content of a digital item or object;
- *Analytical metadata*: sometimes referred to as "subject metadata," information analysing and enhancing access to the resource's contents;
- *Rights management metadata*: information regarding restrictions (legal, financial, etc.) on access to, or use of, digital items or objects;
- *Technical metadata*: particular hardware or software used in converting an item/object to a digital format, or in storing, displaying, authenticating, or securing data;
- *Preservation metadata*: information pertaining to the physical condition of an item/object, and actions (refreshing, migration, etc.) undertaken to preserve and manage physical and digital items/objects/collections;
- *Structural metadata*: information describing the types, versions, relationships and other characteristics of digital items or objects, and/or their component parts;
- *Use metadata*: information relating to the level and type of use of physical or digital items/objects/collections;
- *Other metadata, as determined*: particular metadata elements based on local, regional, and/or organizational requirements, or in accordance with a nationally mandated metadata standard, and not subsumed within any metadata type above.

The concentration of efforts in the development of metadata schemas can be traced to the design of the Standard Generalized Mark-Up Language (SGML) and its adoption as an international standard in 1986 (ISO 8879:1986). Since then, and particularly during the 1990s, as Baker (1999), Caplan (2000), Howarth (2004), and others have noted, there has been steady activity to develop SGML/XML/HTML-based metadata standards for both general applications and specialised information domains. Encoded Archival Description (EAD) (an SGML-based encoding scheme for archive and library finding aids), the Dublin Core (DC) (a simple HTML-based data element set and instructions that authors or publishers can imbed when mounting documents on a network server), the Text-Encoding Initiative (TEI) Header (a SGML-based encoding scheme for complex textural structures), the Visual Resources Association (VRA) Visual Document Description Categories (for describing any entity or event that may be captured in physical form as a visual document of the original work, and including works of art, architecture, and artifacts or structures from material, popular, and folk culture), and the Submissions Data Modeling (SDM) standard emanating from the Clinical Data Interchange Standards Consortium (CDISC), are only a few examples of the many metadata schemes which have been developed. Selecting a schema, and determining which elements (meta tags) to apply will depend, in large part, on the *context* of the digital repository or archive, and attending functional requirements. In general, as Burnett, Ng, and Park (1999, 1212-1213) conclude, the functions or uses of metadata are related to resource discovery–i.e., identifying and locating relevant data–as well as to the levels of the system and end-user, respectively:

> At the system level, metadata can be used to facilitate interoperability and the ability to share among resource discovery tools. . . . At the end-user level, metadata can facilitate the ability to determine:
>
> - What data [are] available;
> - Whether [they] meets specific needs;
> - How to acquire [them]; and
> - How to transfer [them] to a local system

SOUL MATES OR TWO SOLITUDES?

With minimal imagination, one could readily map the preceding functions of metadata with Cutter's three "objects" of the catalogue, or, more currently, with the four user functions[4] outlined in the *Functional Requirements for Bibliographic Records* (*FRBR*) (1998):

- Find (data correspond to search criteria)
- Identify (confirm entity described in record corresponds to entity sought; distinguish between 2 entities with same title)
- Select (language; version)
- Obtain (place order, request; remote access)

This would suggest that, at least from the functional perspective of linking users with information needs to appropriate resources, there was much in common between definitions and concepts of bibliographic control and metadata, respectively. A review of the literature suggests that, at least initially, enmity, rather than equanimity, prevailed.

While metadata schemas developed apace within disciplines or domains unrelated to those of bibliographic control for library resources and collections, there was little need for either comparison or comment. Narrowly confined to its definition within the realm of data management, metadata remained a concept of relevance to computer scientists and those responsible for data warehouses, large data archives, and digital libraries. More broadly defined within the context of a domain, discipline, cultural institution (such as archives or museums), or industry (publishing, pharmaceuticals, manufacturing, etc.), metadata schemas attracted interest but not necessarily engagement from the bibliographic control community. As access to the Web led to an explosive growth in the types and numbers of digital resources that could be readily obtained, the lines between traditional bibliographic control and emerging metadata applications began to blur, legacy systems were subjected to greater scrutiny (spurred by rising costs and skepticism about benefits), and lines appeared to be drawn. Some cataloguers viewed the growing interest in metadata with a curiosity verging on bemusement, as the following excerpt (Milstead and Feldman 1999, 1) illustrates:

> Like the man who had been writing prose all his life without knowing it, librarians and indexers have been producing and standardizing metadata for centuries. Ignoring this legacy, an immense variety of other players have recently entered the field, and many of them have no idea that someone else has already 'been there, done that.' Different systems are being developed for different–and sometimes the same–kinds of information, resulting in a chaotic atmosphere of clashing standards.

At the same time, the bibliographic control community grappled with the proliferation of digital media accessible via the Internet, revising the *International Standard Bibliographic Description for Computer Files* (*ISBD(CF)*) to address remote access materials in its re-titled, *International Standard Bibliographic Description for Electronic Resources* (*ISBD(ER)*), issuing a substantially revised Chapter 9 (Computer Files–renamed, "Electronic Resources") of the *Anglo-American Cataloguing Rules*, and engaging in special projects, such as OCLC's InterCat, for cooperative cataloguing of Internet resources. While these responses were timely and fruitful, the practicalities of facilitating resource discovery through traditional descriptive approaches were severely tested by the sheer volume of digital material. Alternate approaches to describing Internet-resident electronic resources seemed not only desirable, but also necessary, and certainly of high priority.

The brainchild of an informal conversation in a corridor at the 1994 Internet World Conference, Dublin Core with its initial 13-, then 15-, now 18-element set[5] was conceived and articulated as, " . . . an easy-to-create and maintain descriptive format to facilitate cross-domain resource discovery on the Web" (Lagoze 2001). The first invitational Metadata Workshop of March 1-3, 1995, in Dublin, Ohio, brought together, " . . . librarians, archivists, humanities scholars, geographers, and standards makers in the Internet, Z39.50, and Standard Generalized Mark-up Language (SGML) communities . . . " (Weibel 1995, 2). As Weibel (1995, 2) elaborates further:

> Since the Internet contains more information than professional abstractors, indexers and catalogers can manage using existing methods and systems, it was agreed that a reasonable alternative way to obtain usable metadata for electronic resources is to give authors and information providers a means to describe the resources themselves. The major task of the Metadata Workshop was to identify and define a simple set of elements for describing networked electronic resources.

This early incarnation of a simple metadata schema for those creating or providing electronic resources via the Internet was dismissed by some in the bibliographic control community as being simplistic,[6] while others lauded Dublin Core–with its optional, repeatable, and extensive elements–for offering "new options for describing materials that are poorly served by the *AACR2*/MARC suite of standards" (Caplan 2000, 61). As the number of Dublin Core projects steadily increased, the need for richer, more complex, metadata affording finer granularity in resource description also emerged. Observing this shift, Lagoze (2001, 2) explains that, "A notion of 'qualified Dublin Core' evolved whereby the model for simple resource discovery–a set of simple metadata elements in a flat, document-centric model–would form the basis of more complex descriptions by treating the values of its elements as entities with properties ('component elements') in their own right."

As the Dublin Core evolved to become more complex in its structure, and also more inclusive in the types and formats of resources being subsumed within its descriptive framework, the distinctions between it and "traditional" approaches to resource description were becoming less clear. This blurring of lines is nicely summarized in Tillett's (2003, 107-109) comparison of the *Anglo-American Cataloguing Rules*, 2nd edition (*AACR2*), and Dublin Core. She notes that the former is a deliberative rule process, whereas the latter has no rules of its own for syntax or semantics, relying, instead, on the rules of other systems. Since Tillett's article was published, Dublin Core has moved beyond its status as, ". . . a *de facto* standard for metadata on the Web" (Weibel and Koch 2000, 2) to become an international standard (ISO Standard 15836-2003 (February 2003)). As the core fifteen- (now eighteen-) element set and associated qualifiers have matured (Weibel and Koch 2000), applications of Dublin Core have expanded beyond "document-like objects" (DLOs) (Weibel 1995) to deal with more of the types and formats of materials that were previously covered by *AACR2* (and *ISBD*) exclusively. Tillett notes further (2003, 108) that, "*AACR2* prescribes authority control and transcription of information from the item being catalogued. Dublin Core allows both controlled and uncontrolled data. . . . " Her comparison concludes with the observation that cataloguing (using *AACR2*) occurs after a work and its manifestation have been created, whereas, in the world of the Web, "an automatic tool is needed to create basic descriptive metadata at the point an object is created. The metadata that will be part of every future digital object can then be re-used in library catalogs and by search engines worldwide" (Tillett 2003, 109).

The previous discussion has focused to a large degree on the origins and subsequent development of one metadata element set, the Dublin Core. Nonetheless, it should be noted that, "an almost explosive proliferation of metadata schemes" (Caplan 2001, 61) was occurring simultaneously in other disciplines or cultural domains with a particular interest in digital resource description. Cited above, in reference to mark-up syntax (SGML, HTML, XML, etc.), the Text Encoding Initiative (TEI)'s document type definition TEI Header (1990), the Encoded

Archival Description (EAD) (1996), the Visual Resources Association's "Core Categories for Visual Resources" (Version 2.0, 1997), and two metadata specifications derived from Dublin Core for specific domain applications, namely, that of Consortium for the Interchange of Museum Information (CIMI) (1999), and the set for the Gateway to Educational Materials (GEM) (1998) are of relevance to the present discussion. Not only did each schema seek to describe Web-enabled digital resources unique to their respective cultural domains, but they also signaled the beginning of a movement toward greater convergence across formerly diverse and somewhat disconnected disciplines and institutions. The "cross-pollination" of approaches to describing resources and collections was one tangible connection within a series of organizational linkages that have gained in momentum over the past decade. The footprint of the *Anglo-American Cataloguing Rules*, for example, can be discerned within the structure and content of the TEI header. Although inadequate for archival description with its emphasis on organic collections (*fonds*), and collection level finding aids, bibliographic description has provided a logic and structure after which rules for archival description and the derivation of the EAD for finding aids could be modeled.

While differences between the tools of bibliographic control and of metadata application still remain, however minor in nature or interpretation, the similarities have become sufficient–at least in the minds of members of the bibliographic control community–to warrant a confluence in terminology and definition. Note Huthwaite's reference in her title (2003) to *AACR2* and *Other* Metadata Standards [emphasis added], and Tillett's assertion (2003, 106) that, "The standard elements and prescribed order of elements presented in our cataloging rules can be viewed as a *metadata schema*" [emphasis added]. It is not clear whether or not this tendency towards terminological congruence is shared equally in the "digital library" domain. Lynch (1998, 118) has observed that, "It should be clear that 'metadata' is not simply a new, more prestigious term for descriptive and subject cataloging. Traditional bibliographic description is only a small part of the broad range of metadata needed to support the discovery, retrieval, use, and management of digital objects." Likewise, as recently as 2001, Lagoze had commented that, "While the size and changeability of the Web makes professional cataloging impractical, a minimal amount of information ordering, such as that represented by the Dublin Core (DC) may vastly improve the quality of an automatic index at low cost; indeed, recent work suggests that some types of simple description may be generated with little or no human intervention" (p. 1). At second glance, differences in perspective might be more apparent than real, particularly given agreement that a base level metadata record can be automatically generated and, as appropriate or necessary, enhanced subsequently through human intervention.[7]

THE ROAD TO CONVERGENCE

It might have become evident that, in much of the preceding discussion, the focus has been on resource *description*, and the bibliographic codes and metadata schemas that have been devised for that purpose. In conceptualizing the road to convergence, resource description, or describing digital objects for resource discovery, serves as the roadbed on which other layers of convergence have been built. In his introduction to the Resource Description Framework (RDF), Weibel (1997, 1) suggested that, "The Internet can be thought of as a World-Wide Commons in which many previously-distinct resource description communities are mixed together." His observation that globally distributed networking had lessened the barrier of geographic locale as impediment to communication, is equally attributable to cultural institutions, the resources that they preserve and make accessible, and the services that they offer. When museum artifacts, archival *fonds*, and library collections become *digital* documentary evidence of a larger cultural milieu, then the distinctions between and among the institutions that formerly held only physical resources and collections become less precise. Thus, having electronic resources that reside in digital repositories, and can be accessed and shared across a common communications network (Internet, Intranet, etc.) brings together a series of issues and challenges–such as resource description and delivery–that were previously addressed individually by separate cultural institutions. Bibliographic description, archival description, and cataloguing museum artifacts can be seen to be overlapping activities when the item or object shares the same "carrier"–the digital format. Yet, as Dekkers (2001, 1) observed, "Until some time ago, everybody who needed to define a metadata element set (or *schema*) to be used for a particular project or collection of resources, invented their own solution."

Both the logic of, as well as recognition of the potential for, sharing rich metadata for resource description and discovery–the opportunity of schema interoperability–have become apparent as more and more sophisticated projects have been undertaken, element sets have been continuously refined, and applications have matured. At the same time the demand for both digital cultural content, and the structured, standards-based resource descriptions that the overseers of those collections create–both from cognate institutions and more broadly in government, industry, and other knowledge-intensive enterprises–has risen substantially. Gill (2004, 1) provides context for the nature and extent of that demand as follows:

> Unlike much of the information available on the Web, digital cultural content from so-called '*memory institutions*' (Dempsey, 1999) is typically authoritative, high quality, useful for education and research and has a broad appeal to a wide range of audiences. As a result, there is a big impetus to make interoperable digital cultural content available via the Internet.

Given the considerable expense of creating high quality resource descriptions, there are economies of scale to be exploited by identifying domain best practice, harvesting and reusing authoritative records[8] (much as bibliographic utilities have done since the 1970s), and benefiting from the processes and experiences of other cognate institutions.

Yet, as Caplan (2000) notes, there are fundamental challenges to bringing together a heterogeneous group of players who have been working in isolation[9] for a long period of time. There is little or no shared history of working together, and little or no professional vocabulary in common.[10] Each group is associated with different standards organizations, and all have goals and values that are not necessarily aligned. Thus, while the knowledge base is rich, and the potential for collaboration brimming to overflow, fundamental "communal infrastructure and commonality of interest" (Caplan 2000, 2) are lacking. Assuming that these essential gaps can be filled, there remain legitimate reasons as to why a standards-in-common solution poses its own enduring problems, even within the compelling context of interoperability. Competition for market share, anti-trust laws within commercial applications, the inconvenience (and expense) of implementing a standard that is of primary benefit to others, the need for flexibility in innovation and testing, the inherent dynamism (instability and continuous upgrade) of information technology, and the considerable length of time required for developing, implementing, and evaluating a new standard (the standards development life-cycle), may conspire against full collaboration–and particularly international collaboration–among diverse interests and organizational imperatives. Caplan (2000, 2) observes that, "standards are almost by definition the product of compromise," adding that, "It is extremely unlikely that a standards-based solution, whether it be a protocol or data dictionary or procedure or format, can be as efficient and effective for any particular application as a solution tailored to that application. You nearly always give something up when you adopt a standard."

Nonetheless, it must be said that, in the process of giving something up, there is often (usually) something to be gained. Despite the obvious challenges, the allure and perceived benefit of "something gained" seem to be winning out, and the impetus towards greater collaboration gaining momentum. If agreement on standards-in-common remains daunting in the shorter term,[11] interest in, and adoption of, conceptual models and frameworks with the potential for application beyond the domain for which they were initially devised,[12] seem–and are–more readily achievable and now actively underway (see also footnote 9). The Open Archives Initiative Protocol for Metadata Harvesting (OAI-PMH), for example, supports interoperability by defining a minimal or "basic level" of metadata (Dublin Core in the case of OAI) which repositories must use in encoding records for their digital objects in order to facilitate harvesting. Likewise, the Metadata Encoding and Transmission Standard (METS) schema, an initiative of the Digital Library Federation, was developed for encoding descriptive, administrative, and structural metadata for managing objects within a digital library, and exchanging those objects between and among repositories. METS documents can serve as a Submission Information Package (SIP), an Archival Information Package (AIP), or a Dissemination Information Package (DIP) as defined within the Open Archival Information System Reference Model–a standard initially developed for space data systems. In general, then, resource description interoperability is being facilitated where syntax level conversions (XML-rendered metadata) are readily supported through open source or commercial products.

FUTURE DIRECTIONS: POSSIBILITIES AND IMPLICATIONS

While not yet a seamless superhighway, the road to convergence is, nevertheless, under construction and well underway. What does the path laid down so far tell us about where we may be headed? In 1997, an international invitational conference was held in Toronto, Canada, to discuss the principles and future direction of the *Anglo-American Cata-*

loging Rules (1998). Participants analyzed position papers and presentations, formulating a number of bold recommendations for the Joint Steering Committee to undertake as part of its subsequent strategic plan. Among these was the proposed rethinking of the logic and structure of *AACR*, reconsideration of the primacy of physical format ("the carrier") as the basis for resource description, and fundamental restructuring of the rules dealing with serial publications (continuing resources). Within three years, the Library of Congress hosted another international conference, the Bicentennial Conference on Bibliographic Control for the New Millennium (2001), where a broad range of issues related to bibliographic control were assessed alongside of, and in relation to, emerging metadata standards and applications. The interplay of so-called "legacy" and "new" fostered lively discussion, and a set of action items for the Library of Congress to pursue across the short- and longer-term periods.

While important events themselves, within the history of bibliographic control, both conferences illustrate the trend to express or frame the extensive, accumulated body of practice associated with resource description. Notwithstanding Cutter's "objects" (1904), and the Paris Principles of 1961, the standards bodies responsible for the *Anglo-American Cataloguing Rules*, and the *International Standard Bibliographic Description*[13] have been working towards re-articulating bibliographic description within the theoretical or conceptual framework of the *Functional Requirements of Bibliographic Records* (1998). While perhaps seeking to have theory inform practice, engaging in more rigorous modelling[14] provides a framework for resolving problems in a logical, systematic fashion. While in its early stages, it remains to be seen how and how well conceptual modelling will be applied in practice, and interpreted by systems designers and users as a consequence.

For its part, the "metadata community"–assuming such a distinction can and should be made–appears to have been engaging in a process similar to that of the "bibliographic control community" (same *caveat*), although in a different direction. Initially devised as a framework, most metadata schemas have come *de facto* to incorporating the key lessons of application into conceptual underpinnings. Just as if MARC21 had been devised prior to resource description, and was–along with the descriptive cataloguing rules of *AACR* and *ISBD*–the beneficiary of the trial-and-error that comes with a steadily increasing number of "real world" examples, so, too are schemas, such as Dublin Core, enhancing their metadata based on actual use. The introduction of "qualifiers" for selected Dublin Core elements is an example of one such rethinking within the metadata community.[15] Likewise, the focus on developing "application profiles" unique to a particular domain or discipline (Weibel and Koch 2000) indicates a recognition of differences that must be acknowledged and distinguished among general purpose metadata schemas (such as Dublin), regardless of their initial intent. Even the most highly specialized, carefully devised, and meticulously monitored metadata schemas must and do respond to exigencies posed by day-to-day application.[16] Thus, it appears that, while the bibliographic control community is advancing theory to inform its longstanding and extensive application, the metadata community is learning from experience to inform its conceptual frameworks. Hence, opportunities for learning from one another abound, and will prove constructive to enhancing the overall goals of quality description for effective resource discovery.[17]

The efforts toward better theoretical modeling informed by application of standards that are, themselves, iteratively enhanced, will move the processes of electronic resource description–inherent to both bibliographic control and metadata–along the road to a potentially new role beyond the institutional boundaries of libraries, archives, and museums. The need and demand for high quality metadata (and metadata records), well structured and authenticated within a standards-compliant environment, have risen dramatically as more resources come to be added to both Internet and Intranet repositories. For organizations or institutions that have been engaged in the creation and exchange of such records, as the EU-NSF Working Group on Metadata has observed (1999, 2), a role as trusted third-party provider of resource descriptions represents a logical extension. Moreover, such bodies can be counted on to have identified, preserved, and described only those digital objects that are of value, and that represent the more enduring of the vast array of Web-enabled resources available via the Internet. Clifford Lynch (1998, 119), among others, has suggested that, ". . . we are moving into an environment where attention, rather than information, is the scarce resource: There is too much relevant information." Identifying and packaging the best of the most worthy is where cultural institutions have excelled. Extending that expertise into the broader worlds of public and private sector enterprise can surely be of mutual benefit. And while adoption of the role as trusted third-party provider might seem a logical end-point for current activities in the bibliographic control and metadata communities collectively and respectively, the route that cultural institutions ultimately will choose to pursue remains an unknown.

CONCLUSION

Just as internationally determined codes and standards (*ISBD*, *AACR*, authority control, subject access, classification systems, etc.) have fostered the goal of universal bibliographic control, so, too, have syntactic structures, semantic element sets, transmission protocols, cross-schema mappings, and metadata harvesting tools been instrumental to realizing the concept of interoperability. In their respective roles as "change-agents" or catalysts to universal information access and exchange, bibliographic control and metadata seem less like "two solitudes," and more akin to soul-mates. When this comparison in no longer worthy of discussion, we can be assured that the status of the latter has been achieved, and the stairway to interoperable heaven finally climbed successfully!

NOTES

1. Available at URL: http://www.global-reach.biz/globstats/index.php3. Accessed 09/09/04.

2. To put this in perspective, in 2002, Canada, which has the highest percentage of Internet users per capita in the world, reported that 60.8% of its population of 31.4 million was connected, whereas only 5.5% of the 1.3 billion population of the People's Republic of China (PRC) used the Internet. Source: The Economist Intelligence Unit Limited, 22 April 2002, c 2004. Available at: http://www.ebusinessforum.com/index.asp. Click on Global News Analysis and search under "China Internet." Accessed 09/09/04.

3. Available at URL: http://www.pcplus.co.uk/news/default.asp?pagetypeid=2&articleid=5393&subsectionid=360. Accessed 09/09/04.

4. Elaine Svenonius has suggested the addition of "navigate" as a fifth functional requirement.

5. The element "Audience" was added to the core set in 2001; "Provenance" and "Rights Holder" were added in 2004. *See also* URL: http://dublincore.org/documents/dcmi-terms/#H3. Accessed 09/29/04.

6. In his keynote address to the Library of Congress Bicentennial Conference on Bibliographic Control for the New Millennium, Michael Gorman (2001, xxv) referred to metadata as "a fancy name for an inferior form of cataloguing," and as "unstandardized, uncontrolled, ersatz cataloguing."

7. This veritable Electronic Cataloguing-in-Publication (ECIP) is being supported currently by the Library of Congress.

8. The potential reuse–and re-purposing–of authoritative legacy data has been recognized by the Library of Congress through its MARC 21 to XML syntactic mapping (*MARC XML Schema*) and Metadata Object Description Schema (MODS) initiatives. Likewise, OCLC's Web Harvester (part of its Connexion and Digital Archive services) captures and converts (renders) metadata in varying formats.

9. Not to mention others–scholarly societies, academic presses and commercial publishers, computer scientists from a variety of venues, researchers in diverse disciplines, hardware and software vendors, digital media specialists–who are all associated with the digital library community (or un-community, as Caplan (2000, 2) characterizes this heterogeneous grouping).

10. Where vocabulary overlaps, operational definitions may differ. By way of illustration, Caplan (2000, 2) refers to the phrase "digital library" which may invoke "software and applications" for a computer scientist, "organizations and services" for librarians and curators, and "collections of electronic materials" for an academic researcher.

11. That Dublin Core has been designated an ISO standard (2003) represents a significant milestone in the development, implementation, and acceptance of cross-domain (or domain-independent) standards.

12. Witness the extension of the *Functional Requirements for Bibliographic Records (FRBR)* to the archival domain (as one example), and the *CIDOC Conceptual Reference Model* for libraries, archives, and museums, deriving from international standards work by the Comité International pour la Documentation (CIDOC) of the International Council of Museums (ICOM).

13. The ISBD Review Group, chaired by John Byrum, Jr., and under the auspices of the IFLA Cataloguing section.

14. In the case of the *Functional Requirements of Bibliographic Records (FRBR)*, the use of the entity-relationship (ER) model derived from database modeling techniques.

15. A development greeted with mixed reaction (cf. Lagoze 2001).

16. MARBI, the Canadian Committee on MARC, and the Permanent UNIMARC Committee (PUC)–to name a few–are evidence of rigorous and iterative enhancement of communications formats for machine-readable records based on continuous feedback from practitioners using the standards.

17. Notwithstanding the need to resolve persistent problems with spamming technologies that undermine greater exploitation of *existing* metadata by search engines. Until what Tim Berners-Lee (1998) has referred to as "the Web of trust" has been realized more fully, and mechanisms for authenticating and validating trusted third-party metadata implemented, harvesting of metadata-enabled records for digital objects will remain largely confined to Intranets, and to secure third-party sites.

WORKS CITED

Anglo-American cataloguing rules. 2nd ed., 2002 Revision. Amendments 2004. Ottawa: Canadian Library Association.

Baker, Thomas. 1999. Organizing access with metadata. *TIAC White Paper on Appropriate Technology for Digital Libraries* http://www.tiac.or.th/tiacweb/Baker/Section2_3.html. Accessed 09/09/04.

Bearman, David, et al. 1999. A common model to support interoperable metadata. *D-Lib Magazine* 5(1). Available at URL: http://www.dlib.org/dlib/january99/bearman/01bearman.html. Accessed 09/09/04.

Berners-Lee, Tim. 1998. *Realizing the full potential of the web*. Available at URL: http://www.w3.org/1998/02/Potential.html. Accessed 09/09/04.

Burnett, Kathleen, Kwong Bor Ng, and Soyeon Park. 1999. A comparison of the two traditions of metadata development. *Journal of the American Society for Information Science* 50: 1209-1217.

Caplan, Priscilla. 2001. International metadata initiatives: lessons in bibliographic control. In *Proceedings of the Bicentennial Conference on Bibliographic Control for the New Millennium: Confronting the challenges of networked resources and the web: Washington, D.C., November 15-17, 2000.* Edited by Ann M. Sandberg-Fox. Washington, DC: Library of Congress, Cataloging Distribution Service, pp. 61-79.

Caplan, Priscilla. 2000. Oh what a tangled web we weave: Opportunities and challenges for standards development in the digital library arena. *First Monday* 5(6). Available at URL: http://www.firstmonday.dk/issues/issue5_6/caplan/index.html. Accessed 09/09/04.

Chan, Lois Mai. 1994. *Cataloging and classification: An introduction.* 2nd ed. New York: McGraw-Hill.

Consultative Committee for Space Data Systems. Recommendation for Space Data System Standards. 2002. Reference model for an open archival information system (OAIS). Blue Book. Issue 1. January 2002. Available at URL: http://ssdoo.gsfc.nasa.gov/nost/wwwclassic/documents/pdf/CCSDS-650.0-B-1.pdf. Accessed 09/09/04.

Cutter, Charles A. 1904. *Rules for a dictionary catalog.* 4th ed. Washington, DC: Government Printing Office.

De Rijk Spanhoff. 2002. Principle issues: Catalog paradigms, old and new. *Cataloging & Classification Quarterly* 35(1/2): 37-60.

Dekkers, Makx. 2001. Application profiles. or how to mix and match metadata schemas. *Cultivate Interactive* 3 (January 29). Available at URL: http://www.cultivate-int.org/issue3/schemas/. Accessed 09/09/04.

Dempsey, Lorcan. 1999. Scientific, industrial, and cultural heritage: A shared approach. a research framework for digital libraries, museums, and archives. *Ariadne* 22 (December). Available at URL: http://www.aridne.ac.uk/issue22/dempsey/. Accessed 09/09/04.

EU-NSF Working Group on Metadata. 1999. *Metadata for digital libraries: A research agenda.* Available at URL: http://www.ercim.org/publication/ws-proceedings/EU-NSF/metadata.html. Accessed 09/09/04.

Functional requirements for bibliographic records (FRBR). Final Report. IFLA Study Group on the Functional Requirements for Bibliographic Records. Munich: K.G. Saur, 1998. Available on the Web at: http://www.ifla.org/VII/s13/frbr/frbr.pdf. Accessed 09/09/04.

Gill, Tony. 2004. Building semantic bridges between museums, libraries and archives. 2004. *First Monday* 9(5). Available at URL: http://www.firstmonday.org/issues/issue9_5/gill/index.html. Accessed 09/09/04.

Gill, Tony. 2000. Metadata and the World Wide Web. In *Introduction to metadata: Pathways to digital information.* Edited by Murtha Baca. Version 2.0. Available at URL: http://www.getty.edu/research/institute/standards/intrometadata/content.html. Accessed 09/09/04.

Gilliland-Swetland, Anne J. 2000. Setting the stage. In *Introduction to metadata: Pathways to digital information.* Edited by Murtha Baca. Version 2.0. Available at URL: http://www.getty.edu/research/institute/standards/intrometadata/content.html. Accessed 09/09/04.

Gorman, Michael. 2001. From card catalogues to webpacs: celebrating cataloguing in the 20th century. In *Proceedings of the Bicentennial Conference on Bibliographic Control for the New Millennium: Confronting the challenges of networked resources and the web: Washington, D.C., November 15-17, 2000.* Edited by Ann M. Sandberg-Fox. Washington, DC: Library of Congress, Cataloging Distribution Service, pp. xix-xxvii.

Howarth, Lynne C. 2004. Modelling a natural language gateway to metadata-enabled resources. In *Knowledge Organization and the Global Information Society: Proceedings of the Eighth International ISKO Conference, 13-16 July 2004, London, UK.* Edited by Ia C. McIlwaine. Würzburg: Ergon, pp. 61-66.

Huthwaite, Ann. 2003. *AACR2* and other metadata standards: the way forward. *Cataloging & Classification Quarterly*, 36(3/4): 87-100.

International Conference on Cataloguing Principles. 1971. *Statement of principles.* Adopted at the International Conference on Cataloguing Principles, Paris, October 1961. Annotated ed., with commentary and examples by Eva Verona, assisted by Franz Georg Kaltwasser, P. R. Lewis, and Roger Pierrot. London: IFLA Committee on Cataloguing.

International Conference on the Principles and Future Development of AACR. 1998. *The principles and future of the* AACR: *Proceedings of the International Conference on the History and Future Development of* AACR, *Toronto, Ontario, Canada, October 23-25, 1997.* Jean Weihs, editor. Ottawa: Canadian Library Association.

International Federation of Library Associations and Institutions. Cataloguing Section. Working Group on the Use of Metadata Schemes. 2005 in preparation. *Guidance on the structure, content, and application of descriptive metadata records for digital resources and collections: Report of the IFLA Cataloguing Section Working Group on the Use of Metadata Schemas.*

ISBD(G): General international standard bibliographic description. 2004 Revision. The Hague: International Federation of Library Associations and Institutions. Available at URL: http://www.ifla.org/VII/s13/pubs/isbdg2004.pdf. Accessed 09/09/04.

Lagoze, Carl. 2001. Business unusual: How "event-awareness" may breathe life into the catalog. In *Proceedings of the Bicentennial Conference on Bibliographic Control for the New Millennium: Confronting the challenges of networked resources and the web: Washington, D.C., November 15-17, 2000.* Edited by Ann M. Sandberg-Fox. Washington, DC: Library of Congress, Cataloging Distribution Service, pp. 269-286.

Lagoze, Carl. 2001. Keeping Dublin Core simple: Cross-domain discovery or resource description? *D-Lib Magazine* 7(1). Available at URL: http://www.dlib.org/dlib/january01/lagoze/01lagoze.html. Accessed 09/09/04.

Library of Congress. 2001. *Proceedings of the Bicentennial Conference on Bibliographic Control for the New Millennium: Confronting the challenges of networked resources and the web: Washington, D.C., November 15-17, 2000.* Edited by Ann M. Sandberg-Fox. Washington, DC: Library of Congress, Cataloging Distribution Service.

Library of Congress. Network Development and MARC Standards Office. *MARC XML schema.* Available at URL: http://www.loc.gov/standards/marcxml//. (Official Web site) Accessed: 09/09/04.

Lynch, Clifford. 1998. Bibliographic description and digital objects: toward a new discipline of information description and management. In *The future of the descriptive cataloging rules: Papers from the ALCTS Preconference*, AACR2000, *American Library Association Annual Conference, Chicago, June 22, 1995*. Edited by Brian E. C. Schottlaender. Chicago: American Library Association, pp. 107-120.

Lynch, Clifford. 2001. The new context for bibliographic control in the new millennium. In *Proceedings of the Bicentennial Conference on Bibliographic Control for the New Millennium: Confronting the challenges of networked resources and the web: Washington, D.C., November 15-17, 2000*. Edited by Ann M. Sandberg-Fox. Washington, DC: Library of Congress, Cataloging Distribution Service, pp. xxix-xxxvii.

Metadata Encoding & Transmission Standard. *METS schema*. Version 1.3 May 8, 2003. Available at URL: http://www.loc.gov/standards/mets/mets.xsd. Accessed 09/09/04.

Metadata Object Description Schema (MODS). Version 3.0 December 2003. Available at URL: http://www.loc.gov/standards/mods/v3/mods-mapping.html#intro. Accessed 09/09/04.

Miller, P. 1996. Metadata for the masses. *Ariadne*, Issue 5 (September 1995). Available at URL: http://www.ukoln.ac.uk/ariadne/issue5/metadata-masses/. Accessed 09/09/04.

Milstead, Jessica, and Feldman, Susan. 1999. Metadata: cataloging by any other name. . . . *Online* (January 1999). Available at URL: http://www.infotoday.com/online/OL1999/milstead1.html. Accessed 09/09/04.

Reynolds, Regina Romano. 2001. Partnerships to mine unexploited sources of metadata. In *Proceedings of the Bicentennial Conference on Bibliographic Control for the New Millennium: Confronting the challenges of networked resources and the web: Washington, D.C., November 15-17, 2000*. Edited by Ann M. Sandberg-Fox. Washington, DC: Library of Congress, Cataloging Distribution Service, pp. 439-462.

Tillett, Barbara B. 2003. *AACR2* and metadata: Library opportunities in the global semantic web. *Cataloging & classification quarterly 36*(3/4): 101-119.

Weibel, Stuart. 1997. The evolving metadata architecture for the World Wide Web: bringing together the semantics, structure, and syntax of resource description. *ISDL '97: Proceedings of [the] International Symposium on Research, Development and Practice in Digital Libraries 1997, November 18-21, 1997, Tsukuba, Ibaraki, Japan*. Tsukuba: University of Library and Information Science, pp. 16-22. Available at URL: http://www.DL.ulis.ac.jp/ISDL97/proceedings/weibe.html. Accessed 09/09/04.

Weibel, Stuart. 1995. Metadata: the foundations of resource description. *D-Lib Magazine*, 1(1). Available at URL: http://www.dlib.org/dlib/July95/07weibel.html. Accessed 09/09/04.

Weibel, Stuart, and Traugott Koch. 2000. The Dublin Core Metadata Initiative: mission, current activities, and future directions. *D-Lib Magazine*, 6(12). Available at URL: http://www.dlib.org/dlib/december00/weibel/12weibel.html. Accessed 09/09/04.

Metadata, Metaphor, and Metonymy

D. Grant Campbell

SUMMARY. Principles drawn not just from library and information science, but also from structuralist literary theory, provide the beginnings of a flexible theoretical framework that will incorporate not just current metadata activities but those in the future that cannot yet be envisioned. A distinction common in literary studies is used here to distinguish between metadata applications for discovery and metadata applications for use. Metadata systems for resource discovery, such as the Dublin Core, are continuous with the traditions of bibliographic description, and rely on a principle of metonymy: the use of a surrogate or adjunct object to represent another. Metadata systems for resource use, such as semantic markup languages, are continuous with the traditions of database design, and rely on a principle of metaphor: the use of a paradigmatic image or design that conditions how the user will respond to and interact with the data.

KEYWORDS. Metadata, cataloging, bibliographic description, literary displacement, synchrony, diachrony, metaphor, metonymy, synechdoche

---

D. Grant Campbell is Assistant Professor, Faculty of Information and Media Studies, University of Western Ontario, London, Ontario N6A 5B7 Canada (E-mail: gcampbel@uwo.ca).

[Haworth co-indexing entry note]: "Metadata, Metaphor, and Metonymy." Campbell, D. Grant. Co-published simultaneously in *Cataloging & Classification Quarterly* (The Haworth Information Press, an imprint of The Haworth Press, Inc.) Vol. 40, No. 3/4, 2005, pp. 57-73; and: *Metadata: A Cataloger's Primer* (ed: Richard P. Smiraglia) The Haworth Information Press, an imprint of The Haworth Press, Inc., 2005, pp. 57-73. Single or multiple copies of this article are available for a fee from The Haworth Document Delivery Service [1-800-HAWORTH, 9:00 a.m. - 5:00 p.m. (EST). E-mail address: docdelivery@haworthpress.com].

Available online at http://www.haworthpress.com/web/CCQ

doi:10.1300/J104v40n03_04

INTRODUCTION

The rise of the term "metadata" as a means of describing and providing access to electronic resources was cause for celebration in the community of Library and Information Science, in the wake of the first Dublin Core meeting in 1995. As a term that evoked both traditional library services of bibliographic control and new Internet functionalities, the term came to symbolize many good things: a fruitful connection with other disciplines, such as computer science; the potential spread of bibliographic control into the thorny region of Web resources; the emergence of librarians as knowledge experts in the new information economy; and the rise of another Golden Age of cataloguing to replace the one Cutter lamented at the end of the nineteenth century (Cutter 1904, 65).

Like all new concepts, however, "metadata" raised some serious problems in the field of library science in particular, and in information services in general. No one, it seems, has been able to agree on a definition that satisfies all of the uses to which the term is put; nor can they agree on the means by which it should be generated, the expertise required to design it, or the contexts in which it can be employed most usefully. This has had serious consequences for professionals within the LIS community, and for those charged with educating them: what skill sets are necessary for making our graduates capable of working in metadata-related positions, and how can we ensure that our graduates are not radically overselling or underselling their qualifications?

Here I argue that we can only grapple with these questions by creating better and more sophisticated frameworks for comparing the acts of information description and representation that occur both in traditional bibliographic control and in newer metadata applications. Because metadata has emerged from multiple disciplines, we need a theoretical paradigm that will enable us to distinguish between different activities that have the same labels, and to recognize similar activities labeled differently; only then will we be able to locate specific metadata activities within a larger context. By using principles drawn not just from library and information science but also from structuralist literary theory, I hope to provide the beginnings of a flexible theoretical framework that will incorporate not just current metadata activities but those in the future that we cannot yet envision.

BACKGROUND

Metadata is difficult to define as an activity for two primary reasons. First, unlike library cataloging, metadata development involves a large number of varied stakeholders. Metadata is not designed or created by a specially-trained cohort of professionals who have a specific skill set and a common slate of objectives. Instead of proceeding from the articulated principles of Panizzi, Cutter, and Lubetzky, metadata design is prompted by instructions from knowledgeable end users: museum curators, mathematicians, geographers, cartographers, and literary scholars. (At the 2002 International Conference on Dublin Core, for instance, the speakers came from areas as diverse as library and information science, computer science, environmental health science, learning and research technology, mathematics, government, bio-informatics, archives, telecommunications, and health sciences.) "Metadata," therefore, is not confined to the information organizational context that we traditionally call "libraries." While concepts of metadata description are often consistent with library bibliographic control, the term also embraces non-traditional information spaces: corporate intranets, digital libraries of various designs and functionalities, and the World Wide Web as a whole. The cataloger who becomes a "metadata librarian," therefore, works uneasily alongside metadata workers who lack a formal training in *AACR2R* and MARC, and who may not even see the relevance of such training.

Second, metadata has evolved from several different communities, each with its own disciplinary background and objectives. In the library community, metadata is seen as a continuation of the practices of bibliographic control: classification, subject headings, and bibliographic description. Arlene Taylor (1999, 77-99), for instance, uses the term "metadata" to describe the ISBD alongside the Dublin Core, the Text Encoding Initiative, the Encoded Archival Description, and the Government Information Locator Service metadata sets. In database design, on the other hand, "metadata" refers to all of the data supplied by the database designer to facilitate the input, manipulation, and presentation of the data itself: the definitions of entities and attributes, the form and query designs, and the report specifications (Kroenke 2000, 577). Records managers refer to metadata as administrative data intended for the organization and administration of records, including version data and copyright information (Roberts and Wilson 2002). And computer scientists and programmers define metadata as data specifically for electronic objects, containing important documentation and processing instructions, either for the user or the system, such as data dictionaries and HTML meta tags (*Tech-Web Encyclopedia*). Such a definition would include as metadata the markup tags in HTML and XML documents: descriptive metadata that surrounds the actual data, enabling browsers and search engines to find, use, and display the document more effectively.

These complexities have forced professionals in various fields to distinguish between various different types of metadata. Caplan (2003, 3-4), for instance, defines three types of metadata: descriptive metadata to support resource discovery, administrative metadata to support resource management, and structural metadata to support resource use. Of these three, two are the most important for catalogers:

- Metadata for resource *discovery*: data such as bibliographic records or electronic headers, either attached to the document or stored separately, explicitly designed to enhance the resource's "findability" within large information stores.
- Metadata for resource *use*: data such as XML markup and database schema, which determine how a document can be used and manipulated.

As a working distinction between different sets of objectives, this separation of discovery and use is highly useful. We must be aware, however, that the division between the two activities is rarely cut and dried; nor is it always possible to separate the two activities. A bibliographic record is metadata that supports the discovery of the resource it describes; the MARC coding is metadata that enhances the use of the bibliographic record. How can we expand on this distinction to make it more useful and flexible for us?

I would suggest beginning with the features that all of these visions of metadata have in common. To begin with, all fields view metadata as data about data. In that sense, metadata are being used to *represent* other data: to describe that data in ways that serve a specific objective. Second, metadata systems serve their various purposes by functioning as specific languages: these languages are subsets of larger languages–programming languages or natural languages–with special, and usually more rigorous, semantic and syntactical rules governing their use. Hence, a Dublin Core record, whatever the content of its elements, is tagged with standard Dublin Core elements such as "Title" and "Creator." A controlled vocabulary describes a resource according to a subset of terms assembled and combined according to certain rules. And finally, metadata is used in contexts where the information is organized on too broad a scale for an individual to handle: it is therefore designed to serve an information system–be it a traditional library, a corporate intranet, or a Web-based repository–that is handled and maintained by a complex network of operations.

LANGUAGE AND REPRESENTATION

A theoretical framework for metadata, then, should begin from these points of commonality. Metadata are designed to facilitate information systems; they function as a specialized language that is similar to natural language, but employed in unique ways; and they serve the purpose of representing information and information-bearing objects. This view is consistent with Svenonius's theory (2000, 3-6) that information organization is drawn partly from systems theory and partly from linguistics. Foskett also emphasizes the linguistic nature of metadata systems for subject access (1996, 97), referring to controlled vocabularies as specialized "indexing languages" constructed according to both semantic and syntactic relationships.

Even more important, there are any number of other fields, particularly in the fine arts and the humanities, which are also based on the systematic use of familiar objects in a specialized way that serves particular needs of representation. Painters and photographers often render familiar objects according to principles of composition that cause us to view those objects in exciting and startling ways. Composers such as Vaughan Williams and Dvorak took popular folk tunes and rendered them in more complex manifestations in their fantasias, dances, and symphonies. In the early twentieth century, the Russian Formalists introduced the term "defamiliarization" to describe the artist's technique of "'estranging,' 'slowing down,' or 'prolonging' perception and thereby impeding the reader's habitual, automatic relation to objects, situations, and poetic form itself" (McCauley 1997). Surely some of these fields can be used to understand the principles by which metadata systems take the familiar things of this information environment and make them strange.

One particularly fruitful area lies in the field of literary criticism and theory, which studies the use of language in works of poetry, prose, fiction, and drama. Writers of imaginative literature use a rich store of rhetorical and figurative devices for representing entities and ideas. As with controlled vocabularies and other metadata standards, these devices use language in a way that differs from "natural language": "all rhetorical figures," argues Northrop Frye (1990, 71), "have some feature that calls attention to their departure from what is normally taken to be the common-sense (descriptive) use of language." Perhaps the most important of these devices for our purposes is the *metaphor* (Abrams 1981, 63): "In a metaphor a word which in standard ('literal') usage denotes one kind of thing, quality, or action is applied to another, in the form of an identity instead of a comparison." If I declare that my love is a tree whose roots grow ever deeper, I am using the image of a tree, with all of its associations, to describe the emotion of love. The power of the metaphor arises partly from the resemblance: presumably my love is growing more deeply rooted and more difficult to dislodge with every passing year. It also arises from the obvious dissimilarities: my love is clearly *not* a tree, and this lack of identity alerts the reader to the presence of imaginative, figurative language.

Closely connected to the metaphor we find *metonymy*, in which "the term for one thing is applied to another with which it has become closely associated in experience" (Abrams 1981, 64). Hence, a "Conference Chair" is associated with the seat which he or she traditionally occupies, and we understand "reading Shakespeare" to mean "reading the works of Shakespeare." In *synechdoche*, a part of something is used to signify the whole: thus, a breadwinner might refer to having "mouths to feed," using the mouth to represent the entire body.

Before the late 1950s, figurative language in literary theory was generally used to understand "what the author said," or "what the author meant." In the 1960s, however, the rise of structuralism greatly enhanced the sophistication of literary analysis and its discussion of these rhetorical figures. Drawing on Aristotle's distinction between form and content, authors such as Frye, Roman Jakobson, and Roland Barthes drew attention to the fact that literary language, like any other language, has its linguistic rules and practices; that literary works employ structures defined by convention and genre; and that these structures have an intrinsic meaning related to, but distinct from, the semantic content of the words in the document. The dominant relationship, in this view, is not necessarily the literary work's relationship to the physical, social, or psychological reality it is striving to represent, but rather its relationship to other literary works. *King Lear*, for instance, has closer and more meaningful ties to *Oedipus the King*, *The Spanish Tragedy*, and *Death of a Salesman* than to the history of early Britain. Poetics–the study of language used in a literary way–presents the collective body of literature as a coherent system, larger than any one contributor, indeed larger than any single institution of control.

Poetics, then, like bibliographic description, constitutes a series of specialized languages that are embedded in, but distinct from, natural language, that draw attention to their own differences from natural language, and that work within larger systems of meaning that are drawn from their inter-relationships within bodies of literature, in addition to their connections to what lies outside literary systems. Structuralist theory, therefore, which examines linguistic systems as self-enclosed and self-referential structures of meaning, should have some light to shed on the practice of metadata, both in its traditional garb of bibliographic description and its newer manifestations as Dublin Core headers, TEI headers, Encoded Archival Descriptions (EADs), geospatial information, and the like.

Three concepts in particular are worth exploring: synchronic and diachronic views of language, metaphor and metonymy in signification, and literary displacement.

Synchronic and Diachronic Views of Language

This distinction, introduced by Ferdinand de Saussure (1985, 29), suggests that any language at any time can be viewed from two different perspectives. The *diachronic* perspective looks at the historical development of language: the etymology of the vocabulary, the introduction of new concepts, the growth of new distinctions. In literary studies, such a view might involve examining the evolution of such genres as tragedy or romance over time, or the mutations of the heroic poem into the mock-heroic poem. In bibliographic control, such a view could incorporate the growth of cataloguing paradigms over time, tracking the development of authority control, the history of main entry, the revision of the *Anglo-American Cataloguing Rules*, or the development of the International Standard Bibliographic Description. Such a view might also be used to develop a theory of the development of basic bibliographic units: recent research into "the work" as a key entity in library catalogues, such as Smiraglia's "taxonomy of derivation," has used diachronic perspectives to study the ways in which a single work can give birth to any number of derivative works (2001, 41-44).

The *synchronic* perspective examines the relationships between the different elements of a language at a given moment in time. In England, at the end of the eighteenth century, the word "frank" was sometimes used as a verb signifying "to pay one's way." In 1793, therefore, the verbs "to frank," "to fund," and "to pay" would have been considered roughly synonymous. With the passing of that usage, that synonymy has since lapsed, and the English language of 2004 has very different relationships. In bibliographic description, this synchronic perspective is used to establish controlled vocabularies and name authorities: specifying which terms, for the purposes of the catalogue, will be considered either synonymous or related in some hierarchical or associative fashion. In metadata systems, the synchronic perspective occurs through the growing use of namespaces and ontologies: the use of previously defined term sets and the linking of those term sets into defined relationships, to facilitate cross-domain resource discovery.

Metaphor and Metonymy

Roman Jakobson, in 1960, transformed the synchronic/diachronic tension into a distinction between two kinds of signification that has since become seminal in both structuralism and semiotics (1985, 166). When studying specialized uses of language, such as can be found in literary works, we can distinguish on the one hand language that works according to metaphor: the formation of a connection based on simultaneous identity, in which the features of the one entity are used to help the reader interact with the other. When Edward Fitzgerald's translation (1986, 1224) of *The Rubáiyát of Omar Khayyám* states that life is "a checkerboard of nights and days," where destiny "moves, and checks, and slays," the familiar image of the checkerboard "saturates" the reader's perception of life, and the familiar, if ruthless, moves of checkers helps the reader grasp, if not comprehend, the unfamiliar features of life and destiny.

With the rise of graphical user interfaces, HCI specialists have been preoccupied with developing "interface metaphors": visual depictions of the user's tasks, which enable the user to draw on a familiarity with one domain, such as the conventional desktop, to navigate an unfamiliar information space (Toms and Campbell 1999). In bibliographic control, metaphor can be found in the development of standardized paradigms that dictate the structure of bibliographic descriptions, such as the International Standard Bibliographic Description. Similarly, the relationship between a bibliographic record and the MARC coding that makes it readable is a metaphorical relationship; in XML and HTML, the markup tags that pervade the document create an identity between the specific document and a predefined "document type," an identity which enables the browser and other devices to retrieve, manipulate, and present the document in useful ways.

By contrast, some poetic language works according to principles of metonymy, in which the relationship between the two entities is one of contiguity and association, rather than simultaneity and identity. Between you and disaster, declares Shaw's King Magnus to his cabinet, "stands the throne" (Shaw 1956, 77). Clearly, the monarch is not the throne; nor do the attributes of the physical throne of England serve any particular purpose. Instead, the throne is a *surrogate* for the king, with all of his administrative and social power.

Cataloguers know all about surrogates: indeed, the only distinction lies between simple metonymy, in which the two entities are associated but physically separate, and synechdoche, in which a part of the entity is taken for the whole. In creating a bibliographic record, the cataloguer typically selects a source of information, such as a title page, that stands as a synechdochic representative of the whole document: that part which can most effectively "speak" for the whole in a cataloguing situation. The record itself, however, typically is stored separately, and serves as a metonymically-related representative of the resource in the catalogue.

In electronic resources, metadata is sometimes embedded into the headers of the document in a synechdochic relationship: Dublin Core elements can appear in the <META> tags of an HTML header, while the Text Encoding Initiative has an elaborate header for its semantically-coded documents that function as both title page and surrogate for the document for retrieval purposes. Similarly, metadata repositories, such as those using the Open Archives Initiative Metadata Harvesting Protocol, explicitly separate the metadata from the data, creating repositories of Dublin Core records, which are stored in various diverse places.

Displacement

In his work on romance, myth, the Bible, and literature, Northrop Frye incorporates the distinction between metaphor and metonymy into a vast paradigm of human expression. This paradigm rests on the perception of a central core of human thought: the point where the sacred and the secular meet, a point defined by metaphor. The metaphor, which creates an identity that is both apt and yet untrue, connects with the concept of myth, which is historical and yet a-historical (Frye 1977, 72):

> [T]he metaphor conveys an explicit statement, based on the word "is," along with an implicit one that contradicts it. Just as myth

> says both "This happened" and "This can hardly have happened in precisely this way," so metaphor with the "is" . . . conveys implicitly the sense "A is quite obviously not B. . . . " Just as myth is counter-historical, asserting and denying its historical validity at the same time, metaphor is counter-logical.

If myth based on metaphor lies at the heart of Frye's literary, mythological, and spiritual universe, other genres are defined as a series of progressive "displacements" from this core. Romance, for instance, is metonymic, rather than strictly metaphorical; the structures of romance are surrogates of mythical structures, rather than direct expressions of them, displaced "in a human direction and yet, in contrast to 'realism,' [tend] to conventionalize content in an idealized direction" (Frye 1977, 137). And realism, in its documentary adherence to particular times and places, is even further displaced; in realism, the reigning structures of myth and romance are still there, but are obscured, or "displaced," by an often-illusory commitment to "real life." Hence, these structures are much more difficult to identify, and operate on the work in a more subtle and oblique way.

If we used Frye's paradigm as a way of sorting out the various activities of bibliographic description and metadata systems, we see something that looks roughly like Table 1.

At the metaphoric level, whose literary analogue for Frye would be myth, we find those metadata systems that are focused on information resource use. In conventional bibliographic systems, this would include the International Standard Bibliographic Description, which determines the content of bibliographic records, and MARC coding, which enables those records to be transferred and manipulated electronically. Database metadata–the specifications of rows and columns–would also come under this category, as would the semantic markup that pervades an XML document, such as a literary work marked up according to the Text Encoding Initiative or a pathfinder marked up in EAD. In all of these cases, the specific data of the resource has been defined as a particular type: "this document IS A novel"; "this resource IS AN archival pathfinder." The defined document type, recorded in a Document Type Definition (DTD) or an XML Schema, defines and labels the particular parts of a resource, thereby determining how the resource can be used.

At the metonymic level, we have what Frye would term "romance." In conventional bibliographic control, this level would include bibliographic records themselves, which act as surrogates for documents. In electronic metadata systems, this level would include all metadata that

TABLE 1. Displacement in Cataloging and Metadata Systems

Figurative Device	Literary Analogue	Traditional Cataloging Analogue	Metadata Systems Analogue
Metaphor	Myth	Coding issues: MARC ISBD Crosswalks	A TEI vision of XML schemas, marked up documents
Metonymy	Romance	Bibliographic description	Metadata descriptions: TEI Header Dublin Core EAD
----	Realism	Serendipity idea	Free-text searching, formulation of individualized pathways, derived structure

is used to identify and represent another resource, such as a header in Dublin Core, a TEI header, an archival pathfinder itself (regardless of the coding), or a Dublin Core description in a metadata repository. This is the level of resource discovery, rather than use: the metadata descriptions stand in place of the data they describe, frequently because, due to their smaller size, they are more easily saturated with the metaphoric structure than the original document. A bibliographic description, for instance, rearranges the eccentric and frequently ambiguous information in a document into a heavily structured bibliographic description, which is encoded for maximum manipulation.

Beyond this level, we move into what Frye would term realism: where the underlying structures of literature have been displaced to the point of near-invisibility, and the reader's attention is focused on the individual details; in *Oliver Twist*, for instance, the romance structure of quest and homecoming, while still potently present, is submerged in a highly detailed depiction of London in the early 19th century and a deep concern with contemporary social issues of the day. In traditional bibliographic control, this perspective is implicit in the use of classification systems for physical collections. The user may be strolling through the stacks, relying on "serendipity" to discover interesting or useful materials, but behind these apparently chance encounters lies a system that makes the progress along a shelf relevant and meaningful. In metadata systems, this view is most frequently expressed through the various attempts to derive structure, often automatically, rather than imposing it directly through human intervention. The ranking systems of search engines like Google, for instance, attempt to use link frequency to create a hit list that places the most relevant sites at the top; automatic indexing systems attempt to index documents according to word frequency. RSS newsfeeds attempt to harvest blog and news entries into uniform, regularly-updated presentations; bibliometrics seeks to discover unseen patterns in a wealth of seemingly random bibliographic data.

BIBLIOGRAPHIC DESCRIPTION

In a conventional library catalogue, the document acquired for cataloging and storage has generally reached a point where no further alterations are permitted; indeed, this typographical fixity is considered by many to be the feature of the printing press that most powerfully transformed Western thought and scholarship (Eisenstein 1983, 51). Therefore, the distinction between metaphoric metadata and metonymic metadata is relatively straightforward. (See Figure 1.)

The bibliographic record stands in a metonymic relationship to the printed book which it represents; while the description does little to facilitate the use of the book once retrieved, it assists the user in discovering the existence and salient bibliographic features of the book, should it be required. If this metonymic purpose is to be fulfilled, however, the bibliographic record itself needs to be manipulated and used. The record is therefore infused with a standardized structure–The International Standard Bibliographic Description–which ensures that each description in the catalogue will have the same sequence of elements, described and identified in the same way. Furthermore, the record is coded with MARC field delimiters, subfield delimiters and indicator values, which make it machine-readable, as well as human readable, and enable the record to be sorted, displayed, and transferred as required.

METADATA

Because electronic documents often enable machine-readable interpretations of their contents, the relationship between metonymic and metaphoric metadata becomes more complicated. (See Figure 2.)

Here we have an XML version of *Wuthering Heights*, presumably part of a digital collection of literary texts, which has been marked up according to an initiative that has established a standard definition for a novel, with a header that encodes basic bibliographic information in Dublin Core elements. Furthermore, this header has been exported to a

FIGURE 1. Metadata Configuration for Conventional Bibliographic Description

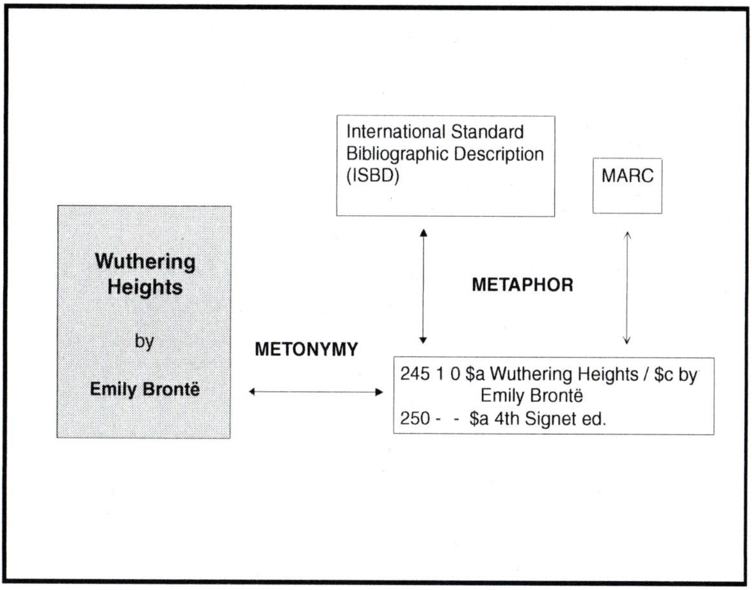

metadata harvesting service, which stores metadata for multiple digital collections in a specialized repository. In this example, we have two pieces of metonymic metadata:

- The description in the metadata repository, which represents the electronic document stored elsewhere;
- The description in the document header, which functions as a synechdoche, representing the entire document of which it is a part.

We also have two sets of metaphoric metadata:

- The semantic XML tags, which surround the actual text of the novel; these tags establish that this piece of XML data is a *novel*, consisting of chapters and paragraphs;
- The semantic XML tags, which surround the metonymic metadata, which identify that the metadata conforms to Dublin Core specifications, and consist, in this abbreviated example, of a title and an author.

FIGURE 2. Metadata in an Electronic Resource

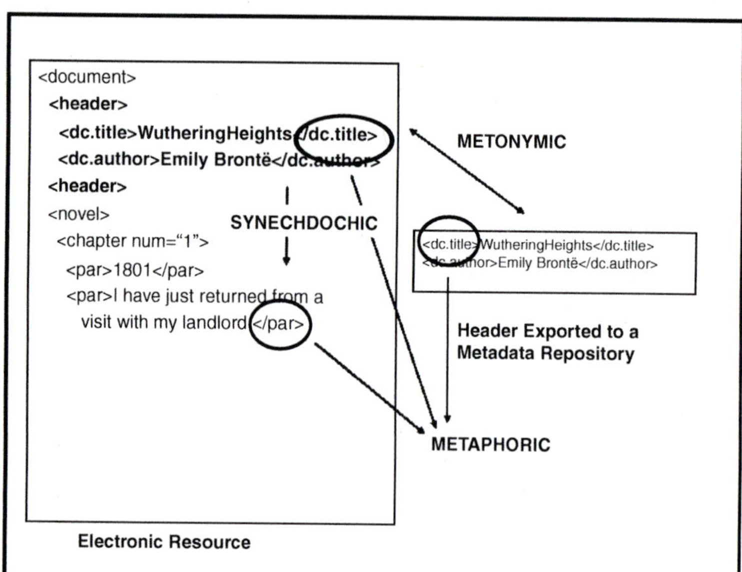

IMPLICATIONS AND LIMITATIONS

This paradigm, linking as it does the range of metadata activities to a model of system, structure, and heightened language use, contains three primary advantages. First, it emphasizes that every activity of information representation and organization involves some mixture of the two extremes of metaphor and metonymy: the most detached surrogate is enshrined in code that makes it operable within large systems, while the most pervasive markup or database metadata exist to represent a structure or model of a specific information domain. It therefore becomes possible to chart various metadata activities along a continuum that represents the various mixes between metaphoric and metonymic metadata. This will hopefully make it possible for employers seeking professionals for metadata projects to specify more clearly the mix of expertise they require, and for various professions to select their preferred position along this spectrum.

Second, the connection to literary language, although by no means the only connection possible, serves to emphasize the complexity and intellectual richness of information representation, both in its traditional library forms or its new metadata forms. Too often, the process of information organization–whether the creation of metadata headers, the design of automatic indexing systems, authority control, RDF schema, or ISBD revision–is seen as the process of stripping away ambiguity and complexity to find the "simple" truth underneath. In fact, the act of information representation is a process of defamiliarization, as surely as are the poetic devices identified by the Russian Formalists. Blindness to this fact has prevented us from accurately assessing the role of automation in information description; by refusing to recognize the intellectual richness of our own field, we are unable to recognize and defend those points where human interpretation can be used to its optimal advantage.

Finally, the complex inter-relationship between metaphoric and metonymic perspectives in modern metadata systems is leading the field of traditional cataloging into a far more intimate relationship with document content than it has ever held previously. Because metadata in the form of markup and database design pervade electronic data, rather than simply pointing to them metonymically, these metadata become an intrinsic part of the document structure, imposing machine-readable classifications of the document's genre, and determining how the document will be machine-processed and machine-understood. As the Semantic Web pioneers new methods and algorithms of document searching, this intimate relationship between data and metadata will have a profound effect on how we manipulate and access the enormous information stores of the future. Tim Berners-Lee dreams of a Web in which we do not enter search criteria: instead, we ask questions, and the spiders read the semantic metadata of various resources to select data from multiple sources that directly answer the question (2000, 185). The answers to our questions, therefore, will be intimately affected by the metadata used to encode all of these data.

This leads us to a potential danger with a structuralist attitude toward information systems: a danger long articulated in literary circles. Because this approach favours the connection of entities within the system, it sometimes gives insufficient attention to other meaningful and important relationships. Frye was attacked long ago for perceiving his mythological paradigm as a transcendent literary system and ignoring the political views–"somewhere between liberal Republican and conservative Democrat"–that underlie the paradigm: "it is remarkable," noted Terry Eagleton acidly (1983, 94), "that literature, severed from any sordid practical concern as it is, is in the end more or less capable of telling us which way to vote." Similarly, an excessive focus on finding structural relationships within information systems can lead to blindness towards important issues. Creating interoperable namespaces and crosswalks between metadata systems can ignore the highly specific cultural, social, and intellectual contexts in which many of these metadata systems arose. Cross-domain resource discovery is a fine ideal, as long as we recognize that no two domains are alike, and that there will be occasions when preserving the social context of an information space is more important than designing a system that pulls data from its context into a distorted or over-simplifying structure.

CONCLUSIONS

Bibliographic control has traditionally imposed order upon the seeming chaos of the bibliographic universe, by subjecting individual documents to a rigorously-structured set of metonymic descriptions that enable these documents to be found under various useful circumstances. Catalogers have traditionally had little influence over how these documents are read and used once retrieved. However, with the rise of new metadata systems, which infiltrate the documents themselves and affect the way they are used, cataloging has moved into new and daunting territory, in which our traditional role as information intermediaries has become less rigidly defined and more subtly powerful. A "metadata librarian," of the sort described in modern job advertisements, is moving into regions where it will be impossible to hide behind the rationale of resource discovery. This new professional will be moving into the realm of document use, and will need, in addition to new software, new training, and a new vocabulary, a new theoretical frame to navigate this realm effectively and ethically.

WORKS CITED

Abrams, M.H. 1981. *A Glossary of Literary Terms*. 4th ed. New York: Holt, Rinehart and Winston, p. 63.

Berners-Lee, Tim, with Mark Fischetti. 2000. *Weaving the Web: The Original Design and Ultimate Destiny of the World Wide Web*. New York: HarperBusiness, p. 185.

Caplan, Priscilla. 2003. *Metadata Fundamentals for All Librarians*. Chicago: American Library Association, p. 3-4.

Cutter, Charles. 1904. "Rules for a Dictionary Catalog: Selections." 4th ed. Reprinted in *Foundations of Cataloging: A Sourcebook*. Edited by Michael Carpenter and Elaine Svenonius. Littleton: Libraries Unlimited, 1985: p. 65.

de Saussure, Ferdinand. 1985. "The Linguistic Sign." *Semiotics: An Introductory Anthology*. Edited by Robert E. Innis. Bloomington: Indiana University Press, 1985: p. 29.

Eagleton, Terry. 1983. *Literary Theory: An Introduction*. Oxford: Blackwell, p. 94.

Eisenstein, Elizabeth L. 1983. *The Printing Revolution in Early Modern Europe*. Cambridge: Cambridge University Press, p. 51.

Fitzgerald, Edward. 1986. "The Rubáiyát of Omar Khayyám." *The Norton Anthology of English Literature*, Vol. 2. 5th ed. Edited by M. H. Abrams et al. New York: Norton, p. 1224.

Foskett, A.C. 1996. *The Subject Approach to Information*. 5th ed. London: Library Association Publishing, p. 97.

Frye, Northrop. 1977. *Anatomy of Criticism: Four Essays*. Princeton: Princeton University Press, p. 137.

Frye, H. Northrop. 1990. *Words with Power: Being a Second Study of 'The Bible and Literature.'* Markham: Viking, p. 71.

Jakobson, Roman. 1985. "Closing Statement: Linguistics and Poetics." *Semiotics: An Introductory Anthology*. Edited by Robert E. Innis. Bloomington: Indiana University Press, p. 166.

Kroenke, David M. 2000. *Database Processing: Fundamentals, Design & Implementation*. 7th ed. Upper Saddle River: Prentice Hall, p. 577.

McCauley, Karen. 1997. "Russian Formalism." *The Johns Hopkins Guide to Literary Theory and Criticism*. [online]. [cited 6 July 2004]; available from: http://www.press.jhu.edu/books/.

"Meta-data." *Tech-Web Encyclopedia*. [online]. [cited 6 July 2004]; available from http://www.techweb.com.

Roberts, John, and Wilson, Andrew. 2002. *International Recordkeeping/Records Management Metadata Initiatives: Report and Recommendations for DC Advisory Board*. [online] April 23, 2002. [cited 6 July 2004]; available from http://dublincore.org/groups/government/DCMIResourceManagement.html.

Shaw, George Bernard. 1956. *The Apple Cart*. Middlesex: Penguin, p. 77.

Smiraglia, Richard P. 2001. *The Nature of "A Work": Implications for the Organization of Knowledge*. Lanham: Scarecrow Press, p. 41-44.

Svenonius, Elaine. 2000. *The Intellectual Foundation of Information Organization*. Cambridge: MIT Press, p. 3-6.

Taylor, Arlene G. 1999. *The Organization of Information*. Englewood: Libraries Unlimited, p. 77-99.

Toms, Elaine G. and Campbell, D. Grant. 1999. "Genre as Interface Metaphor: Exploiting Form and Function in Digital Documents." *Proceedings of the Hawaii International Conference on System Sciences*. IEEE.

An Exploratory Study of Metadata Creation in a Health Care Agency

Leatrice Ferraioli

SUMMARY. Traditional paper documents, as containers of information, remain a primary source of organizational knowledge, and function as vehicles of communication. Despite the increasing use of electronic mail and other digital technologies, the entrenchment of paper documents in the fabric of work practices demands that attention be paid to how they are managed for organizational effectiveness. The workplace is likened to an information-ecology where the study of personal classification schemes can be firmly positioned within an epistemological framework. Temporal, spatial, and contextual factors influenced the creation of three levels of personal metadata along a continuum of abstraction. Loss of intellectual content may occur equally as a result of both high and low levels of abstraction. Personal metadata were also found to reflect the participant's situational and domain specific knowledge.

Leatrice Ferraioli is Performance Improvement Coordinator, VNA of Long Island Inc., 100 Garden City Plaza, Suite 100, Garden City, NY 11530 (E-mail: LeaFerraioli@aol.com).

[Haworth co-indexing entry note]: "An Exploratory Study of Metadata Creation in a Health Care Agency." Ferraioli, Leatrice. Co-published simultaneously in *Cataloging & Classification Quarterly* (The Haworth Information Press, an imprint of The Haworth Press, Inc.) Vol. 40, No. 3/4, 2005, pp. 75-102; and: *Metadata: A Cataloger's Primer* (ed: Richard P. Smiraglia) The Haworth Information Press, an imprint of The Haworth Press, Inc., 2005, pp. 75-102. Single or multiple copies of this article are available for a fee from The Haworth Document Delivery Service [1-800-HAWORTH, 9:00 a.m. - 5:00 p.m. (EST). E-mail address: docdelivery@haworthpress.com].

Available online at http://www.haworthpress.com/web/CCQ

doi:10.1300/J104v40n03_05

KEYWORDS. Knowledge domains, discourse communities, information ecologies, personal metadata

INTRODUCTION

The act of classification is a primary tool in knowledge organization. Classification, therefore, is a central activity engaged in by the individual to impose order and structure upon his information or knowledge universe. The ultimate goal for which classification strives is the future retrieval of information or knowledge for use by the individual. Therefore, an effective classification scheme necessarily overlays a consideration of information seeking and retrieval. The identification of classification as a central activity in documentary organization has been noted by Marco and Navarro (1993, 126). Further, document seeking and retrieval, as a crucial area for information science, proceeds from the searching of supplementary information about an item or the identification of items that correspond to certain formal document attributes (Albrechtsen and Hjørland 1997, 137).

However, classification, as a scholarly activity and integral part of the profession or science of information studies, would seem to suffer from something of an identity crisis. A prevailing practice is for indexers, who are "subject experts," to classify documents through seemingly ad hoc methods (Hjørland 2002b, 450). Such subjectivity on the part of the individual indexer, therefore, necessarily introduces a bias in the classification process (Quinn 1994, 140). On the other hand, attempts to introduce a level of objectivity to classification methodology fail to offer a fully satisfactory solution. An objectivist approach aims to discover the objective rules used by indexers while, at the same time, it is known that the current state of modern information retrieval is one that, oftentimes, is unable to successfully meet user needs based on the mismatch between indexer terms and user queries. If one accepts the inherently social and pragmatic nature of classification, it becomes evident that classification research needs to be nested within an epistemological framework that supports a paradigm shift towards historicism and pragmatism.

What becomes of interest in the study of the methodology of classification, therefore, are several elements: the notion of document, the mechanism by which knowledge organization is accomplished through representation, the personal human factors that mediate the process of classification, and the placement of classification within an epistemological framework. Each of these concerns will be discussed as a backdrop for the rationale of this study.

Traditional paper documents, as containers of information, remain a primary source of organizational knowledge, as well as function as vehicles of communication. Despite the increasing use of electronic mail and other digital technologies, the entrenchment of paper documents in the fabric of work practices demands that attention be paid to how they are managed for organizational effectiveness. While many conceptions of "document" have evolved from the nineteenth century documentalists' to contemporary views, documents in this study refer to text records manifested in paper form within an office setting. One important comparison, however, between the views of the documentalists and more modern viewpoints will be seen to have significance in this study. That is, emphasis is now placed on the social construction of meaning and the user's perception of significance and evidential character of documents. In particular, the notion of relevance is considered to be situational and ascribed by the viewer (Buckland 1998, 218).

Rationale for the study of how effectively paper documents are classified finds support in the fact that, over the course of the year 1999, global paper output increased by 4.6% to a total of 316 million tons. The top producer was North America, with an output of 108 million tons in 1999. Specifically, office paper use constitutes 30%-40% of total paper consumption (Sellen and Harper 2002, 10, 11). The widespread use of paper documents also comes at a cost. One such cost relates to the filing and retrieving of documents in light of the estimate that 3% of all paper documents are filed incorrectly, and almost 8% are eventually "lost." Such intellectual loss is compounded by a monetary cost of upward to $120 per misfiled document (Sellen and Harper 2002, 28, 29).

The effective management of paper documents, therefore, requires the imposition of some classificatory structure. The subsequent representation and organization of documents, then, becomes a chief task of knowledge organization. The concept of document representation, in the form of metadata, takes on central import in this study as its role in effective classification and retrieval is highlighted. Many purposes of metadata have been recognized, among them the description of the attributes of a resource that ultimately support its discovery, management, and effective use (Vellucci 2000, 34). It is this function of metadata, that of resource description for discovery, that is the focus of this study, as metadata are critical components in the context of knowledge representation (Ercegovac 1999, 1165).

The process whereby metadata are created by the individual human indexer in a paper-based environment has not been the focus of scholarly inquiry compared to that of automated metadata generation for the digital environment. Therefore, in the absence of an overarching system of information organization and management, documents can be poorly classified leading to ineffective retrieval. Thus, how documents are ultimately represented through human-created metadata and subsequently classified is the primary research question to be addressed by this exploratory study. With no structure at all, people find it difficult to categorize documents and often get lost in their own filing systems (Sellen and Harper 2002, 37). The lack of an organizational schema is compounded by the human factors that influence the classification process. Perception of document contents, representation of the knowledge, and the assignment of a storage spot is accomplished by the individual without benefit of guidelines or training in knowledge organization or classification theory (Mackenzie 2000, 408).

How then does, or indeed can, the study of personally constructed classifications be a legitimate scholarly pursuit in information studies? The grounding of user-created metadata studies and socially constructed classification schemes within an epistemological framework of historicism and pragmatism can provide the foundation for the continuing study of such context-dependent inquiry. A classification always reflects some values, priorities, and views of what is classified and what goals the classification is intended to support (Hjørland and Albrechtsen 1999, 134).

The purpose of this paper is to explore how metadata are created by the individual for the purpose of document representation and organization for retrieval. As little is known concerning the personal metadata creation process by individuals, methodologies of the qualitative paradigm were employed. A case study approach in a health care agency employed semi-structured interviews, structured observations, and verbalizations with two administrative staff members. It is hoped that the preliminary data obtained concerning the cognitive processes brought to bear on the representation of documents based on individual background, perspective, knowledge, and situation will inform the study of personal metadata development as a legitimate concern within the field of information studies. The study of such personal classification schemes might, therefore, have implications for future developments in digital technologies that support effective information retrieval. Further, the embedding of a unique line of scholarly inquiry within an epistemological paradigm can advance information science as well as inform differing views of knowledge.

THE PHILOSOPHY-EPISTEMOLOGY LINK

How one conceives of knowledge and its representation and classification will have an impact on how scholarly research progresses and what are deemed legitimate avenues of inquiry. A constraining effect is thus created, which might lead to missed opportunity and discovery. Worse might be the pursuit of any inquiry without integration into an epistemology. The shift from the classical idea of a universe of knowledge reflected in a perfect classification scheme to one that embraces the individual in a context-dependent environment where social and cultural factors are influential has been discussed by several scholars (Hjørland 1998b; Mai 1999; Jacob 2000).

The theories of classical empiricism and rationalism view knowledge as neutral or value-free and as something that exists and can be classified outside the scope of human influence. As such, the classic tradition of classification theory posits a separation between man and nature and has as its task the description of an objective non-human nature. The underlying premise is that there is such a universe of knowledge that can be mapped (Mai 1999, 549). In its espousal of a fundamental dichotomy between subject and object, the modernist philosophy assumes the ability of rational science to uncover the underlying laws of cause and effect (Jacob 2000, 16). The role of language in this philosophical stance becomes significant in that it, necessarily, must be rational and, in essence, prescribed. Such a universal language refers to a tongue that would have the ability to provide every representation, and every element of every representation (Foucault 1970, 84). Likening a classification scheme to a well-constructed language, then, supports the effective representation and organization of knowledge by establishing a standardized and invariant pattern of universal reality (Jacob 2000, 17).

In his case study of the classification of psychology, Hjørland (1998b) demonstrates how different approaches to classification have been applied to the classification of psychology. Although the field tends to see itself as a "natural kind," it is, perhaps, better understood as a "social construction." He further asserts that classifications cannot be neutral regarding approaches or theories about its subject matter. On the contrary, the classification of a subject field requires a conception or view of that particular field (Hjørland 1998b, 164). Therefore, the belief that classifications are not neutral leads to a consideration of a shift toward historicism and pragmatism as a fruitful underlying epistemology for classification research.

Historicism is a philosophy that emphasizes that perception and thinking are always influenced by our language, culture, by our pre-understanding and "horizon" (Hjørland 1998a, 608). The notion of context, then, factors heavily into such an approach. The term "contextualizing" stands for the process of how people come to know or make sense of their situation (Solomon 2000, 254). A classification system within an historicist epistemology, therefore, is based on the development of knowledge producing communities. Knowledge domains as discourse communities rather than the individual, then, become the focus of information science research. According to Hjørland and Albrechtsen (1995, 400), knowledge organization, structure, cooperation patterns, language and communication forms, information systems, and relevance criteria are reflections of the objects of the work of these communities and of their role in society.

Closely tied to historicism is the pragmatic philosophy, which is oriented to the future and toward the fulfillment of human goals. Hjørland (1999, 134) states that research must be built on a historical and pragmatically oriented epistemology as information science seeks to organize knowledge for optimizing human learning and utilization of knowledge. Knowledge must, therefore, be examined within its historical, social, and cultural context. The exploration of the metadata creation process by human indexers, whose subjectivity comes to the fore as a consequence of their particular situation, would, therefore, seem to fall most reasonably within the epistemological framework of historicism and pragmatism. The discussion to follow will expand on the notions of discourse community, knowledge domains, and the influence of culture on classification methodology.

DOMAIN ANALYSIS

The domain-analytic paradigm in information science states that the best way to understand information in information science is to study the knowledge-domains as thought or discourse communities (Hjørland and Albrechtsen 1995, 400). The behavior of the individual as a primary research focus is, therefore, subsumed to his membership in a working group. Further, the domain-analytic perspective necessarily invites inquiry into the social and functional aspects of informational behavior.

As such, this paradigm is consistent with the epistemological framework of historicism and pragmatism. To classify a knowledge field is, thus, to take part in the dialog and evaluation of goals, values, and consequences of doing science in one way or another. It is to examine the "cultural warrant" of both knowledge production and its organization (Hjørland and Albrechtsen 1999, 135). Cultural warrant, as described by Beghtol (2002, 45), posits that every classification system is based on the assumptions and preoccupations of a certain culture and that a knowledge organization system is more likely to be useful and appropriate for those who are members of a culture. Rejection of a universal classification scheme in favor of a plurality of knowledge, thus, occurs at both the individual and group level.

The domain-analytic approach would seem to lend itself to consideration of the notion of ontologies based on specific knowledge domains or work communities. Knowledge representation, if viewed as a way to codify domain knowledge, must take into account both subject knowledge and conscious choice about what one deems to be relevant. Therefore, some concepts will necessarily be rejected in favor of others. This notion of "ontological commitments" views knowledge representations as imperfect approximations of reality, thereby forcing the selection of what one sees as meaningful and sufficient to interpret the world through representations adequate to a certain task or goal (Binwal and Lalhmachhuana 2001, 6).

What this means for the present discussion of classification theory within a historical and pragmatic epistemology is that information studies should respond to the emerging and continual influences of cultural and social factors that mediate the classification of knowledge. Historicism, also known as social constructivism, views knowledge as the product of historical, social, and cultural factors where fundamental concepts are, in turn, culturally determined and domain-dependent (Albrechtsen and Jacob 1998, 296). This approach has led to research on work-based classification schemes that is particularly relevant and lends theoretical support to this study of personal metadata creation.

Likening the workplace to an ecology broadens the view of classification to include the structuring of knowledge base contents to suit the individual's information needs during decision making. Thus, ecological schemes require field studies of the search questions and the need formulations as they occur in the work situation (Pejtersen and Albrechtsen 2000, 98). It is suggested that ecological theory may inform the human metadata creation process through a consideration of the social constructivist theory of semantics, which implies that meanings are constructed in social discourse (Hjørland 1998c, 23). The enactment of a diverse information ecology in which interacting machine and human resources collaborate to serve users will, like a natural ecology, provide the most robust, balanced system in which life flourishes to the fullest (Nardi and O'Day 1996, 86). The study of personal classification schemes can, therefore, occupy a legitimate place on the information science research agenda as such inquiry finds support in the study of work domains and ecologies within the historic and pragmatic traditions.

METHOD

Assumptions and Rationale for a Qualitative Design

This exploratory research was conducted within the qualitative paradigm using the case study method. The nature of the research question, which is to discover the ways in which individuals create metadata, necessitated a qualitative approach in that the influence of values, meaning, interpretation, and context played a primary role in data collection and in the ultimate explanation of the phenomena being investigated. Qualitative researchers are interested in meaning–how people make sense of their lives, experiences, and their structures of the world (Creswell 1994, 145).

The intent of qualitative research is to understand a particular situation by the researcher placing himself or herself in the natural setting where human behavior and events occur. Therefore, participant's perceptions and experiences become the focus and meanings and interpretations are negotiated. The resultant investigative process will be focused on the researcher's goal to make sense of a phenomenon. Use of the qualitative paradigm was also supported as little is known about the research topic under investigation.

The Case Study Approach

The case study method was appropriate in that a single entity or agency was examined within the constraints of time and activity. This can be likened to the instrumental case study whereby a particular case is examined mainly to provide insight into an issue (Denzin and Lincoln 2000, 437). This single case will be seen to be a complex entity grounded within a number of contexts: interpersonal, cultural, heuristic, etc. The holistic case study, therefore, calls for an examination of these complexities. The research question posed and the observations made formed the organizational structure within which the research occurred. Both methods addressed user perception, cognition and behavior and, thus, attempted to orient the researcher to complexities connecting ordinary practice in the natural setting to abstractions (Denzin and Lincoln 2000, 440).

The Researcher's Role

One assumption of the qualitative paradigm is that the researcher is the primary instrument in data collection. As such, it becomes necessary to identify any personal values and biases at the outset of the study. From 1995-2000 this researcher was employed at the research agency as a senior level administrator, second in line to the CEO. In that capacity the researcher worked with both participants. The work unit to which both participants are assigned is that of performance improvement and staff development. In their roles as the Director and Assistant Director, they occupied a "subordinate" position to the researcher although there was no direct organizational reporting relationship. In the researcher's prior position, responsibility for daily operations, regulatory compliance issues, and human resource functions allowed for directives to be given and responded to by the participants as their work unit fulfilled an organizational support function. The researcher is currently employed at the research agency in a consultant and special projects capacity on a per-diem basis.

However, the researcher believes that personal and professional understanding and knowledge of the organizational context and culture enhances researcher awareness and knowledge of the processes examined in the exploration of the research question. It is recognized, however, that the introduction of certain biases is inevitable. Such biases may shape interpretation of the data but reasonable effort has been made to ensure an acceptable level of objectivity. With consent of the Long Island University Institutional Review Board, data collection occurred on November 15, 2002, and November 18, 2002.

Data Collection

This study was conducted on-site at a not-for-profit certified home health agency located on Long Island, New York. The agency employs approximately 100 employees (professional and non-professional) and provides diverse health care services to approximately 3,000 eligible clients per year in Queens, Nassau, and Suffolk counties. The participants were the Director of Performance Improvement/Staff Development and the Assistant Director of Performance Improvement/Staff Development of the research agency who have been employed in this capacity for 2 years and 4 months and 6 years and 9 months, respectively. These participants were chosen based on the likelihood that they would, necessarily, interact with a large volume of paper documents and, therefore, maintain a large paper document filing system.

A face-to-face interview was conducted with each participant in her private office during a regular working day. An interview guide was developed to explore the personal construction of classification schemes as expressed through participant description and explanation. Predetermined questions were formulated by the researcher to elicit participant description of cognitive interpretation of behaviors with, and decision making concerning, documents. The researcher employed probing, as needed, to seek clarification or otherwise augment researcher understanding. Prepared questions were asked in the same order to each participant and did not contain any terminology likely to be unfamiliar to the participant, i.e., metadata. Handwritten notes were recorded by the researcher during the interview. The notes consisted of both selected verbatim participant responses and initial researcher comments and reflections. Immediately following the interview session, the researcher added additional personal comments and interpretations upon a review of the interview data in its totality for later analysis.

At a second session on another day following the interview, each participant was asked to interact with their incoming documents in their usual manner while the researcher observed. In addition, each participant was asked to verbalize as she interacted with the documents. The researcher, again, recorded handwritten notes of the participants' actions, verbalizations, and decisions. Researcher interpretation and comments were, again, noted during the observation period, which lasted approximately 25 minutes. The researcher also received permission to review each participant's work files, both paper and electronic, where applicable. The researcher noted such things as number of files, subject headings, duplications, and location.

A second observation occurred later on the same day. In this observation, each participant was given a document, selected by the researcher, and instructed to process it as a normal incoming document while verbalizing their thoughts. The subject matter of the documents was selected especially so as not to be directly within the work domain of the participant, i.e., health care related, performance improvement/quality assurance, education/training issues, etc. The rationale for this decision on the part of the researcher was to "force" participant evaluation of the document at a more granular level. Therefore, any "standardized" response by the participant, as might be expected with documents related to usual work issues, would be ameliorated. The researcher, again, recorded handwritten notes of the participants' behaviors and verbalizations. It is noted, however, that each person who conducts observational research brings distinctive talents and limitations to the enterprise; therefore, the quality of what is recorded becomes the measure of usable observational data rather than the quality of the observation itself (which is, by definition, idiosyncratic and not subject to replication) (Denzin and Lincoln 2000, 676).

Ethical Considerations

Several safeguards were employed to protect the participant's rights and confidentiality as well as that of the organization. Written authorization was obtained from the CEO allowing the research to be conducted on-site at the research agency and granting the researcher the right to review confidential organizational documents and files. Consent was also obtained from each participant agreeing to be the subject of an interview and structured observations. Explicit information outlining the participant's rights, use of the data by the researcher in reporting, and the protection of confidential data by the researcher were also provided as part of the written consent.

Data Analysis Procedures

Data analysis proceeded simultaneously with data collection and interpretation. Initial researcher comments and interpretations were noted during the interview as well as during the observations. A content analysis of the data was performed whereby data were "reduced" and interpreted as the researcher re-examined data to begin to sort it into emerging categories for further analysis. Multiple iterations were performed on the data as researcher interpretations were formulated. The following strategies were employed to ensure data quality (Creswell 1994, 142): (1) Triangulation of data: data were collected through interviews, verbalizations, and observations; (2) Member checking: the participant served as a check throughout the collection and analysis process. On-going validation of the researcher's interpretation of the participant's meanings occurred and ensured the truth value of the data; and (3) Clarification of researcher bias: researcher bias was articulated in a previous section of this paper. The intent of the study was to form a unique interpretation of events at the research agency. Therefore, concerns for generalizability were not preeminent. However, the themes that emerged during data analysis, as well as through the data collection protocol, are replicable.

METADATA AND RELATED ISSUES

Metadata

The ability of metadata to fulfill the goal of high level contextual meaning in the digital environment is less certain than in the uniquely creative intellectual process brought to bear by the individual during interaction with a document (Ferraioli 2001, 3). It is this belief that provides an underlying impetus to the study of human-created metadata for use in personalized classification schemes. Metadata inserts a layer of human intervention and interpretation where words are actual bearers of meaning and significance. Documents are seen as relevant to a given search because their value and purpose is assessed only according to the way they are represented and interpreted in the metadata that describe them (Friesen 2002, 1). Therefore, the process by which documents are represented through metadata that are the product of a uniquely individual process has merit for continuing inquiry by the scholarly community.

The concept of meaning, then, takes on a primary role in effective document representation and classification. Meaning, however, is not static or consistent either among different individuals or, indeed, for a single individual. Documents remain the same but contextual meaning and use will vary. One reason for an expected variability in meaning relates to the use or expected use of documents and information by different groups. Any terms used to describe a document are necessarily a reflection of the individual indexer's interpretation. Interpretation, in turn, evolves from the indexer's "contextual place" within a larger group. This position has been recognized by Wenger (1998, 4) who discusses social participation that shapes not only what we do, but also who we are and how we interpret what we do. Extending this notion to metadata, then, suggests that static description and technical document representation, likely, fails to capture the essence of rich meaning and context. The meaning of any set of terms, therefore, can be evaluated only in the context of a community whose members are involved in similar activities and share similar values (Wenger 1998, 53). A mismatch or inconsistency between index terms created by a user and indexer is assumed to be higher than that between or among indexers because of the difference in perceived meaning of the document between them (Park 1996, 420). This further supports the significance of communities of practice as an influential factor in the construction of meaning.

One study that examined the practices associated with metadata creation for a collection of physical slides and digital images (Marshall 1998, 10) can provide some insight as well as support for the methodology used in this study. In this ethnographic study, interviews were conducted with and observations made of staff at a university library and educational technology center. A significant conclusion was that at the field site, naturally occurring metadata that arise out of a collection's development and use show great promise of enhancing the collection's description and access.

Subject Determination

Closely linked to the practice and conception of document representation is that of subject analysis. Determining what a document is about, however, can be problematic and less than satisfactory as a basis for metadata development and ultimate resource discovery. The Dublin Core Element Set aims to provide a framework for the creation of metadata that is consistent. The Guidelines for the Creation of Content for Resource Discovery Metadata of the National Library of Australia (2002, 4) are based on the Dublin Core and define *subject* as the topic of the content of the resource. Ten guidelines for *subject* are given, such as the recommended use of a thesaurus, use of unstructured keywords (if a thesaurus is not used), avoidance of broad terms, and use of names if the item is *about* a person or organization.

However, these guidelines operate from the assumption that subject determination is a neutral and static process, something that can be accomplished from some compression of the semantics of a document. The ever changing complex and rich tapestry that is everyday individual experience and interaction with the world cannot, in such a scheme, be brought fully to bear on this issue. A more useful and fruitful conception of subject analysis recognizes the reality that user needs are not static nor are they the product of a unidimensional intellectuality.

Hjørland (1998a, 611) posits a "sociological-epistemological paradigm" or "domain analytic" approach that recognizes that any given document may serve different purposes for different user groups. This approach embraces contextual meaning as central to subject definition and, necessarily, supports the belief that a document has an infinite number of subjects. Therefore, the process of subject analysis is one of giving priority to those subjects that best serve the needs of users of the information system in question (Hjørland 1998a, 610).

A notable illustration of a social construction of a subject can be seen in Huber and Gillaspy's (1998) treatment of HIV/AIDS. The inherent complexity of this disease, which embodies a myriad of physical, psychological, social, and political manifestations, cannot be contained in a single description or definition. The authors recognized that social perceptions of this disease, coupled with an exponential growth of information, converged to create an information environment in need of some control while maintaining a degree of fluidity so as to appropriately meet the needs of users. The organizational schema of a controlled vocabulary was intended to facilitate knowledge organization relative to HIV/AIDS while being reflective of the biomedical and non-biomedical complexities associated with the disease. Similarly, the structure needs to remain flexible enough to accommodate discourse evolution while the controlled vocabulary is representative of the intricacies that define the body of knowledge associated with the disease (Huber and Gillaspy 1998, 206).

Finally, the firm embedding of subject fluidity within a philosophical framework is expressed by Hjørland's (1998a, 610) definition of the subject of a document as the epistemological potentialities of that document.

Relevance

The prior discussion on subject analysis suggests that *subject* is not an objective notion. Correspondingly, the idea of an objective relevance, as judged by "subject experts," falls short of providing satisfactory information retrieval outcomes. An important point is made by Harter (1992, 603) in distinguishing between the notion of relevance as related to topicality and how relevance is actually used in an everyday sense. He indicates that in ordinary language usage, relevance does not mean "on the topic." Rather, it implies a relationship between an assumption and a given context. This relationship, then, adds or decreases information, offers a new perspective or, otherwise, causes a cognitive change. Thus, a subjective or user-based relevance is the antithetic notion put forth. However, Harter extends this notion to one of psychological relevance as manifested through the retrieval of documents that "bear on the matter at hand."

Picking up on the thread of Hjørland's position on the definition of a subject, one can posit a relationship between subject and relevance. Namely, if a subject is an "epistemological potentiality," then a subject can have different relevances. This relationship is supported through Hjørland's (2002a) analysis of four schools of psychology and their implicit relevance criteria, which are different even when addressing the same subject. His results demonstrated that if one regards behaviorism, cognitivism, neuroscience, and psychoanalysis as different approaches to psychology, each with their own core journals, then those views overwhelmingly determine the use of information sources, information needs, and relevance in library and information science. He concluded that an epistemological approach is necessary and that such "mental models" are historical, cultural, and social products (Hjørland 2002a, 267).

RESULTS

The primary aim of this exploratory study was to determine the ways in which an individual creates personal metadata for the purpose of classification and organization of documents in the work setting. The data suggest that both physical document attributes and non-document attributes affected how documents were represented for classification. This result finds support in an earlier study by Kwasnik (1991) who found that physical attributes, form, author, topic, and title were used in making classificatory decisions. In addition, situational attributes, time and other non-document dimensions were also found to factor into classification decisions. Figure 1 illustrates document attributes and Figure 2 illustrates non-document attributes that were broadly developed from the interview, verbalization, and observational data. Identified categories are not mutually exclusive across attribute type. *Subject/topic* as a document attribute is related to *intellectual content* as a non-document attribute. *Time* also emerges under each category of attribute but in differing contexts.

FIGURE 1. Document Attributes Affecting Metadata Creation

Sender/author of document	Use of headers, title lines, etc.
Perceived subject/topic/title	Use of title lines, bolding, etc.
Time	Due dates, formatting cues
Genre	Newsletters, journal articles, memos, etc.
Formatting	Use of bold, italics, etc.

FIGURE 2. Non-Document Attributes Affecting Metadata Creation

Location within work space:
- -close proximity (on desktop)
- -bookcases
- -filing cabinets ("archives")
- -in computer (electronic files)

Time sensitivity issues (work imposed time constraints, deadlines, etc.)

Intellectual content

Perceived relevance:
- -immediate, personal, and to others
- -future, personal, and to others

Perceived value:
- -interesting
- -relevant
- -important

Reading behavior:
- -skimming
- -scanning
- -reading

Document Attributes

Sender/Author/Title was identified by both participants as an attribute that engages their attention immediately and consistently upon initial document interaction. Judgments concerning the sender were seen to result in three activities: retention and filing of documents in a discrete collection; discarding documents; or retention and filing in a "holding pattern" file. Of particular significance was the identification of a perceived power component attached to the document based on the sender. For example, both participants indicated that if the document's sender was the CEO, it would be read fully and immediately at the initial interaction. One participant then filed these documents in a file labeled with the CEO's name, while the other participant filed such documents in a file labeled "Memos" as this is the primary form of inter-agency communication. Neither representation would appear to be of sufficient granularity to effect the retrieval of specific documents based on their intellectual content. Both participants stated that they "would have to go through the entire file to find something."

Documents were perceived as "junk mail" based on the sender, i.e., conference organizations (particularly if not health care related), book publishers, consulting services, etc. Such documents were sometimes not opened at all, the decision to discard based on the sender as indicated on the envelope, and discarded immediately.

A final activity involved filing documents in a file labeled as "Miscellaneous." Although the sender might not be judged as important, the subject or content of the document, having been determined by either reading fully or scanning, can result in the document being retained. Again, retrieval effectiveness is seriously affected by the lack of a sufficiently specific document representation. Although one participant verbalized that her intention is to review the documents in the miscellaneous file periodically to make final disposition decisions, this is, in fact, not done with any regularity. The potential "loss" of documents is, therefore, a real concern. However, on occasion, when this review of documents is done, they might be classified differently and moved to a discrete file or else discarded. Time constraints during the work day were cited by both participants as the primary reason for creating a file labeled as "Miscellaneous."

Subject/Topic/Title attributes are discussed in the aggregate as they formed a general construct of interpretation for both participants. Title lines, and use of bolding and other formatting features assisted both participants in making a decision as to the topicality of documents. Subject determination was made from the title of documents, such as journal articles, work-based newsletter articles, and on the basis of the participant's judgment of intellectual content. One participant was observed to use physical document cues, primarily, while the other participant tended to read more upon initial interaction with documents and, therefore, determine subject matter apart from total reliance on a document's title. The investment of more time in reading up front resulted in the integration of information within the participant's mental framework. One participant verbalized that a particular professional newsletter article, whose title contained the words "patient privacy," was, in fact, "about" and applicable to the Health Insurance Portability and Accountability Act (HIPAA) regulation. Therefore, the subject of this particular document was determined to be "HIPAA" and was filed under this heading. This level of specificity in the file name was seen to be the result of the participant's immediate work related situation. This participant was charged with the responsibility for preparing a continuing education program for all agency staff on this regulation as required by state and federal mandate.

The *Genre* of documents seen in the work setting primarily fell into the categories of internally generated memoranda, state and federal communications, which take the form of administrative memoranda or bulletins, industry specific professional newsletters, and internally generated reports, which are manifested in a variety of standardized agency formats.

Genre, as a specific variable, was not seen to be particularly instrumental, in and of itself, in the metadata creation and classification process. Rather, it was the work-related use of particular documents and reports and their relationship to the current work situation of the participants that affected the metadata created. A similarity was seen between both participants when their work file names were compared. Most file names were descriptively related to work-based tasks, projects, and reports for which the participants were responsible. Examples of file names that correspond to work-related reports were "Exit Interview Tracking," "Infection Control," "Competency Evaluations," "Case Conferences," "Needs Assessment Surveys," etc. Based on the particular report or genre, these documents were filed in the participant's filing cabinet or in binders located on bookshelves. The relevance to the work situation was determined to be the primary influence on how such documents were represented.

Non-Document Attributes

File Location–both participants utilized a filing cabinet, bookcase(s), and desk-top files. Functionality of files across physical location parameters was similar for both participants and denoted a time-sensitive work-based relevance. File cabinets contained "archival" files and were used the least. Examples of these files included "Memos," "Forms," and prior years' documents and reports of any type. Documents falling into a mid-range of use were stored in binders on bookshelves. Reference books, policy and procedure manuals, continuing education records, committee meeting minutes, etc., were the typical documents stored in this location.

Paper files located on each participant's desk were those that were interacted with on a daily to weekly basis. They represented current work projects in progress or those pending, typically, within a month's time at a maximum. These files were mostly duplicates of computer files for the one participant who utilized electronic files, and of files located in the filing cabinet of the other participant who only worked with traditional paper documents. File names of the desk-top files were the same as their counterparts. Only their physical location, in close proximity to the user, indicated their prominence within the participant's work schema. For example, the file named "Infection Control–Monthly Reports 2002" was kept in the file cabinet of one participant. The desk-top file was named "Infection Control" and contained information and data being collected for the current month in preparation for report completion.

A clear hierarchical relationship was seen in file location between both participants: desk-top (weekly or daily use); bookcases (less frequent use, less current information); and filing cabinets ("archival" documents, used least frequently).

The assessment of *Intellectual Content* was found to be related to the reading behavior of the participant and a determination of the perceived relevance of the document. This practice was seen more in one participant who, based initially on document cues of subject, sender, and time sensitivity information, for example, engaged in more reading behavior. Becoming more informed allowed for the internalization of information and the engagement of active thinking resulting in the creation of less abstract metadata.

Relevance judgments concerning documents were also tied to whether the participant indicated that a document was "interesting" or "important." The translation of relevance, however, into a decision about metadata was linked to how a document and the information it contained was situated within the participant's work-related environment. One participant indicated that documents "personally relevant to my own job" were identified by their intellectual content and given file names that were highly descriptive of a work-related task or report to be produced.

The lack of or perceived lack of *Time* was seen to be a primary determinant in the extent to which reading, scanning, and skimming behavior occurred. Time sensitivity issues regarding deadlines and other work-imposed constraints also affected where files were kept physically in the work environment and how they were subsequently represented. The use of less granular metadata resulted in "catch all" files and subsequent loss of documents and their intellectual content. Therefore, the failure to create more effective metadata at the time of document evaluation and interaction is a practice that can result in poor retrieval effectiveness.

The relationship that emerged whereby differing levels of term specificity were used for document representations across a work functionality dimension is illustrated in Figure 3. General metadata tended to be used for documents that required no immediate action and whose perceived relevance was indeterminate at the time of initial interaction. More specific metadata were used for documents that were interacted with on a more frequent basis, being related to current work projects. These documents were also mobilized more within the work environment. Specific metadata were reserved for those documents that did not fall within the functional model of the other two categories.

ANALYSIS AND DISCUSSION

The findings of this study, although limited in scope, indicated that the use of physical document and non-document cues interacted within the mental framework of the participants based on their work situation. Evaluation of documents and subsequent creation of document representations for organization and classification were bound to temporal, spatial, and contextual factors related to the participant's activities. These findings contribute to grounded theory in light of similar studies on classification behaviors.

Temporality factors in the classification of electronic mail were exhibited by managers in a study by Mackenzie (2000b). A first level of classification based on immediate need was identified where time emerged as a major factor. Mail was determined to relate to something the manager needed to do, what others needed to do, and what was of interest but required no action. These messages remained in the in-box to facilitate task management through periodic review until tasks were completed or there was a change in their status. A second level of classi-

FIGURE 3. Metadata Abstraction Levels

Primary level metadata (high abstraction)

- -least specific terms
- -time dependent creation
- -relevance indeterminacy
- -skimming

***Benefits*: Ease of creation**

"When I don't have time to read something but want to keep it because it might be useful I just file it in the Misc. file until I can get to it."

***Liabilities*: Ineffective retrieval, "lost" documents**

"I have to look through the whole file to find something."

"Sometimes I forget what I put in it."

Examples: "Memos," "Computers," "Legal Issues," "Misc."

Secondary level metadata (intermediate abstraction)

- -more specific
- -time dependent work-based projects
- -relevance dependent
- -reading, scanning, skimming

***Benefits*: Fast, accurate retrieval, information mobilization**

"All quarterly infection control reports are filed together by year."

"I use post-its to mark things in a file that I need for another report."

***Liabilities*: None**

Examples: "Infection Control Reports," "Utilization Review," "Case Record Reviews"

Tertiary level metadata (low abstraction)

- -most specific
- -relevance indeterminacy
- -reading, skimming

***Benefits*: Ease of creation, facilitates browsing**

"This article's title caught my interest so I read the first two paragraphs. I wanted to keep it–I'll probably read it all at some point."

***Liabilities*: Memory dependent for future retrieval**

"I may not remember that I have this article or what it's about. But, I could find it easily enough by just going through the files."

Example: "Journal article on electronic records"

fication was also identified that was driven by future need. These messages were stored in a more stable scheme (Mackenzie 2000b, 181-2).

A hierarchical schematization was also seen in the present study as participants categorized documents based on time factors and perceived relevance. The assignment of secondary level metadata to current work project files that participants kept on their desk top would seem to align with Mackenzie's findings that managers actively task-manage their in-box. Similarly, her second level of classification, based on future need where messages are classified in a more stable scheme, corresponds to the present study's findings whereby tertiary level metadata were assigned to documents that the participant believed might be useful at a later time.

In the present study, time limitations imposed upon or perceived by the participants were found to influence the rapidity with which metadata were assigned to documents as well as to influence its quality for retrieval effectiveness. This resulted in a high level of abstraction in the document representation. The potential for "loss" of documents and intellectual content was exhibited and such document representation was assigned to documents whose relevance was indeterminate at the time. Documents, thus classified by primary level metadata, were just as likely to include irrelevant information that would be discarded at a later time and documents whose relevance related to a future, but not as yet, unidentified need. While a striking similarity is seen in the influence of time as a variable, in both this and the Mackenzie study, the participants in this study did not consistently engage in in-depth discriminatory cognitive processing at the time of initial document interaction. Therefore, it is suggested that an initial investment of time and attention at the point of document interaction might be necessary in order to create quality metadata capable of aiding in the retrieval process.

Literature on the environment as a factor in organizing schemas is fairly extensive and would seem to have some applicability to the findings of this study. As personal collections of information are the most used of all information resources, it becomes necessary for the individual to be able to create and store such collections in addition to decorative items. Collections are noted to be things like document photocopies, journals, notes, manuals, computer files, etc. (Mann 1993; Barreau 1995; Kwasnik 1991). In this study, the classification of collections of documents was spatially determined. More current and frequently used files were located in close proximity to the participant in desk-top files, while less used and "archival" documents were located on bookshelves and in filing cabinets. Similarly, Hert (1999, 8, 9) found that old files were rarely referred to, individuals did not necessarily know what was in them, or that they were not organized in useful ways. Malone (1983) found that the difficulty of classifying diverse items is an important mediating factor as to where they are physically located in the work space, e.g., the most pressing work is front and center.

In this study, documents relating to current projects were kept on the participant's desk in colored file folders named for the task or report or in the computer as an electronic file. In such a schema, the metadata were clearly visible and allowed for quick access, retrieval, and mobilization. The contextual basis for metadata creation within the physical setting of the workplace has also been noted by other researchers. Context was seen to be an important factor in the interpretation and re-use of documents. In the electronic environment, the date and time information created by the computer added contextual detail beyond the limitations of brief file names (Neumann 1999, 580). The context of the physical and organizational spaces within which metadata systems exist is also cited by Hert (1999, 8). She found that physical aspects such as space and color are routinely used to provide context to enable understanding of information.

Within the framework of temporal, spatial, and contextual influences, there also emerged a tentative schema of metadata creation arranged along a continuum of varying levels of abstraction in terms chosen for document representations. This was seen, in part, to be a function of the process used by the participant in order to comprehend documents during interaction. When dealing with time constraints, participants tended to skim documents, noting document attributes such as the author or title line. The assessment was made, at this point, to either retain the document or discard it. However, for those documents retained, document representation oftentimes failed to progress beyond a generic label. Scanning, on the other hand, which carries a connotation of searching, occurred more frequently in the creation of secondary and tertiary level metadata. Here, the participants engaged in a more intimate relationship with documents, extracting intellectual content and perceiving immediate information relevance in relation to their work tasks and their own domain knowledge. The metadata created as a result of this process tended to be highly specific, corresponding to narrowly prescribed areas such as report names, etc. The conceptual aspect of scanning has been noted to result in the making of inferences and the use of information to produce a coherent representation (Farrow 1991, 153).

The retrieval of intellectual content via the documents in which it is contained requires metadata that possess a certain degree of determinacy. However, it has been suggested by this study that varying degrees of abstraction were used based on reading behavior, time factors, and physical workspace environment. This finding is corroborated by Blair (2001, 285) who states that document representations can vary greatly in their level of determinacy–their ability to precisely identify a given document or set of documents. He cites the example of a document's title as being a highly determinate representation. He then contrasts this with keywords, which represent the intellectual content of a document far less precisely since many documents can, in fact, be represented by the same keyword(s). Although no operational distinction was made in this study between a representation and a keyword, the use of the term metadata encompasses both notions, for all practical purposes.

A low level of metadata abstraction (high level of specificity) may be seen to correspond to Blair's keyword. In both instances, intellectual content is represented. However, one study participant, in using a summarization of the title of a journal article as the file name, achieved a more precise representation than Blair seems to attribute to keywords.

CONCLUSION

In summary, participants in this study exhibited similar behaviors when interacting with documents for the purpose of comprehension and subsequent representation for organization and classification. Time was an influential factor in the metadata creation process in terms of its quality and retrieval effectiveness. Participants tended to devote less attention to the comprehension of a document's subject, meaning, and use when under time constraints. This behavior is expected as deadlines will always dictate the amount of effort expended on any given activity. However, making decisions within a time compressed environment often leads to a greater possibility of satisficing and use of heuristics (Higgins 1999, 134).

Subject determination by the participants was made through the processing of a combination of document and non-document cues. The highly interpretational process of subject analysis was seen as participants evaluated documents against the framework of their work related environment. The involvement in current work projects provided a contextual backdrop against which documents were evaluated more thoroughly, thus, resulting in document representations of less abstraction.

The use of the physical workspace environment was also seen as an integral component of the participants' behavior in organizing documents. Hjørland (1996, 2) treats subject analysis as an interpretational process by which documents are analyzed and explicit subject retrieval data are created. Viewed from a realistic philosophy of knowledge, Hjørland (1996, 3) goes on to posit that the interpretation of a document's "epistemological or informative potential" is a never-ending process. Further, he states that the individual subject's behavior in relation to use and representation of information should be interpreted in light of a disciplinary context. Indeed, the participants in this study were shown to represent documents within the context of their own immediate sphere of activity within a defined domain of knowledge.

Personal metadata, as an ordering device, is a rich and complex compendium of the individual's knowledge, perception, situational boundedness, and membership within a knowledge domain. As such, it is not easily amenable to analysis but the potential it presents in terms of document organization and the enactment of knowledge work far outweighs any expressed disregard for its study within the scholarly community.

Documents retain organizational information and are the repositories of organizational memory and intelligence. The consequences of poor document retrieval can be striking when one considers that it is estimated that one billion documents are created each day in North America and that executives spend 40% of their time dealing directly with documents that might contain as much as 90% of a corporation's information (Blair 2002, 274). How effectively individuals interact with and are able to use documents, therefore, is an important issue to be addressed through continuing study of document representation within an epistemological framework of pragmatism. A pragmatic viewpoint for the study of personal metadata is supported by the fact that there is an inherent creativity to natural language and that document representations are linguistic in nature. Therefore, meanings of keywords that may be extracted from text are not equivalent in meaning to those same terms when used in everyday language. Therefore, language has a pragmatic context, but as has been recognized, a pragmatic context has no equivalent in computerized information retrieval (Blair 2002, 376).

The study of human-created metadata, therefore, represents an opportunity to position this field of inquiry within a philosophy of information studies. Personal metadata are uniquely qualified to articulate the scope, intent, and function of a particular collection of documents. In addition, their ability to describe documents in terms of expected use as well as reflect the fluidity of classification, even as documents remain fixed (Marshall 1998, 1, 2), highlight their potential as a fertile area of scholarly attention.

WORKS CITED

Albrechtsen, Hanne and Birger Hjørland. 1997. Information seeking and knowledge organization: The presentation of a new book. *Knowledge organization* 24: 136-44.

Albrechtsen, Hanne and Elin K. Jacob. 1998. The dynamics of classification systems as boundary objects for cooperation in the electronic library. *Library trends* 47: 293-312.

Barreau, D. K. 1995. Context as a factor in personal information management systems. *Journal of the American Society for Information Science* 46: 327-39.

Beghtol, Clare. 2002. Universal concepts, cultural warrant, and cultural hospitality. In *Challenges in knowledge representation and organization for the 21st century, Integration of knowledge across boundaries, Proceedings of the 7th International ISKO Conference, 10-13 July 2002, Granada, Spain* ed. Maria J. Lopez-Huertas. Advances in knowledge organization v. 8. Wurzburg: Ergon, pp. 45-9.

Binwal, Jagdish Chandra and Lalhmachhuana. 2001. Knowledge representation: Concepts, techniques and the analytico-synthetic paradigm. *Knowledge organization* 28: 5-16.

Blair, David C. 2002. The challenge of commercial document retrieval Part I: Major issues, and a framework based on search exhaustivity, determinacy of representation and document collection size. *Information processing and management* 38: 273-91.

Blair, David C. and Steven O. Kimbrough. 2002. Exemplary documents: A foundation for information retrieval design. *Information processing and management* 38: 363-79.

Buckland, Michael. 1998. What is a document? In *Historical Studies in Information Science*, ed. Trudi Bellardo Hahn and Michael Buckland. Medford, New Jersey: Information Today, pp. 215-20.

Creswell, John W. 1994. *Research design: Qualitative and quantitative approaches.* Thousand Oaks: Sage Publications.

Denzin, Norman K. and Yvonna S. Lincoln, ed. 2000. *Handbook of qualitative research.* Thousand Oaks: Sage Publications.

Ercegovac, Zorana. 1999. Introduction: Integrating multiple overlapping metadata standards. *Journal of the American Society for Information Science* 50: 1165-68.

Farrow, John F. 1991. A cognitive process model of document indexing. *Journal of documentation* 47: 149-66.

Ferraioli, Leatrice. 2001. Genres, personal metadata, and private knowledge. Unpublished paper.

Foucault, Michel. 1970. *The order of things: An archeology of the human sciences.* New York: Random House.

Friesen, Norm. 2002. Semantic interoperability and communities of practice. Accessed at: http://www.cancore.ca/documents/semantic.html.

Guidelines for the creation of content for resource discovery metadata. 2002. Accessed at: http://www.nla.gov.au/meta/metaguide.html.

Harter, Stephen P. 1992. Psychological relevance and information science. *Journal of the American Society for Information Science* 43: 602-15.

Hert, Carol A. 1999. Studies of metadata creation and usage. Accessed at: http://www.fcsm.gov/01papers/Hert.pdf.

Higgins, Margaret. 1999. Meta-information, and time: Factors in human decision making. *Journal of the American Society for Information Science* 50: 132-9.

Hjørland, Birger. 1996. Subject representation and information seeking: Contributions to a theory based on the theory of knowledge. Accessed at: http://www.db.dk/NHS/ARTIKLER/EMNEREPR/eng_sum.html.

Hjørland, Birger. 1998a. Theory and metatheory of information science: A new interpretation. *Journal of documentation* 54: 606-21.

Hjørland, Birger. 1998b. The classification of psychology: A case study in the classification of a knowledge field. *Knowledge organization* 25: 162-201.

Hjørland, Birger. 1998c. Information retrieval, text composition, and semantics. *Knowledge organization* 25: 16-31.

Hjørland, Birger. 2002a. Epistemology and the socio-cognitive perspective in information science. *Journal of the American Society for Information Science and Technology* 53: 257-70.

Hjørland, Birger. 2002b. The methodology of constructing classification schemes: A discussion of the state-of-the-art. In *Challenges in knowledge representation and organization for the 21st century, Integration of knowledge across boundaries, Proceedings of the 7th International ISKO Conference, 10-13 July 2002, Granada, Spain* ed. Maria J. Lopez-Huertas. Advances in knowledge organization v. 8. Wurzburg: Ergon, pp. 450-56.

Hjørland, Birger and Hanne Albrechtsen. 1995. Toward a new horizon in information science: domain-analysis. *Journal of the American Society for Information Science* 46: 400-25.

Hjørland, Birger and Hanne Albrechtsen. 1999. An analysis of some trends in classification research. *Knowledge organization* 26: 131-39.

Huber, Jeffrey T. and Mary L. Gillaspy. 1998. Social constructs and disease: Implications for a controlled vocabulary for HIV/AIDS. *Library trends 47*: 190-208.

Jacob, Elin K. 2000. The legacy of pragmatism: Implications for knowledge organization in a pluralistic universe. In *Dynamism and stability in knowledge organization: Proceedings of the Sixth International ISKO Conference, 10-13 July 2000, Toronto, Canada*, ed. Clare Beghtol, Lynn C. Howarth, Nancy J. Williamson. Advances in knowledge organization v. 7. Würzburg: Ergon Verlag, pp. 16-22.

Kwasnik, Barbara H. 1991. The importance of factors that are not document attributes in the organization of personal documents. *Journal of documentation* 47: 389-98.

Mackenzie, Maureen. 2000a. The personal organization of electronic mail messages in a business environment: an exploratory study. *Library and information science research* 22: 405-26.

Mackenzie, Maureen. 2000b. The classification, storage and retrieval of electronic mail: two exploratory studies. In *Proceedings of the 63rd Annual Meeting of the American Society for Information Science* 37: 177-89.

Mai, Jens-Erik. 1999. A postmodern theory of knowledge organization. In *Proceedings of the 62nd Annual Meeting of the American Society for Information Science* 36: 547-56.

Malone, T. W. 1983. How do people organize their desks? Implications for the design of office information systems. *ACM transactions on office information systems* 1: 99-112.

Mann, T. 1993. *Library research models: A guide to classification, cataloging and computers*. New York: Oxford University Press.

Marco, Francisco Javier Garcia and Miguel Angel Esteban Navarro. 1993. On some contributions of the cognitive sciences and epistemology to a theory of classification. *Knowledge organization* 20: 126-32.

Marshall, Catherine C. 1998. Making metadata: A study of metadata creation for a mixed physical-digital collection. Accessed at: http://www.csdl.tamu.edu/~marshall/d198-making-metadata.pdf.

Nardi, B. and V. O'Day. 1996. Intelligent agents: What we learned in the library. *Libri* 46: 59-88.

Neumann, Laura. 1999. Physical environment as a resource in information work settings. In *Proceedings of the 62nd Annual Meeting of the American Society for Information Science* 36: 572-86.

Park, Hongseok. 1996. Inferential representation of science documents. *Information Processing and Management* 32: 419-29.

Pejtersen, Annelise Mark and Hanne Albrechtsen. 2000. Ecological work based classification schemes. In *Dynamism and stability in knowledge organization: Proceedings of the Sixth International ISKO Conference, 10-13 July 2000, Toronto, Canada*, ed. Clare Beghtol, Lynn C. Howarth, Nancy J. Williamson. Advances in knowledge organization v. 7. Würzburg: Ergon Verlag, pp. 97-110.

Quinn, Brian. 1994. Recent theoretical approaches in classification and indexing. *Knowledge organization* 21: 140-47.

Sellen, Abigail J. and Richard H. R. Harper. 2002. *The myth of the paperless office*. Cambridge, Massachusetts: The MIT Press.

Solomon, Paul. 2000. Exploring structuration in knowledge organization: Implications for managing the tension between stability and dynamism. In *Dynamism and stability in knowledge organization: Proceedings of the Sixth International ISKO Conference, 10-13 July 2000, Toronto, Canada*, ed. Clare Beghtol, Lynn C. Howarth, Nancy J. Williamson. Advances in knowledge organization v. 7. Würzburg: Ergon Verlag, pp. 254-60.

Vellucci, Sherry L. 2000. Metadata and authority control. *Library resources and technical services* 44: 33-43.

Wenger, Etienne. 1998. *Communities of practice: Learning, meaning, and identity*. Cambridge University Press.

The Defining Element–A Discussion of the Creator Element Within Metadata Schemas

Jennifer Cwiok

SUMMARY. The attribution of authorship in the context of electronic works is complex. Defining the semantic content of the element that denotes authorship or responsibility for an electronic resource must adhere to the prescribed definition of the elements within metadata standards. The Creator element is a kind of catchall element for the designation of responsibility for a resource's content. The Creator element or its equivalent in individual metadata schemas is examined: (1) to understand how the element is treated and functions within each specified schema, and (2) to eventually decipher similarities and differences of the Creator element across different schemas, which shall indicate defining attributes of the element. Standardization of the definitions within various element sets is suggested. In the case of the Creator element, attribution should reside with the entity primarily responsible for the resource.

Jennifer Cwiok is Keywork Librarian, The Granger Collection, 381 Park Avenue South, Suite 901, New York, NY 10016 (E-mail: jrcwiok@gmail.com).

[Haworth co-indexing entry note]: "The Defining Element–A Discussion of the Creator Element Within Metadata Schemas." Cwiok, Jennifer. Co-published simultaneously in *Cataloging & Classification Quarterly* (The Haworth Information Press, an imprint of The Haworth Press, Inc.) Vol. 40, No. 3/4, 2005, pp. 103-133; and: *Metadata: A Cataloger's Primer* (ed: Richard P. Smiraglia) The Haworth Information Press, an imprint of The Haworth Press, Inc., 2005, pp. 103-133. Single or multiple copies of this article are available for a fee from The Haworth Document Delivery Service [1-800-HAWORTH, 9:00 a.m. - 5:00 p.m. (EST). E-mail address: docdelivery@haworthpress.com].

Available online at http://www.haworthpress.com/web/CCQ

doi:10.1300/J104v40n03_06

KEYWORDS. Electronic resources, metadata schemas, Creator element, authorship attributes

INTRODUCTION AND BACKGROUND

Due to the rapid growth of electronic resources, information retrieval systems have had to develop, adapt, and innovate in order to keep up with an ever-changing array of digitally based resources. Consequently, new standards and methods for describing electronic and other non-print works have been established. In order to contend with the saturation of information that the Internet and electronic resources have given way to, international metadata initiatives are consistently proposing revisions to already existing metadata standards and new metadata schemas are in constant development.

The attribution of authorship in the context of electronic resources is complex and problematic for metadata representation. How does one determine authorship of a complex electronic resource, which is the culmination of the work of a myriad of entities? How does one determine the authorship when the content of the electronic resource may change at any moment without warning? What is the semantic content of the element that denotes authorship or responsibility for an electronic resource and how does the term used determine the element's meaning? These questions are at the crux of our discussion of the Creator element within metadata schemas. Before we can discuss the Creator element and its function within certain metadata schemas, we must first define metadata.

Defining Metadata

The most common and, at this point, exhaustively used definition of metadata is "data about data." While this definition is completely accurate, it does little to convey the purpose and function of metadata within the context of information organization and retrieval. Paul Miller (2004, 4) offers a more elaborate definition:

> In essence, metadata is the extra baggage associated with any resource that enables a real or potential user to find that resource; to decide whether or not it is of value to them; to discover where, when and by whom it was created, as well as for what purpose; to know what tools will be needed to manipulate the resource; to de-

> termine whether or not they will actually be allowed access to the resource itself and how much this will cost them. Metadata is, in short, a means by which largely meaningless data may be transformed into information, interpretable and reusable by those other than the creator of the data resource.

Miller's definition also reflects the fact that metadata is not a new concept, nor is it meant to only describe electronic or non-print materials. The card catalog was a type of metadata, but was not referred to in this manner. However, the migration of bibliographic records from print to MAchine Readable Cataloging (MARC) formats gave rise to terms such as "cataloging data" and "bibliographic data," which eventually evolved into the term "metadata" as catalogers began describing networked electronic resources. A convergence of library science, computer science, and information science and their respective methods of information organization gave sway to this transformation. No longer was the description of a resource limited to *AACR2* (*Anglo-American Cataloguing Rules*) and MARC formats; the term "metadata" accounted for this broader world of information organization (Vellucci 1999).

Since the mid-1990s, the establishment of various metadata standards has been on the fast track. International initiatives with discipline-specific intentions (electronic resources, archival finding aids, art objects, etc.) began work to develop metadata standards that would improve the organization and retrieval of resources. Presently, the goal is less that of the establishment of a standard, but more of maintenance, refinement, and overall enhancement of current standards.

As metadata schemas become more sophisticated, the focus of implementers shifts to issues of interoperability, authority control, and semantics. In his description of the EAC (Encoded Archival Context) schema, an enhancement to the EAD (Encoded Archival Description), Daniel Pitti (2001, 5) shares his vision for the possibilities for describing complex entities and the need to reflect not only the description of the resource itself, but its relationship to other entities as well.

> Relations between records, creators, and functions and activities are dynamic and complex, and not fixed and simple. Creators are related to other creators. Records are related to other records. Functions and activities are related to other functions and activities. And each of these is interrelated with the others. Markup and relational database technologies enable the development of flexible and dynamic descriptive systems. By developing dedicated semantics and structures for describing each descriptive component and its complex interrelations, we can build de-

scriptive systems that are far more efficient and effective than those we realize in print.

In order for this multi-level, multi-relational description to exist and function, there must be a certain adherence to the prescribed definition of the elements within a metadata standard. Crosswalks, authoritative mappings from the metadata elements in one schema to the elements of another, allow for interoperability without schemas having to share the same semantics (Caplan 2003). This works fine when equivalent elements with different semantic representation have an equal definition governing them. However, if there is ambiguity in an element's definition, attribution of the element is completely up to the individual implementing the schema. It is here that we find our difficulty with the Creator element.

The Creator Element: A Case of Good Intentions

All metadata schemas include some kind of internal framework composed of a variety of elements, attributes, components, and/or aggregates. The Creator element is a kind of catchall element for the designation of responsibility for a resource's content. Within the Dublin Core schema, the Creator element is defined as "an entity primarily responsible for making the content of the resource" (DCMI 2004). This definition may be interpreted in many different ways, especially in the description of electronic resources.

Indeed, it was the intention of the Dublin Core (DC) originators and others who have modeled the DC schema to establish a loose set of guidelines to describe electronic resources. Electronic resources are unpredictable and volatile in nature; the stringency of *AACR2* did not accommodate the description of an electronic work whose scope, content, and webmaster could change in a matter of minutes. Unfortunately, it's the very nature of the electronic work that makes it so difficult to describe and to adequately provide reliable access. Loose language and the optional, repeatable elements are characteristic of many metadata schemas.

The Creator element is also problematic due to the status accorded to authorship of a work. Electronic resources are indeed works; thus, it is difficult to separate our concept of "authorship" in the print world from our analyses and description of electronic resources. Smiraglia (2001, 10-11) illustrates this point in his description of electronic resources and the erosion of information "gatekeepers" that dominate the print world:

> Some have suggested that the problem of the work will not obtain in the digital universe. Yet the brief history of the world-wide-web has shown us that a key characteristic of websites is volatility–and that is a desirable characteristic. This will lead, no doubt, to shifts in the power structure in the dissemination of knowledge. Where once gatekeepers such as publishers and editors decided what was published and therefore allowed into the public's domain of exploitation, the constantly changing world-wide-web allows little room for such control. Webmasters control what appears on their sites and for those in the receiving role the rule is ever caveat emptor–"buyer beware."

The gatekeepers that govern what enters the public realm of knowledge in the print world are all but gone in the electronic domain. Webmasters compose, download, scan, and transcribe content onto their sites, but what role are they fulfilling–creator, author, publisher? Certainly, a webmaster can fulfill all or none of these roles. A webmaster is the creator of a website, but might not be the originator of the content–therefore, is the creator of the website simply a contributor, while ultimately being the entity intellectually responsible for the content of the site itself?

In a description of the Creator element in *Creating and Documenting Electronic Texts* (2000, 51), the following definition is asserted:

> Author or Creator
>
> Label: Creator
>
> The person or organization primarily responsible for creating the intellectual content of the resource. For example, authors in the case of written documents, artists, photographers, or illustrators in the case of visual resources. Note that this element does not refer to the person who is responsible for digitizing the work; this belongs in the CONTRIBUTOR element. So in the case of a machine-readable version of King Lear held by the OTA [Oxford Text Archive], the CREATOR remains William Shakespeare, and not the person who transcribed it into digital form. Again, standard authority files should be consulted for the content of this element.

This interpretation works if we are limiting the types of electronic resources to straight digital representations of works that have appeared in print. However, this is rarely the case with present day electronic resources. Content can be pulled from various sources and manipulated to suit the needs of the webmaster; there can be JPEGs created from actual photos as well as straight digital graphics by different artists included on one website. So then, how do we proceed? Do we describe each component from each "creator" separately or do we describe the electronic resource as its own work? In the end, does it matter how responsibility for the resource is delineated as long as adequate access is provided?

In order to formulate a sense of what a "creator" might or might not be and what purpose defining the element might serve, we must look at the treatment of access points and authorship in *AACR2*.

AACR2: *Authorship, Main Entry, and Access Points*

An exploration of the treatment of authorship in *AACR2* is necessary to understand how librarians have traditionally attributed responsibility for works in print and electronic formats. It is also essential in understanding why schemas like the Dublin Core were created as a loose language, rather than a more structured, rule dependent language like *AACR2*.

AACR2 defines a "personal author" as "the person chiefly responsible for creation of the intellectual or artistic content of a work" (*AACR2* 2002). The *AACR2* concept of main entry illustrates the importance of the role of personal author in bibliographic description. *AACR2* defines main entry as "the complete catalogue of an item, presented in the form by which the entity is to be uniformly identified and cited" (*AACR2* 2002). This essentially means that the entire literary unit may be attributed to a single authoritative entity. Therefore, the objective is to provide access to all works emanating from a particular entity under the appropriate personal name or corporate name.

Long ago Pettee traced the history of two fundamental principles underlying the Anglo-American cataloging codes: the authorship principle and the literary unit principle. The authorship principle states that the personal author entry should take precedence over any other entry form. In Pettee's view, the author principle is, in essence, a construct of the Western world–works are primarily known by their creators (Carpenter and Svenonius 1985). Pettee ([1936] 1985, 75) asserts:

> The attribution of authorship is the first principle of American catalogers. But why this tireless search? A second principle, even more fundamental, which necessitates the search, emerges. The

> book in hand is considered not as a single item but as a representative of a literary unit. It is the province of the catalog to assemble these literary units, issued in various forms, under a single caption.

Therefore, historically, the concept of authorship has been central to bibliographic description and organization of the catalog to promote collocation.

In addition to personal authorship, corporate authorship also plays a substantial role in the nature of an author within the catalog. Origination is one model for ascribing authorship; a second model for ascribing authorship is centered on the concept that an author is in some way *responsible* for the work (Carpenter 1981). Carpenter theorizes, "The author of a work is the one who is responsible for the work. This responsibility may be transferred" (Carpenter 1981). In the instance of corporate authorship, there is an attribution of responsibility rather than a concern over where the work originated. This concept is especially important when considering the description of electronic resources since they often emanate from corporate entities or a revolving door of webmasters.

In order to understand how electronic resources fit into this framework, we must look at how *AACR2* deals with the modification of a work. A work is considered to be "modified" when the content and nature of the original work has changed substantially or if the medium of expression has been changed (*AACR2* 2003). Translations, reproductions of works of art, illustrated texts, and musical arrangements for different instruments are not considered to be modified works; therefore, *AACR2* prescribes that attribution go to the originator and not the modifier (*AACR2* 2003).

While the rules governing modified works in *AACR2* are specific and complex, they are not necessarily representative of the content of the work. When one reads Coleman Barks' translation of a Rumi poem, one is not reading Rumi, but Barks' interpretation of Rumi. After all, Rumi wrote in Arabic; therefore, the translation not only involves going from one language to another, but from one alphabet to another. Patrick Wilson ([1987] 1989, 10-12) asserts: "A translation of a work is a different work; if you've read Plato or Marx in translation, you haven't read any work by Plato or Marx, but a different work by someone else, though directly derived from works of Plato or Marx." The same logic pertains to the digitization of a work–it is, in a sense, a translation.

The rules for attribution and access are quite complex in *AACR2* in order to account for the complete range of a work and its instantiations.

Smiraglia (2002, 70-71) illustrates the complexity of the rules governing attribution and access in *AACR2* and the perceived necessity of such rigorous rules:

> We must be aware that the purposes of these rules in *AACR2* are many and complex–they are intended as much to promote collocation as a means for retrieval as they are to individuate given works. However, we may observe in these fairly complex instructions some of the variety of volatility of works. Whatever we may think of these provisions, the fact is that they have come about for very pragmatic reasons to guide catalogers who encounter works in which attribution is complex, or in which the creative role has shifted from one individual to another.

The three main points here regarding the purpose and function of the Creator element within metadata schemas are: collocation, individualization, and the collaborative nature of electronic resources. These factors are influencing the shift of creative responsibility from originator to moderator. The collocation function of *AACR2* is dependent on the concept of main entry and a rigorous prescription for how to delineate origination for the intellectual content of a work. The establishment of schemas like the Dublin Core that utilize a loose language and have elements that are repeatable and optional implies that collocation is not necessarily a concern in the description of electronic resources. In fact, where once collocation was the ultimate objective, the desire for interoperability has become the focus. So then what is the Creator element's role within these schemas and should there be a move to limit the element more severely to ensure that equivalent elements ("author," "originator," etc.) contain like content?

Conception of Authorship

The nature of authorship and creation has historically influenced the way in which knowledge is perceived and organized and it continues to do so today. Both Roland Barthes and Michel Foucault argued for a critical movement away from viewing works as mere products of their authors, but as valuable entities in their own right. The Barthesian analysis called for a 'death of the author,' asserting that a "work" lives as long as it is read. Therefore, the origination is simply a component in a work's existence, rather than its most defining attribute. Barthes' analysis decentralizes the author and encourages a conceptual shift to how a work is perceived by the reader; thus, the work becomes a part of a larger body of knowledge, rather than an isolated product of an individual.

Rather than take the author completely out of the equation like Barthes, Michel Foucault put forth the notion that the cultural conception of "authorship" was a direct outgrowth of the commodification of literature (Finkelstein and McCleery 2003) and is, in fact, an important component in the assessment of the "creation" of a work itself and the status attributed to its creator. We cannot begin to have a conversation regarding "creatorship" without examining the edification of the author and its correlation with the establishment of intellectual property. Foucault (1984, 222) asserts:

> Although, since the eighteenth century, the author has played the role of the regulator of the fictive, a role quite characteristic of our era of industrial and bourgeois society, of individualism and private property, still, given the historical modifications that are taking place, it does not seem necessary that the author function remain constant in form, complexity, and even in existence. I think that, as our society changes, at the very moment when it is in the process of changing, the author function will disappear, and in such a manner that fiction and its polysemous texts will once again function according to another mode, but still with a system of constraint–one which will no longer be the author, but which will have to be determined or, perhaps, experienced.

Essentially, the author function to which Foucault refers is becoming obsolete in the digital environment. The lines defining authorship are blurring due to the growing complexity of digital resources and the non-commodified nature of the Internet and digital libraries. In the digital domain, anyone may create a resource–some even for free. Content is often pulled from a variety of sources with different originators and content and creator may change at any moment without warning.

Individualization of works and the creation of literary property under copyright legislation have made the establishment of "authorship" a lucrative commodity within our culture. Again, *AACR2* parallels our laws of copyright in its rules of attribution. Smiraglia (2001, 72) points out that:

> The individual creator of a work once fixed in a tangible medium earns the right to be called its author. But as the work finds its place in society and evolves over time, modifications to it displace

> the author in favor of those who continue to exert creative influence over the signifying ideational and semantic content.

While electronic resources may be copyrighted, there is often no relationship between the copyright holder and who is actually responsible for the content of the resource. Electronic resources may also contain a wide range of individually copyrighted materials. For instance, a fairly complex, scholarly website contains a JPEG of a Jeff Wall photo. The original photo is the artistic property of Jeff Wall, but the JPEG image is protected under the copyright statement on the website. I am drawing this example not as a way of illustrating the intricacies of copyright law, but as a means of revealing the complexities of attribution of an electronic work along the lines of commodity.

In addition to a decreased level of individualistic importance, electronic resources have proven to be the most volatile of works. A website's content and scope may change within minutes as can the entity responsible for the site's content. As Eggert has asserted, the focus is shifting from "who did it" to "who is doing it now."

Whether or not the attribution of responsibility of electronic resources is best under the stringency of *AACR2* or the loose framework of a metadata schema like Dublin Core has yet to be seen. It is clear though that the concept of "authorship" is shifting within our society and electronic resources have had a great impact on this trend. In essence, what we are seeing is a pull away from the concept of traditional authorship within the context of electronic resources. The ambiguity of the definition of the Creator element within metadata schemas reflects a kind of indifference to whom we are to attribute responsibility. Michel Foucault (1984, 205) expressed this sentiment when he echoed Beckett's assertion, "'What does it matter who is speaking,' someone said, 'what does it matter who is speaking.'"

REPRESENTATION AND FUNCTIONALITY OF THE CREATOR ELEMENT OR CORRESPONDING ELEMENTS WITHIN INDIVIDUAL METADATA SCHEMAS

Moving forward, we may now look at the Creator element or its equivalent in individual metadata schemas. The purpose of exploring the element in different metadata schemas is twofold: (1) to understand how the element is treated and functions within each specified schema, and (2) to eventually decipher similarities and differences of the Creator element across different schemas, which shall indicate defining attributes of the element. The metadata schemas discussed in this part are as follows:

1. DC (Dublin Core)
2. VRA Core (Visual Resources Association)
3. GEM (Gateway to Educational Materials)
4. EAD (Encoded Archival Description)
5. ONIX (Online Information Exchange)
6. TEI (Text Encoding Initiative)
7. GILS (Global Information Exchange)

This by no means is a comprehensive list of metadata schemas, but rather a selection of schemas that demonstrate the role of the creator and equivalent elements in other schemas.

The discussion of the Creator element within metadata schemas is broken down into two sections according to semantic representation. The first section consists of the metadata schemas that contain the Creator element: DC, VRA, and GEM. The second section discusses the metadata schemas that employ a term other than Creator as one of the prescribed elements: EAD, ONIX, TEI, and GILS. Each section contains a brief overview of the schema being discussed in order to provide context and purpose of the metadata schema itself. After an initial explanation of the metadata schema, we explore the Creator or corresponding element within the schema.

Creator Element: Discussion of Schemas

In this section, the Creator element within the DC (Dublin Core), VRA (Visual Resource Association), and GEM (Gateway to Educational Materials) schemas is discussed respectively. Each subsection seeks to explore the Creator element and how it functions within each schema. It should be noted that VRA and GEM are both modeled after the Dublin Core and therefore, have many of the same issues surrounding the attribution of the Creator element. Both the VRA and GEM have made modifications to the element by addition of qualifiers to the element, but as we shall see, these modifications have done little to alleviate the conceptual problems inherent to the application of the element.

The aim of this section is to raise questions regarding the Creator element, which ultimately informs the meta-analysis of the element in the next part. Questions to consider: How is the Creator element designated in regard to the traditional concept of authorship and/or intellectual responsibility? How does use of the term Creator affect the other elements within the schema? Is there an authority of form of the name that governs the element? Is the element repeatable and/or optional and if so, how does that effect the description of the object?

The Creator Element in the DC (Dublin Core) Schema

The DCMI (Dublin Core Metadata Initiative) is made up of an international network of working interest groups and committees (Howarth 2003), engaged in an open forum for the development of interoperable online metadata standards that support a broad range of purposes and business models (DCMI 2004). While DC strives to achieve semantic interoperability, it is also a model for facilitating and enhancing resource discovery and description on the Web (Howarth 2003). The DC Metadata Element Set contains a set of fifteen core data elements. In addition to the fifteen elements, there are two classes of qualifiers: element refinements and encoding schemes. All of the elements in the DC schema are optional, repeatable, and extensible, which adds increased functionality to the simple core of set descriptors (Howarth 2003). The schema itself is also format-independent; thus, it is not tied to any single type of data representation (Caplan 2003).

When the DC element set was first created, it was intended to provide a framework for the description of electronic resources. At this time, the development of e-resources was in its infancy and the developers of the DC were uncertain regarding the stringency of the rules governing the description of electronic resources. The volatility of electronic resources lends itself to the establishment of a loose definition of elements and it is here that we find our difficulty with the Creator element. In her description of the Dublin Core schema, Priscilla Caplan identifies certain problems that are inherent in the application of the DC. The overlap of meaning in the definitions of the elements Creator, Contributor, and in some cases, Publisher, has led to confusion among implementers in regards to which element to use and when to use it (Caplan 2003). The Dublin Core Metadata Element Set designates the following definitions for Creator, Contributor, and Publisher:

Identifier: Creator

Definition: An entity primarily responsible for making the content of the resource.

Identifier: Publisher

Definition: An entity responsible for making the source available.

Identifier: Contributor

Definition: An entity responsible for making contributions to the content of the resource.

There have been suggestions that Creator, Contributor, and Publisher be rolled into one single element called "agent," which was considered, but rejected (Caplan 2003). According to Caplan, the bibliographic community has always accorded authorship special status. This has always been reflected in the *AACR2* concept of main entry and since the Dublin Core has been an important resource in retrospective conversion projects, there has been a tendency with implementers to try and mirror *AACR2* concepts of authorship and attribution within the Dublin Core (Caplan 2003). However, employing the *AACR2* concept of authorship and main entry in the description of e-resources is a complex issue simply because of the nature of electronic works.

The complexity of the issue surrounding the assignment of the Creator element may be illustrated by an exploration of the Duke University's online archival collection, "Documents from the Women's Liberation Movement" (http://scriptorium.lib.duke.edu/wlm/). The introduction to the site states, "The items in this online collection are scanned and transcribed from original documents held in Duke's Special Collections Library. We are making these documents available online in order to support current teaching and research interests related to this period in U.S. history" (Duke University 2004). We may infer from the introduction that there are going to be several entities involved in the creation and maintenance of this resource. The site credits the following individuals for their work on the site:

Rosalyn Baxandall–material selection

Catherine Boulle–scanning, transcriptions, HTML coding

Lydia Boyd–scanning, HTML coding

Ginny Daley–material selection, categorization, background notes, HTML coding and editing

Linda Gordon–material selection

Paolo Mangiafico–project coordination, web page design and editing, HTML coding

Laura Micham–transcriptions, OCR scanning and editing, HTML coding

Anne Valk–material selection

In addition to the determination of Creator or Contributor status of the individuals listed above, there are also reproductions of documents by a range of authors to consider.

In the "Documents of the Women's Liberation Movement" example, we see the problematic nature of the element. Paolo Mangiafico is credited with the design and editing of the page, HTML coding, and project coordination–should he be the considered the "creator"? Should all of the individuals credited with HTML coding be considered "creators" as well or should they be considered "contributors"? On one of the subsidiary pages of the site, Roxanne Dunbar's essay "Who Is the Enemy?" has been transcribed or scanned as a part of the project. Roxanne Dunbar undoubtedly wrote this essay, which originally appeared in *No More Fun and Games: A Journal of Female Liberation* and has most likely appeared elsewhere. Now it exists in a digital format–should Roxanne Dunbar be considered the "creator" or should it be the individual who transcribed or scanned the essay? Who is primarily responsible for making the content of the resource? These are all difficult questions to answer and ultimately, there may not be an answer that satisfies the complexity of the issue of according authorship or intellectual responsibility in the context of electronic resources.

Designating the Creator element is also compounded by the fact that the DC schema does not utilize the one-to-one principle. The one-to-one principle states that if multiple versions of a resource exist, there should be separate records that accurately describe each of them (Caplan 2003). For example, if a photographer takes a photograph, the photographer is generally recorded as the creator of the photograph. However, if the photograph is digitized and now exists as a JPEG, the scanner of the photograph would be considered the creator (Caplan 2003). The JPEG and the photograph are two complete and separate entities and if the one-to-one principle were to be applied in the DC schema, there would have to be two separate records to describe the images. In the next section we explore the VRA Core. Implementers of the VRA Core utilize the one-to-one principle in the description of works and images.

The Creator Element in VRA Core (Visual Resources Association) Schema

The VRA Core was developed by the Visual Resources Association as a means to describe visual works of art and their surrogates. The VRA Core was modeled on the Dublin Core with the intent to supply a core set of elements that all implementations could share and could be supplemented by additional elements at the local level (Caplan 2003). In addition to trying to establish semantic interoperability, there is no prescribed syntax and the elements are optional and repeatable like the DC, but it's not explicitly stated that this is the case with the VRA (Caplan 2003).

The current version of VRA Core is comprised of seventeen categories that may be applied to works of art and to their surrogates or representations. The intent here is to designate separate records (sets of metadata elements) for each work and representation respectively. Within the VRA schema a "work" is defined as "a physical entity that exists, has existed at some time in the past, or that could exist in the future. It might be an artistic creation such as a painting or a sculpture; it might be a performance, composition, or literary work; it might be a building or other construction in the built environment; or it might be an object of material construction" (VRA Core Categories 2002). Hence, conceptually, the visual representation of a "work," the "image," which consists of slides, photographs, and digital files, needs to be treated as a complete and separate entity. Of course, it should be noted that a photograph of an object by a noted photographer might be considered a "work" in its own right.

The delineation between a "work" and an "image" has great implications for the role of the Creator. The same prescribed elements apply to both a "work" and an "image" and both employ some form of a Creator element. Contrary to the Dublin Core element set, VRA provides for a more specific framework for ascribing responsibility. According to the VRA element set, the breakdown of the Creator element looks like this:

Creator.Role

Creator.Attribution

Creator.Personal name

Creator.Corporate name

Unlike the Dublin Core schema, it is assumed that the implementers of VRA will honor the 1:1 principle; thus, one record would be created to represent a single entity. If a drawing were scanned to create a JPEG image, the drawing would be fully described on one record and the JPEG on another (Caplan 2003). Therefore, the original object and its surrogate could potentially have different creators. The implication for the attribution of responsibility in the context of e-resources is less ambiguous than in the Dublin Core.

The Creator Element in the GEM (Gateway to Educational Materials) Schema

GEM (Gateway to Educational Materials) is a metadata schema that was created as a project of the U.S. Department of Education and the ERIC Clearinghouse on Information and Technology at Syracuse University. The project's aim is to "provide 'one-stop, any-stop' access to the substantial, but uncataloged, collections of Internet-based educational materials available on various federal, state, university, non-profit, and commercial Internet sites" (GEM 2004). The creation of "The Gateway" was a method the GEM Initiative implemented as a solution to the resource discovery problem being experienced by many educators. "The Gateway" is a database that essentially provides access to quality collections of educational resources, such as lesson plans and similar curriculum resources.

Like the VRA Core, the metadata schema behind the "The Gateway" is also modeled after the Dublin Core. From its inception, the GEM Initiative has worked closely with the Dublin Core Metadata Initiative to create GEM's core element set, which consists of Dublin Core elements as well as their qualifiers extended with a set of GEM-specific elements and qualifiers. All of the elements are repeatable and in theory, the GEM element set is syntax-independent and its semantics may be represented in a variety of formats like the Dublin Core (Caplan 2003).

One modification to the DC element set is that the GEM profile extends the Dublin Core with element refinement qualifiers. Due to the inherent problems in ascribing responsibility with the Creator element in the Dublin Core, the GEM schema adds a Role qualifier to Creator, Contributor, and Publisher elements (Caplan 2003). Therefore, implementers of the GEM schema may qualify the role of the Creator. For example, if the content of a lesson plan is included in a digital library for educational resources, the webmaster may be considered the Creator. Within the schema, the element would look like this:

<meta name="DC.creator" content="(type=role)Webmaster">

<meta name="DC.creator" content="(type=namePersonal)Jane Doe">

Yet, even with the element refinement qualifiers, we still lack an appropriate guideline for assigning the elements of Creator, Contributor, and Publisher. In the context of the digital library, is the author of one of the ten lesson plans included in the electronic resource to be considered a Creator or a Contributor? Is the webmaster who actually constructs the resource a Creator or a Publisher? In a sense, the element refinements alleviate these problems by allowing implementers to code for the role an individual had in making a resource available; however, it also complicates matters by raising the questions regarding intellectual responsibility, authorship, and accurate resource description. In essence, all of the issues regarding the Creator element in the DC and VRA schemas are ever present within this context as well.

Summary

This closes our discussion of the metadata schemas that employ the creator element within their element sets. Even with element refinement qualifiers, there is still overlap between the elements and a good deal of ambiguity in establishing a standard definition of what a Creator actually is. The difficulty demonstrated in the application of these schemas to describe electronic resources implies a need to reassess how we think of the attribution of "authorship" in the electronic domain. With the advent of these resources, there has been a shift from "where did this resource originate?" to "who is responsible for this resource?" The volatile nature of electronic resources makes the "responsibility" aspect of the equation a substantial consideration. In addition, the collaborative nature of e-resources also complicates matters.

In the print world, the standard possible entities involved in the creation of a "work" are author, publisher, editor, illustrator, translator, and photographer. As illustrated in the Dublin Core discussion, a complex, scholarly electronic resource may be a creation made possible by the collaboration of a multitude of entities. This is a substantial jump from the traditional concepts of authorship and access inherent in *AACR2*. In the next section, we shall discuss metadata schemas that utilize an element other than Creator to attribute authorship or responsibility in order to assess whether a different semantic representation offers any solutions to this problem.

Elements Equivalent to the Creator Element: Discussion of Schemas

The schemas included in this discussion are EAD (Encoded Archival Description), ONIX (Online Information Exchange), TEI (Text Encoding Initiative), and GILS (Global Information Exchange). This section is structured similarly to the previous section with a brief overview of the schema and an analysis of the element. Since the purpose of this paper is to explore the Creator element, we analyze the schemas in this section according to the implications for defining the Creator element and for the attribution of authorship in the context of electronic resources.

The Author Element in the EAD (Encoded Archival Description) Schema

The EAD (Encoded Archival Description) was developed as a means of encoding traditional print finding aids in a digital format. At its inception, there was no universal standard for the creation of finding aids; therefore, the originators of the EAD gathered sample finding aids from a variety of repositories in order to uncover the range of practice found among them (Caplan 2003). SGML was the original syntax for the EAD DTD (Document Type Definition) because it could handle the lengthy narrative text and multi-level hierarchy required to sufficiently encode the finding aids; there is now an XML EAD DTD as well. The EAD DTD has three sections:

<eadheader> contains information about the EAD itself

<frontmatter> gives a formatted description of the finding aid for publications

<archdesc> describes the archives or manuscripts collection

The Author element is included in the Title Statement portion of the EAD Header and may also be included in the Title Page element in the Front Matter. The definition of the Author element prescribed in the *EAD Tag Library* follows (EAD 2002):

<author> Author

Description:

Name(s) of institution(s) or individual(s) responsible for compiling the intellectual content of the finding aid. May include a brief statement indicating the nature of the responsibility, for example, archivist, collections processor, or records manager. Because acknowledgement of such individuals or institutions often appears on the title page of a finding aid, the <author> element is available in both the required <titlestmt> portion of the <eadheader> and the optional <titlepage> element in <frontmatter>.

In addition to the Author element, there are four other elements within the EAD DTD for the designation of responsibility for the resource (EAD 2002).

> Use the <creation> element found under <profiledesc> to designate the encoder of the finding aid. Use the <persname> or <corpname> element with the ROLE attribute to designate the author in a Biographic Reference <bibref> citation. Use the <origination> element to designate the compiler, collector, or creator of the materials being described.

In contrast to the DC, VRA, and GEM, the EAD DTD prescribes a very clear delineation between potential types of authors that may have to be considered in the construction of the EAD schema.

ONIX (Online Information Exchange) Schema

The ONIX (Online Information Exchange) schema was originally developed as a method for publishers to exchange trade information electronically with retailers, online retailers, wholesalers, distributors, and other entities in the book and journal market. ONIX International is a product of the union between the Association of American Publishers' *Guidelines for Online Information Exchange* (ONIX) and EDItEUR's EPICS Data Dictionary, which were two independently developed metadata specifications for exchanging information regarding the book trade (Goreman 2004).

ONIX may be mapped to MARC; however, it does not support *AACR2* cataloging. The actual ONIX record is an XML representation of bibliographic, trade, and marketing information. The ONIX schema relies heavily on coded values, use of composites, data sets that must occur together, and multiple options for representing the same data (Caplan 2003). The ONIX schema does not prescribe rules for choice of content, which allows the format of the item being described in a variety of ways.

ONIX does employ many of the elements that are characteristically used in traditional library cataloging; however, these elements are treated quite differently within the ONIX schema. For instance, authorship is represented by use of the Contributor composite, which must include a contributor role code (Caplan 2003):

> Elements are defined for representing personal names in unstructured normal order, in unstructured inverted order, and in structure form separately delimiting parts of the name, such as prefixes and titles. A person's name can be given in one, two, or all three forms with the same composite.

The Contributor composite utilizing the unstructured inverted for the personal name looks like this within the schema:

```
<Contributor>
    <ContributorRole>A01</ContributorRole>
    <PersonNameinverted>Doe, Jane</PersonNameinverted>
    <BiographicalNote>Jane Doe has an MFA in English from Yale.
    She is currently the head of the English Graduate Studies Program
    at UC Berkley. She has four cats.</BiographicalNote>
</Contributor>
```

In the example above, Jane Doe's name might also have been represented as "Jane Doe." There is virtually no authority or guidance for the formulation of personal or corporate names within the ONIX standard.

The lack of authority within the Contributor composite is a perplexing issue considering that the ONIX standard shares the *AACR2* concept of authorship. The special status accorded to authorship within the ONIX schema is reflected in the presence of the Biographical Note element. The community utilizing this standard, the publishing industry, cares about who wrote the book being described and who that person is within the industry. Yet, regardless of authorship's import within this schema, it is designated to a "Contributor" composite with no structure. Why not use the term <Author> in defining the composite? Why not mirror the *AACR2* concept of Name Authority?

The use of the term "Contributor" to define the element is also an interesting characteristic within the ONIX schema. The ambiguity inherent in the definition of the Creator element is not present within ONIX's Contributor composite. We know who the author of the book being described is; we know who the editor of a journal is, which is why the *AACR2* concept of authorship works so well for the ONIX schema. However, the Contributor composite may become problematic in the description of e-books and e-journals. Is the author of the book still the primary party responsible for the resource or is it the individual who digitized the book? The digitization of the book makes it a completely separate entity from the book itself. The same rings true in the description of e-journals. In the context of electronic resources, the Contributor composite is really just as ambiguous as the Creator element.

The Author Element in the TEI (Text Encoding Initiative) Header

Under the joint sponsorship of the Association for Computers and the Humanities, the Association for Computational Linguistics, and the Association for Literary and Linguistic Computing, the TEI (Text Encoding Initiative) was established in order to "develop guidelines for the consistent SGML encoding of electronic texts and to encourage their use and exchange for humanities scholarship" (Caplan 2003). The *TEI Guidelines* attempts to deal with the mark-up of several different kinds of texts for many types of historical, literary, and linguistic analysis; however, the only part of the *TEI Guidelines* that is of concern to us is the TEI Header which is defined in part five of the *Guidelines*.

The TEI Header is the part of the TEI Standard that precedes all of the marked-up text of a resource. The TEI Header, in essence, describes the text, including its source, revisions, bibliographic description of the text, etc. (Howarth 2003). The TEI Header is comprised of four sections, which is defined as an SGML DTD. Here are the four sections with their SGML tags:

<fileDesc> contains the bibliographic description of the electronic text

<encodingDesc> describes the relationship between the electronic text and the source(s) from which it was derived

<profileDesc> describes the non-bibliographic aspects of the text, specifically the languages used, the situation in which it was produced, and topical and genre descriptors

<revisionDesc> contains the revision history of the file (Caplan 2003).

Most of the elements in the TEI Header are optional and in most cases, there are alternative methods for representing the same content. Therefore, the TEI Header provides for some complexity and offers many options in the description of the text. The scholars responsible for designing the TEI Header were aware of its potential within a library context. This awareness encouraged them "to design the header in congruence with ISBD" (International Standard Bibliographic Description) (Caplan 2003). While adhering to the ISBD, the TEI Header does not require adherence to *AACR2* standards in the provision of content.

The <fileDesc> is the only portion of the TEI Header that is required; it is also the only section of the TEI Header that was explicitly designed to conform to ISBD. Within the <fileDesc> section of the TEI Header, there are seven subsections. Caplan (2003, 67) defines them as:

<titleStmt> information about the title and those responsible for the intellectual content

<editionStmt> information relating to the edition of the text

<extent> the approximate size of the electronic text

<publicationStmt> information on the publication or distribution of the electronic text

<seriesStmt> information about the series to which the text belongs

<notesStmt> notes providing additional information about the text

<sourceDesc> a bibliographic description of the source text(s) from which the electronic text was derived

It is important to note that the first six sections of the <fileDesc> correspond to six areas of bibliographic description within *AACR2*. The eight areas prescribed in *AACR2* for bibliographic description are: Title and statement of responsibility area, Edition area, Material (or type of publication) specific details, Publication, distribution, etc. area, Physical description area, Series area, Note area, Standard number and terms of availability area (Caplan 2003). The correlation between the areas in the TEI Header and *AACR2* bibliographic description reflects, to a certain extent, that the manner in which intellectual responsibility is treated within the TEI Header.

Within the TEI Header, authorship is expressed as a sub-element within the Title Statement <titleStmt> and the Source Description <sourceDesc> subsections, which fall under the File Description <fileDesc> section (TEI 2004). The Author sub-element is defined as the author of the *original* work. Therefore, the entity responsible for the text in its electronic form is not represented in this element. However, the entities responsible for the electronic text are represented in the <sponsor>, <funder>, <principal>, and <respStmt> sub-elements. Using the example of Roxanne Dunbar's essay, "Who Is the Enemy" from the online archival collection, "Documents of the Women's Liberation Movement," the structure of the Author and Statement of Responsibility sub-elements looks like this:

```
<titleStmt>
   <title>Who is the Enemy</title>
   <author>Dunbar, Roxanne</author>
   <respStmt>
      <resp>Creation of machine-readable text:</resp>
      <name>Paolo Mangiafico, Duke University</name>
      <resp>TEI markup</resp>
      <name>Jennifer Cwiok</name>
   </respStmt>
</titleStmt>
```

The ascription of intellectual responsibility in the TEI Header is much more straightforward due to the delineation of specific roles–author of the original and the creator of the digital form of the work.

In addition to the Author sub-element within the <titleStmt> element, there is an Author sub-element within the Source Description <sourceDesc> element as well. The <sourceDesc> is a required element, which describes the source from which the electronic file was derived (Caplan 2003). Therefore, in the case of Roxanne Dunbar's essay, "Who Is the Enemy?" the <sourceDesc> would look like this:

```
<sourceDesc>
  <biblFull>
    <titleStmt>
      <title>Who is the Enemy?</title>
      <author>Roxanne, Dunbar</author>
    </titleStmt>
  </biblFull>
</sourceDesc>
```

Again, the attribution of authorship is relatively clear. We know that we are describing the *original* version of the essay and not the digital version.

The Originator Element in the GILS (Global Information Locator Service) Schema

The GILS (Global Information Locator Service) evolved out of the Government Information Locator Service, which served the federal departments and agencies in the United States. The original goal of GILS was the establishment of "a federation of interoperable agency-based locator services giving the public access to agency-produced resources" (Caplan 2003). Presently, GILS is an international standard that operates on the Internet and other networks, making GILS interoperable with many information resources.

The GILS schema is defined dependent of the Z39.50 protocol, which specifies the core set of GILS elements (GILS 2004). Annex E of the Profile defines the GILS Core Element Set and specifies the name of the element and its repeatability along with its definition. Within the GILS schema, all elements are optional and there is no specification regarding content. However, some of the elements require values to be recorded in a particular format or controlled vocabulary (Caplan 2003).

The basic elements within the GILS framework are defined very broadly since the intent of GILS locator records is to describe the full range of agency resources, which includes print and electronic resources as well as nontraditional resources such as job searching services and programs. Authorship is expressed in the Originator element, which is a repeatable element. The Originator element is defined as "the element that identifies the information resource originator" (GILS 2004). In addition to the Originator element, there is also a Contributor element, which is also repeatable. The GILS Core defines the Contributor element as the element "used if there are names associated with the resource in addition to the Originator, such as personal author, corporate author, co-author, or a conference or meeting name" (GILS 2004).

Again, with the Originator and Contributor elements, we see a certain level of ambiguity. For instance, if a resource is created by an individual, but emanates from an agency, which entity is determined to be the Originator? GILS, like the Dublin Core, has a very loosely defined element set to allow the schema to function in the description of a vast array of information resources. As we have seen with the DC Creator element, the attribution of intellectual responsibility is not always clear cut. The Originator element is problematic because it does not specify if the element is suppose to reflect intellectual responsibility on any level or if it is simply reflecting from which agency the resource emanates.

Summary

This closes our discussion of the metadata schemas, which incorporate an element other than the Creator to express attribution of authorship or responsibility. A fundamental difference between the schemas that do not include the Creator element and the schemas discussed in the previous section is that the schemas in this part were not modeled after the Dublin Core. As a result, we did not see many of the same difficulties in the application of these schemas as we did with the DC, VRA, and GEM schemas.

The TEI Header, EAD, ONIX, and GILS are very complex schemas, which seems to lessen the ambiguity surrounding the definition of elements. There is a direct correlation between the complexity of the schema and the specificity of the element set it employs. While there still remains some difficulty in the attribution of responsibility within the schemas, it is substantially less of a problem which suggests that refining the element sets with more stringent guidelines may be a possible solution in the delineation of intellectual responsibility.

META-ANALYSIS OF THE CREATOR ELEMENT

Questions regarding the purpose and function of the Creator element have been raised throughout the course of our discussion of the element. In the previous part, the breakdown of schemas according to the semantic representation–the actual term used–in the element revealed that the problems for attributing responsibility were not necessarily specific to the schemas that incorporate the Creator element. The schemas that incorporate the Creator element, DC, VRA, and GEM, are more simplistic in their structure than those that use another term to denote responsibility. The EAD, ONIX, TEI, and GILS schemas are relatively complex–therefore, there is a bit more guidance in the attribution of responsibility within the standard. The simplicity of the DC, VRA, and GEM schemas is precisely the reason why the elements are defined so loosely. While the simplistic structure of these schemas allow them to describe a wide range of resources, there appears to be a need for more stringent guidelines in the establishment for what should be delineated as Creator, Contributor, and/or Publisher.

The addition of qualifiers within the DC, VRA, and GEM schemas restricts the meaning of an element in order to aid in the attribution. For instance, within the VRA Core, the Creator element qualifiers: Role, Attribution, Personal Name, and Corporate Name delineate the possible types of responsibility the "creator" may have in the making of the resource. The qualifiers do make the assignment of responsibility easier on a practical level. However, on a theoretical level, there is still a lack of proper designation for the Creator element.

The following tables illustrate the elements, qualifiers, and sub-elements in the Dublin Core-based schemas and their counterparts. Table 1 includes the schemas that incorporate <Creator> and its related elements; Table 2 contains the schemas in which the "Creator" appears as a related element or a sub-element.

It is clear that the more complex schemas, EAD and TEI from Table 2 for instance, have well-defined element sets, which alleviates some of the difficulty in the designation of intellectual responsibility. It is also evident that the creation of schemas with a loose framework, as in Table 1, was intended to allow for malleability when describing various resources. However, as electronic resources become more complicated themselves, it is necessary to refine existing metadata schemas and to critically analyze our intentions in their implementation. Are we intending to describe the electronic resource and exploit the electronic domain or are we going to treat digitization like a translation of sorts? How much

TABLE 1. Dublin Core-Based Schemas Containing the Creator

Schema	**Element and Enhancements**	**Related Elements**	**Sub-Elements**
Dublin Core	Creator	Publisher Contributor	
VRA Core	Creator.Role Creator.Attribution Creator.Personal name Creator.Corporate name		
GEM	Creator.Role	Contributor.Role Publisher.Role	

TABLE 2. Schemas That Do Not Contain the Creator Element

Schema	**Element and Enhancements**	**Related Fields**	**Sub-Elements**
EAD	Author		<profiledesc> <creation> <bibref> <persname> <corpname> *(used with ROLE attribute)* <origination>
ONIX *(Authorship is represented in a Contributor Composite)*		<Contributor> <ContributorRole> <PersonName> <BiographicalNote>	
TEI Header			<TitleStmt> <author> <respStmt> <resp> <name> <sourceDesc> <bib1Full> <titleStmt> <author>
GILS	Originator	Contributor	

does origination matter when credit may be ascribed in an access point like <contributor>? Users will still be able to retrieve the desired resource and know who is responsible for the resource.

We know that the creation of the Dublin Core schema was an initial response to the growing need to describe electronic resources effectively. It intentionally broke from the stringency of *AACR2* to formulate a loose set of guidelines to facilitate description. The notion of breaking with the *AACR2* concept of main entry and the strict framework of MARC was on point. However, the establishment of the DC schema and schemas modeled after it have done little to shake many in the library community from its dependence on the concept of main entry and the flat file system.

Rather than run in the other direction from *AACR2*, we should take a nod from its development and incorporate it in the evolution of metadata schemas. In the context of electronic resources, there has been exponential growth and change with which those in the information profession have tried to contend. Instead of trying to play catch-up with the Internet, we need to take a step back and analyze the medium itself–it is not a book and the rules that we have implemented to describe bibliographic entities are not necessarily applicable or appropriate for the electronic domain.

TOWARD THE FUTURE: SOME SUGGESTIONS

The conceptual difficulty in the definition of the Creator element is deciphering what exactly the metdata schema should be describing. We also need to establish what purpose the element is intended to serve. Murtha Baca (1998, 15) raises an interesting issue in trying to establish what the role of metadata is:

> What exactly should metadata describe? Strictly speaking, metadata should describe the properties of an object that itself is data, for example a Web page, a digital image, or a database–which is analogous to the librarian's practice of cataloging "the thing in hand." For networked resources, however, these properties are not very interesting or useful for the purpose of discovery; for example, if researchers are interested in discovering images of famous artworks on the Web, they would generally search using the properties of the original artworks (e.g., CREATOR = Picasso, DATE = 1937), not the properties of the digital copies or "surrogates" of them (e.g., CREATOR = Scan-U-Like Imaging Labs, Inc., DATE = 1998).

In essence, we are at a crossroads. It is clear that once a work is digitized it exists in a significantly different medium, but how do we provide access to it? As Baca asks, are we providing a description of what we have in hand–digital data, or are we mimicking the print world and offering descriptions of electronic resources in ways that the masses may understand and use?

In a sense, these concerns go back to Patrick Wilson's theory of the bibliographic control and the descriptive and exploitative domains (Wilson 1968). We are concerned with adequately describing the electronic resource we "have in hand," yet we want to describe it in such a way that it may be discovered by those seeking the information. Using Baca's example of a Picasso image is informative. True, the information about the entity responsible for digitizing the image might not be of immediate concern to the individual searching for the information, who just wants the image, period. However, there needs to be a realization that the fact that the image *is* a digital surrogate is of great import.

It is necessary to critically assess the accuracy of digital surrogates and to note that webmasters have a significant amount of intellectual responsibility invested in the sites they create. The solution to the problem in the Creator element might lie in moving from the concept of "authorship" and "origination" to a concept of intellectual responsibility.

Perhaps the problematic nature of the Creator element allows us to move forward in our assessment and treatment of knowledge. The evolution of the Internet and the availability of electronic resources completely reflect Barthes ([1977] 2002, 24) idea of "death of the author":

> The reader is the space on which all the quotations that make up a writing are inscribed without any of them being lost; a text's unity lies not in its origin but in its destination. Yet this destination cannot any longer be personal: the reader without history, biography, psychology; he is simply that *someone* who holds together in a single field all the traces by which the written text is constituted.

I am not suggesting that we completely abandon the concept of authorship or origination in the description of electronic resources. I do think there needs to be a reassessment of what exactly we are describing and a deeper consideration of electronic resources as works unto themselves.

The exploration of the Creator element and issues of "authorship" in the electronic domain becomes increasingly important as electronic resources become more prevalent in scholarly research. One of the criticisms of electronic resources as a research tool is that students and scholars alike are ceasing to view the source of the information with a critical eye. Falsification of information on the Internet is a common problem and one that needs to be addressed since many in the academic community are looking no further than their computers for desired data. It is essential that we begin to address the fact that webmasters and the compilers of digital information have great power and our gaze must shift from origination of content to responsibility for content.

One solution might be to standardize the definitions within various element sets. In the case of the Creator element, attribution should reside with the entity primarily responsible for the resource. Responsibility for the content contained within the resource may be credited in a sub-element–<creator.origination>. Another solution might be to mimic the EAD and TEI schemas. The specificity within the element sets makes delineating responsibility and creatorship roles a straightforward process.

As the semantic web continues to grow and librarians strive to catalog electronic resources, the establishment of standard definitions for elements is becoming more relevant and important. True, metadata schemas may interoperate regardless of shared semantics, but the information contained in equivalent elements must be the same. This initial discussion of the ascription of authorship and intellectual responsibility within the context of electronic resources illustrates the need for further discussion and examination of how we view and respond to works in a digital framework.

WORKS CITED

American Library Association. 2002. *Anglo-American cataloguing rules*. Chicago: American Library Association.

Baca, Murtha. 1998. *Introduction to metadata: Pathways to digital information*. [Los Angeles]: Getty Information Institute, 1998.

Barthes, Roland. [1977] 2002. Death of the author. In *The book history reader*, ed. by David Finkelstein and Alistair McCleery. London; New York: Routledge, pp. 221-24.

Caplan, Priscilla. 2003. *Metadata fundamentals for all librarians*. Chicago: American Library Association.

Carpenter, Michael. 1981. *Corporate authorship: Its role in library cataloging*. Westport: Greenwood Press.

Carpenter, Michael and Elaine Svenonius eds. 1985. *Foundations of cataloging: A sourcebook*. Littleton: Libraries Unlimited.

DCMI. 2004. *Dublin core metadata initiative*, 18 July 2004. <http://www.dublincore.org/>.

Editeur, *ONIX for Books*, 16 July 2004. <http://www.editeur.org/onix.html> (December 2003).

Foucault, Michel. 1984. What is an author? In *Foucault reader*, ed. by P. Rabinow. Harmondsworth: Penguin, pp. 101-20.

GEM, *Gateway to Educational Materials*, 20 July 2004. <http://www.thegateway.org/> (2003).

GILS, *Global Information Locator Service (GILS)*, 18 July 2004. <http://www.gils.net/index.html>.

Gorman, G.E. and Daniel G. Dorner. 2004. *Metadata applications and management.* Lanham: Scarecrow Press.

Howarth, Lynne C. 2004. "*Modelling a metalevel ontology*," 26 June 2004. <http://www.fis.utoronto.ca/special/metadata/mmo/overview.htm>.

Jones, Wayne, Judith R. Ahronheim, and Josephine Crawford. 2002. *Cataloging the web: Metadata, AACR2, and MARC 21.* Lanham: Scarecrow Press.

Library of Congress. 2004. *Encoded Archival Description*, 18 July 2004. <http://www.loc.gov/ead/> (12 August 2004).

Library of Congress, *MARC Standards*, 15 July 2004. <http://www.loc.gov/marc/> (16 September 2003).

Miller, Paul. 2004. Metadata: What it Means for Memory Institutions. In *Metadata applications and management*. ed. G.E. Gorman and Daniel G. Dorner. Lanham: Scarecrow Press, pp. 4-16.

NISO. 2004. *Understanding Metadata.* Bethesda: National Information Standards Organization.

Pitti, Daniel V. 2001. *Creator Description: Encoded Archival Context.* Charlotteville: University of Virginia.

Smiraglia, Richard. 2001. *The nature of "a work": Implications for the organization of knowledge.* Lanham: Scarecrow Press.

Svenonius, Elaine. 1989. *The conceptual foundations of descriptive cataloging.* San Diego: Academic Press.

TEI Consortium 2003, *Text Encoding Initiative*, 18 July 2004. <http://www.tei-c.org/> (6 September 2003).

Vellucci, Sherry L. 2000. Metadata and authority control. *Library resources & technical services* 44: 33-43.

Visual Resources Association, *Visual Resources Association*, 18 July 2004. <http://www.vraweb.org/> (13 August 2004).

Wilson, Patrick. 1968. *Two kinds of power: An essay on bibliographic control.* Berkeley: University of California Press.

Content Metadata–An Analysis of Etruscan Artifacts in a Museum of Archeology

Richard P. Smiraglia

SUMMARY. Metadata schemes target resources as information-packages, without attention to the distinction between content and carrier. Most schema are derived without empirical understanding of the concepts that need to be represented, the ways in which terms representing the central concepts might best be derived, and how metadata descriptions will be used for retrieval. Research is required to resolve this dilemma, and much research will be required if the plethora of schemes that already exist are to be made efficacious for resource description and retrieval. A preliminary study was designed to see whether the bibliographic concept of "the work" could be of any relevance among artifacts held by a museum. The "works metaphor" is extended from the bibliographic to the artifactual domain by altering the terms of the definition slightly, thus: instantiation is understood as content genealogy.

Richard P. Smiraglia is Professor, Palmer School Library and Information Science, Long Island University, 720 Northern Boulevard, Brookville, NY 11548 (E-mail: Richard.Smiraglia@liu.edu).

The author would like to acknowledge the contribution of Alessandro Pezzati, Museum Archivist, who provided access to all museum records concerning the artifacts under study, and to Lynn A. Grant, Conservationist, University of Pennsylvania Museum of Archaeology and Anthropology.

[Haworth co-indexing entry note]: "Content Metadata–An Analysis of Etruscan Artifacts in a Museum of Archeology." Smiraglia, Richard P. Co-published simultaneously in *Cataloging & Classification Quarterly* (The Haworth Information Press, an imprint of The Haworth Press, Inc.) Vol. 40, No. 3/4, 2005, pp. 135-151; and: *Metadata: A Cataloger's Primer* (ed: Richard P. Smiraglia) The Haworth Information Press, an imprint of The Haworth Press, Inc., 2005, pp. 135-151. Single or multiple copies of this article are available for a fee from The Haworth Document Delivery Service [1-800-HAWORTH, 9:00 a.m. - 5:00 p.m. (EST). E-mail address: docdelivery@haworthpress.com].

Available online at http://www.haworthpress.com/web/CCQ

doi:10.1300/J104v40n03_07

Case studies of Etruscan artifacts from the University of Pennsylvania Museum of Archaeology and Anthropology are used to demonstrate the inherence of the work in non-documentary artifacts.

KEYWORDS. Artifacts, cultural information resources, instantiation, content genealogy, content metadata

INTRODUCTION

Even in the short life-span of the term "metadata," many complex schemes have been developed rapidly to assist in the description of resources, so as to facilitate retrieval. Yet, like their bibliographic counterparts–cataloging rules–metadata schemes have emerged with two major (if traditional) difficulties. The first is that the schemes target resources as information-packages, without attention to the distinction between content and carrier, elsewhere described as item and work (Smiraglia 2001). The second difficulty is that most schema are derived without empirical understanding of the concepts that need to be represented, the ways in which terms representing the central concepts might best be derived, and how metadata descriptions will be used for retrieval. Regardless of the complexity or the modernity of metadata schemes, the historical problem is perpetuated–once again we are creating retrieval tools based on resources in hand, selected essentially by chance, without knowledge of the characteristics of other, similar resources. Research is required to resolve this dilemma, and much research will be required if the plethora of schemes that already exist are to be made efficacious for resource description and retrieval. Even more research will be required to facilitate cross-walks for knowledge sharing.

This paper represents one small step toward such research. I will report the results of a preliminary study, which was designed to see whether the bibliographic concept of "the work" could be of any relevance among artifacts held by a museum. To do so, I begin by posing "the work" as a metaphor for the content of an information-package. The empirical portion of the study is qualitative, involving case study analysis of artifacts, and unstructured interviews of museum staff. A preliminary report appeared in Smiraglia (2004), from which much of the introductory material here is derived.

THE "WORKS" METAPHOR

"Works" are key entities in the universe of recorded knowledge. (Works are sometimes also described by these key terms: opera, oeuvres, Werke, etc.) Elsewhere (Smiraglia 2001, 2002) I have demonstrated that substantial proportions of works in the bibliographic universe exist in multiple instantiations, which can be understood epistemologically as falling into two categories: works whose instantiations are derivative, and those that are mutations from the progenitor. Taxonomies that can classify instantiations of works have been developed by Tillett (1987), IFLA (1998), Smiraglia (2001), and others, and several authors have contributed differing sets of language to describe works (see Smiraglia 2003). Smiraglia (2001), Vellucci (1994), Yee (1993), and others have demonstrated the vast potential for variant instantiation (i.e., mutation, derivation, etc.).

Works mutate and derive across time and culture in response to their entrance into a canon of cultural meaning. That is, works that become somehow associated with meaning beyond their own texts–such as the *Bible*, or *Gone with the wind*–will be reproduced in a wide variety of editions, adaptations, performances, and so forth. Systems for information retrieval must be designed with this in mind, to facilitate gathering of the instantiations of a given work, as well as selection of one from among many. The metaphor of the work and its instantiations is not a uniquely documentary phenomenon; it can be extended into other domains of recorded knowledge. (For instance, Coleman (2003) has demonstrated the application of the "works" metaphor to scientific models.) The present study represents an attempt to extend the works metaphor into the realm of natural artifacts that might be held by museum repositories.

The characteristics of bibliographic works are as follows (see Smiraglia 2001):

1. "Work" is an abstract concept (immaterial, conceptual);
2. A work is a new synthesis of knowledge that consists of ideational content and semantic content;

3. Once expressed, a work may take a variety of physical instantiations;
4. The expression of a work may change freely in either ideational or semantic content or both;
5. Relationships among works are complex; and
6. A work's essential role is as a vehicle of communication between its creator and its consumers.

Instantiations (often referred to as "versions" or "editions" or even "manifestations" of a work) are the artifacts of the individual points in time when a given work is set down, or recorded either for preservation or for dissemination. A concrete example: an author creates a story, writes it out as a manuscript (first instantiation), has an edited version of it published as the first edition (second instantiation), and when it becomes a hit it is translated into another language (third instantiation, this time a mutation), and also sells it to be made into a screenplay (fourth instantiation, another mutation). The motion picture is also a hit (fifth instantiation) and is sold on DVD (sixth instantiation, or second instantiation of the motion picture). This fame encourages repeated new editions of the original novel both in expensive hardback editions and in paperback editions (seventh and eighth instantiations, these are considered derivations). A mutation is an instantiation in which the semantic or ideational content or both have been altered; a derivation is an instantiation, subsequent to the first, in which no semantic or ideational content has changed. IFLA's FRBR model with some confusion refers to these as "expressions" and "manifestations."

From Documents to Artifacts, from Instantiation to Content Genealogy

To carry the metaphor from the bibliographic domain to the artifactual domain we alter the terms of the definition slightly. What we have heretofore called "instantiation" is now understood as content genealogy, and we expect there might be many categories of mutation and derivation. A new term, "re-presentation" (hereafter rendered simply as "representation"), is used to describe images or descriptions of otherwise unique artifacts (fine art, natural science)–representation clearly precedes instantiation. Artifacts, real-world information objects, have distinct ideational and expressive content apart from their carriers as do bibliographic works. Artifacts are unique and immutable, but their representations are potentially many and are infinitely mutable. Further, whereas in the documentary domain no particular instantiation can be claimed to be concurrent with the work, in the artifactual domain the unique artifact is itself concurrent with the work. We begin with a simple model (see Figure 1). The artifact is unique and immutable. Its representations, such as a photograph, can be contained on websites or in books. The book itself is subject to derivation, such as multiple editions, all of which will contain the representation of the artifact. For each representation$_n$ there can be many sites of reproduction (representations in print)$_n$ all of which might be subject to multiple instantiation$_n$.

CASE STUDY OF ETRUSCAN ARTIFACTS

To date there is little or no evidence about the instance or extent of the representation of artifacts. Case study in the qualitative vein is an appro-

FIGURE 1. Content Genealogy Model

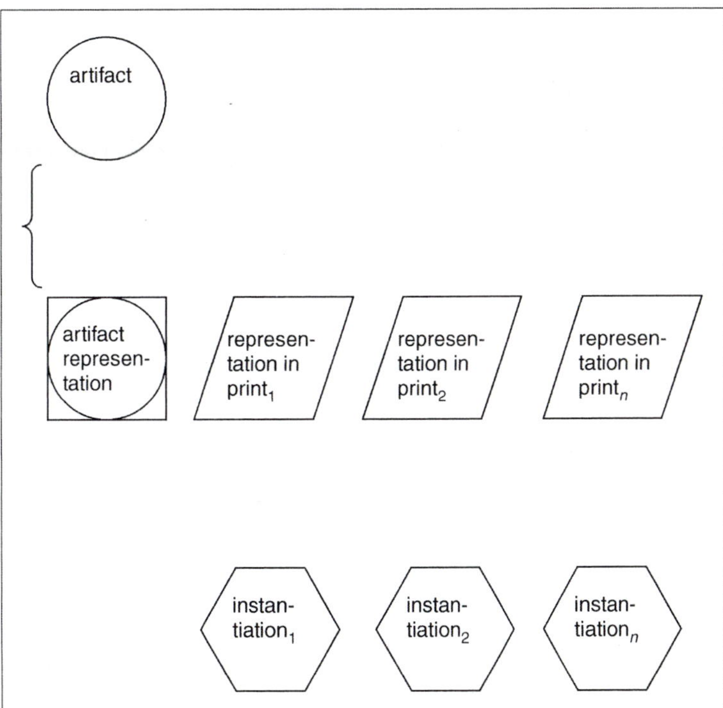

priate first step in unexplored territory. Essential research questions boiled down to whether multiple representations of an artifact might be extant and might therefore need to be represented in an information system, and whether the "works" metaphor might be useful for describing sets of representations. Therefore, a set of artifacts was sought that would be easily available to the researcher and that would be likely to have appeared in representations in print as well as in digital form. Etruscan artifacts from the University of Pennsylvania Museum of Archaeology and Anthropology were selected to provide qualitative evidence of the content genealogy of representations of non-documentary artifacts. These artifacts are housed in a popular exhibition that is also well-represented in digital form on the Web (http://www.museum.upenn.edu/new/worlds_intertwined/etruscan/main.shtml) and in a published *Guide* (2002). Eight artifacts (represented in Table 1) were selected based on their prominence in the exhibit, and with attention to their diversity.

TABLE 1. The Eight Artifacts as Described by UPM

Material	***Artifact***	***Source***	***Date***	***URL****
Terracotta	Hut urn	Said to have come from the area between Albano and Genzano	8th c. BC	earliest.shtml
Impasto	Kotyle	Narce, Tomb I	7th c. BC	orientalizing.shtml
Impasto**	Footed bowl	Narce, Tomb 19M	early 7th c. BC	faliscan.shtml
	Etrusco-Corinthian Olpe	Vulci, Tomb B	6th c. BC	daily.shtml
	Nenfro Lintel***	Ovrieto, Crocifisso del Tufo Necropolis	ca. 550 BC	language.shtml
	Bucchero Kantharos	Vulci, Tomb B	6th c. BC	technology.shtml
Terracotta	Antefix with Satyr Head	Caere (Cerveteri)	4th c. BC	architecture.shtml
Alabaster	Cinerary urn		3rd-2nd c. BC	final.shtml

*http://www.museum.upenn.edu/new/worlds_intertwined/etruscan/main.shtml
** "Craftsmen often made ceramic copies of the bronze conical stands used by rulers for banquet wine. The more economical material allowed large scale, extravagant forms."
*** "These 'talking objects' seem to express magically the power that ancient peoples felt came from the ability to read and write."

Specifically, operational research questions were:

1. How many representations in-house can be found for these eight artifacts?
2. Does their inclusion in the exhibit indicate the possibility of greater representation or instantiation?
3. Are the representations instantiated outside the museum (in literature, on the Web, etc.)?
4. Is there a difference between representation of an artifact that is deliberately informative (one that bears text) and one that is merely persistent?

We can begin, then, with reference to our model as the base set. For each artifact, it is apparent that the artifact is represented by one photograph, which in turn has been digitized for use on the Web. This, therefore, is the minimum set (A, AR_1, AR_2) among our cases.

Representation Taxonomy

The Museum Archivist was the gatekeeper for this study, the one person with access to all internal records about the artifacts. We began with an interview, from which a meta-level taxonomy of representation emerged. At the top level the taxonomy resembles our initial model, except that representation now can take one of two categories–metadata (textual description) or representation (image or model):

Artifact

- Metadata
  - Instantiation
- Representation
  - Instantiation

For each artifact in the museum, both textual descriptions (metadata) and representations (images or models) exist. Both metadata sets and representations are commonly reproduced in a variety of ways, thus yielding instantiations. In fact, the two nodes–metadata and representation–can be broken down into more specific information-object sets. These are:

- Metadata
  - Finding aid
  - Field notes
  - Letters
  - Conservation treatment notes
  - Register descriptions
    - Object cards
  - Image order invoices
  - Museum database records
  - Catalog card records
- Representation
  - Field photos
  - Drawings
  - Working images
  - 3D models
  - Exhibition color images
    - Digitized images
  - Conservation photos
  - Photo archives
    - Negatives
    - Prints
    - Transparencies
  - Object reproductions

This, then, is the meta-level set of metadata and representation instantiations that might exist for any given artifact within the repository. It is important to note that each of these information-objects serves a specific purpose within the museum.

The Eight Artifacts

For each artifact, every record in-house was examined and noted. The taxonomy served to guide the research. That is, finding aids were examined first, then field notes and registers, and so forth. Ultimately several divisions of the museum were visited, as each holds its own unique records. Whenever possible records were copied, yielding (ironically) yet another set of instantiations. It was no surprise to discover that for each artifact both metadata and representations exist. Table 2 contains the total numbers of representations and metadata sets that were found for each artifact, both in-house and outside the repository. We compiled a bibliography of 150 texts on the Etruscans from the collections of research libraries in New York. Unfortunately, examination of those texts yielded no representations of these eight artifacts. Likewise, Web searches revealed no representations (not even those on the museum's own Website). But internal records indicated the presence of several publications in which both metadata and images could be found.

The symbols appearing in the columns for in-house metadata and representations correspond to terms in the taxonomy. The symbols for external sources correspond to publications on a short list:

The Robert H. Coleman Collection of Archaeological Objects. 1897. *Catalogue*. Philadelphia: Davis and Harvey's Gallery.

Bates, William N. 1905. University of Pennsylvania. *Transactions. Dept. Archaeology* I, Pt. III: 165-168.

The University of Pennsylvania. 1905. *Transactions of the Department of Archaeology, Free Museum of Science and Art*, vol. I, Part III.

Luce, Stephen Bleecker, ed. 1921. *Catalogue of The Mediterranean Section*. Philadelphia, The Museum.

The Gallery of Italic and Etruscan Art. 1933. *The University Museum bulletin* v. 4 no. 6 (Nov.): 6.

Dohan, Edith Hall. *American Journal of Archaeology* 1934.

Dohan, Edith Hall. 1942. *Italic tomb-groups in the University Museum*. Philadelphia: University of Pennsylvania Press; London: Humphrey Milford; Oxford Press.

Edwards, G. Roger. 1958. Italy and Rome. *University Museum bulletin* 22 no. 2 (June) 5-11.

Publications of the University Museum 1973. Philadelphia: University of Pennsylvania.

Moser, M.E. 1984. *Etruscan pottery: the meeting of Greece and Etruria*. Dickinson College.

Horne, Lee, ed. 1985. *Introduction to the collections of The University Museum bulletin*. Philadelphia: The Museum.

Herrmann/Gottfried Semper 1985 MIT Press.

Horne, Lee, ed. 2002. *Guide to the Etruscan and Roman worlds at the University of Pennsylvania Museum of Archaeology and Anthropology*. Philadelphia: The Museum.

The list is in chronological order, which is itself informative. Note that there are periodic clusters around exhibits, catalogs, and journal articles. (Because the list was compiled from museum sources, some of the citations are incomplete and could not be verified independently.) Each of these publications appears to be unique–a search on OCLC's Worldcat in July 2004 turned up no additional editions or other instantiations.

The chief feature of Table 2 is the fact that there is disparity among the artifacts in the quantity of metadata and image representations. That is, beyond the initial set of register description and exhibit image, certain of the artifacts have substantial sets of information-objects, both in-house and outside the museum. The Etrusco-Corinthian olpe has the most, and the lintel has the fewest. Because all eight artifacts were selected from the Web version of a popular exhibition, and all are included in the exhibition catalog, these factors must not contribute to the size of the representation set. The next factor checked was the presence of field notes–it seemed reasonable to consider whether the extent of notes created at the time of excavation might have any influence on the size of the representation set. But, as Table 2 demonstrates, no field notes were found for three of the artifacts–the Etrusco-Corinthian olpe, the hut urn, and the lintel. The olpe (with no field notes) has the largest representation set in the study, and the cinerary urn, which has the next largest set, has extensive field notes. So the presence of field notes was ruled out as a factor contributing to size of the representation set. Finally, whether the artifacts is a deliberately signifying object–one that has writing on it–also can be ruled out in this study. The lintel, with few representations, and the cinerary urn, with many, are the two signifying objects in the study.

Earlier I used the term 'content genealogy' to describe the succession of representations that occur along a chronological continuum. There are several rich examples in this study. The easiest to understand, perhaps, is the content of the museum's database, which includes verbatim

TABLE 2. Artifacts and Representations: Totals

Artifact	Representations in house	Representations in publication	Metadata in house	Metadata in publication
Etrusco-Corinthian Olpe	Wb,LS^1,LS^2,Ng^1,Ng^2,Ng^3,Ng^4,Ng^5,CRp	Gu,GS,Do,DC	AC,OR,AR,CRp,LR,Wb	Ex,DC
Footed bowl	Wb,FN,Cy,Ng	Do,Gu	AC,OR,AR,FN,LR,Wb	Ex,DC,Do
Kantharos	Wb,FN,Cy,Ng	Gu	AC,OR,AR,FN,LR,Wb	Ex,DC
Hut urn	Wb	MB'33,Gu	AC,OR,AR,CRc,Wb	Ex
Antefix/Satyr Head	Wb,FN,Cy,Ng,CRp	AJA'24,MB'33, Gu	AC,OR,AR,FN,CRc,Wb	Ex,Lu,AJA'24
Cinerary urn	Wb,CRp^1,CRp^2,CRp^3,FN,Cy,Ng	Gu	AC,OR,AR,Wb,CRp,FN	Ex,Lu,Tr,Ba,Fb,Pa
Kotyle	Wb,FN,Cy,Ng	Gu	AC,OR,AR,Wb	Ex,Do
Lintel	Wb	Gu	AC,OR,OR,IR,AR,Wb	Ex

the content of the object record cards; this creates a simple set: M, M^1. In addition to forming a linear sequence in time (a parallel to the bibliographic successive relationship), this relationship is one in which the original metadata set is embedded in a new set; this "embedding" parallels the amplification relationship demonstrated in the bibliographic arena. Another simple example is the digital image that appears on the website, which is the same as that which appears in the printed *Guide*; for each artifact there is a set: R^1, $R^1{}_1$. The olpe yields some more complex examples. A lantern slide image, for which there is also a nitrate negative, a 35 mm. negative, and 3 copies of the 35 mm. negative, appears as a photograph in Dohan (1934); this yields the set: $R^1{}_{ls}$, $R^1{}_{nn}$, $R^1{}_{35n\,(35n1\text{-}3)}$, $R^1{}_p$, $R^1{}_{p2}$. There are two such (different) images of the olpe. And, in fact, all of the images listed in the column headed "representations in print" come from images held in the museum, with similar genealogies. The problem for metadata is to describe each representation accordingly and to allow linkage for collocation.

The last part of the analysis involved removing all of the functional metadata and representations–those created in-house–to see whether any difference might emerge in the size of the representation set. The reasoning here was that the in-house metadata sets seemed nearly identical across all eight artifacts. Given that, an obvious question is: what would the distribution look like without those sets? The answer, as before, is ambiguous. The olpe and the cinerary urn have the largest sets of representations in print, followed closely by the satyr head antefix.

In sum, the olpe and the cinerary urn have the most representations and instantiations, and the satyr head is close behind. The other five artifacts have much smaller representation sets. Presence in the exhibit or on the Web, field notes, and signifying content all could be ruled out as contributors to the size of the representation set. However, the three artifacts with substantial representation sets all seem to have appeared in published volumes soon after their acquisition.

This observation was confirmed in an interview with the Conservationist, who called these items "frequent flyers." According to her, once an object has been published it gets requested for loan, photos of it are requested, and so forth, even if the museum has better or more interesting exemplars items in its collections. These items spend more time on loan than they do in the museum on exhibit. Each time the artifact is loaned an entirely new set of before- and after-metadata and photographs are generated to insure the continued integrity of the artifact. And, while on loan, the artifact is likely to have metadata and image representations published in the loan-exhibition catalog, which will likely generate more attention over time.

Metadata Forms and Information Ecologies

Earlier we noted that the artifacts all had more or less equivalent metadata sets in-house. These sets can be summarized at the meta-level in terms of their sources (field notes, accession ledgers, object records, conservation records and reports, and online catalog records) and data types (object entities, and activity-based descriptors). In fact, each division of the museum that deals with the artifact generates its own metadata set and might generate its own image representations as well. Object-type metadata sets tend to include a common set of descriptors, but activity-based descriptors differ from division to division depending on the work that has taken place. The accession ledger contains information about where and when the artifact was found, the object record contains terms that locate the artifact in culture (people, time, place), the conservation records related precise physical characteristics and actions taken, loan records indicate the time and place to which the item was loaned along with any special care requirements, and condition reports (used to note a breakage or other anomaly) include a narrative about the incoming and outgoing condition of the artifact. The museum's online catalog uses a complex template that includes "tabs" for all of the above, within which each division's own metadata set can reside.

But as noted before, each artifact also seems to carry its own unique identifier set from division to division. This set, which I call the "object entity," includes:

Object type

Material

Culture

Source

Collector

Date acquired.

This, then, can be said to be the base metadata set uncovered in-house. In this museum, at least, this set of identifiers is found useful across divisions and has the capability to uniquely identify each artifact.

However, there was little authority control–what was called "Etruscan" in one place might have been called "Etrurian" or "Italic" in another, for instance. These terms are not quite synonyms, but each was considered a useful identifier in one context or another. One artifact, the lintel, had two object records with two different numbers. The second record was uncovered during this research, but it was not the record used by the museum to represent the artifact in the exhibition or elsewhere.

The most interesting observation was the degree to which each division of the museum generates its own metadata and representations. Albrechtsen (2000) has written about what she calls "information-ecologies," groups of people working together who generate their own domain-specific vocabulary and ontology. This museum is a perfect example. While a meta-level description exists in-house and is useful across the institution, each division of the museum is also encouraged to use its own information ecology to generate useful metadata, all of which eventually reside together in the online catalog.

CONCLUSIONS

The research questions for this study focused attention on whether there would be many representations for each artifact in-house (there were), whether there might also be many representations externally (and again there were), and whether mitigating factors concerning the size and diversity of the representation set could be identified. We found that these artifacts had in-house representations at a fairly predictable rate based on internal museum functions. Each artifact was represented in each division of the museum as it passed from accession to conservation to exhibit to loan, and so forth. Divergence in the size and diversity of the representation set appeared to be a function of the "popularity" of the artifact–popularity here defined as the aftermath of having appeared in print. Thus popularity, at least among these eight artifacts, was a function of publication and not of exhibit. We found that the object-entity has a stable and consistent metadata set. But we also discovered that specific ecologies within the museum contribute varying but related metadata sets as well.

All of this suggests that a meta-theory of content genealogy is possible. Such a meta-theory would harmonize the "works" metaphor from the bibliographic domain with a "representation" metaphor from the artifactual domain. Instantiation, or the evolution and reproduction of representations is observed in both domains. Canonicity, which seems to contribute to the size of instantiation sets in the bibliographic domain, is mirrored in the artifactual domain by what we have here called "popularity." At a meta-level, cultural acceptance of a work or an artifact creates public demand for more representations. This is in line with Eggert's suggestion that works are collaborations over time–participatory entities that incorporate the "agencies" of those who encounter them (1994, 76).

Much more empirical evidence is necessary. The results here represent a preliminary analysis of a preliminary study–we have seen some interesting concepts emerge that might help formulate a larger-scale empirical study. The evolution, derivation, mutation, and dissemination of ideational and expressive content across time, culture, and linguistic boundaries must be the subject of further investigation. And any meta-theory must describe the interaction of signification (meaning) and reception (or perception).

Nash (2002) narrates the history of early Philadelphia, interpreting artifacts and archival evidence to compile the untold story of the first capital of the United States, which was also the largest and most racially diverse city of colonial America. He lends credence to our effort with this observation concerning a coffeepot (Nash 2002, 66-68):

> Such a piece as a coffeepot . . . provides an example of how such an artifact can have multiple meanings. It can be viewed most directly as a handsome example of high-style eighteenth-century craftsmanship, as an intrinsically valuable work of decorative art. Through a second lens, the coffeepot can be seen as a crucial piece of evidence in tracing the new meaning of gentility in the eighteenth century. Amid rising consumerism, in both England and its colonies, genteel people developed a new sense of refinement, acted out in elegant manners, witty conversation, and graceful movements on occasions that depended on the importation of new beverages from exotic ports of call–in this case coffee beans from South America. Through a third lens, the Richardson coffeepot can be considered, although not actually seen, with regard to the organization of rhythms of work of the artisan who crated the object. Behind the coffeepot lay several work processes involving African cultivation of the coffee beans, the sailors who shipped them to Philadelphia, and the small silversmith workshop production that linked together the labor of apprentices, journeymen, and master craftsmen. Finally, behind the coffeepot, absent from the

view of the lovely pot itself, resided the role of the crafts worker in the political and social life of a port town such as Philadelphia.

The richness of artifactual evidence belies the simplicity of the metadata that describe them. An artifact, like a "work," is greater than the sum of its perceptions. Sitting in the focal point, an artifact can help a scholar tell a story that helps us better understand the world in which we live. The collectivity of the representations of the artifact, joined together in a virtual museum, offer the scholarly world a potentially much richer information resource. We will continue to need better empirical understanding to aid in the development of content metadata to meet that challenge.

WORKS CITED

Albrechtsen, Hanne. 2000. The dynamism and stability of classification in information ecologies–problems and possibilities. In *Dynamism and stability in knowledge organization: proceedings of the Sixth International ISKO Conference 10-13 July 2000 Toronto, Canada*, ed. Clare Beghtol, Lynne C. Howarth, Nancy J. Williamson. Würzbuerg: Ergon Verlag, pp. 1-2.

Coleman, Anita S. 2003. Scientific models as works. In *Works as entities for information retrieval* ed. Richard P. Smiraglia. Binghamton, N.Y.: The Haworth Press, Inc., pp. 129-59.

Eggert, Paul. 1994. Editing paintings/conserving literature: The nature of the 'work.' In *Studies in Bibliography* v.47 ed. by David L. Vander Meulen, pp. 65-78. Charlottesville, Pub. for The Bibliographical Society of the University of Virginia by The University Press of Virginia.

Guide to the Etruscan and Roman Worlds. 2002. Philadelphia: The University of Pennsylvania Museum of Archaeology and Anthropology.

International Federation of Library Associations, Study Group on the Functional Requirements for Bibliographic Records. 1998. *Functional requirements for bibliographic records*. München: K. G. Saur.

Nash, Gary B. 2002. *First city: Philadelphia and the forging of historical memory*. Philadelphia: University of Pennsylvania Press.

Smiraglia, Richard P. 2001. *The nature of "a work:" Implications for the organization of knowledge*. Lanham, Md.: Scarecrow Press.

Smiraglia, Richard P. 2002. "Works as signs, symbols, and canons: The epistemology of the work." *Knowledge organization* 28 (2002): 192-202.

Smiraglia, Richard P. ed. 2003. *Works as entities for information retrieval*. Binghamton, NY: The Haworth Press, Inc.

Smiraglia, Richard P. 2004. Knowledge sharing and content genealogy: Extending the "works" model as a metaphor for non-documentary artifacts with case studies of Etruscan artifacts. In McIlwaine, Ia ed., *Knowledge organization and the global in-*

formation society, proceedings of the Eighth International ISKO Conference 13-16 July 2004 London UK. Würzburg: Ergon Verlag, pp. 309-14.

Tillett, Barbara Ann Barnett. 1987. Bibliographic relationships: Toward a conceptual structure of bibliographic information used in cataloging. PhD dissertation, University of California, Los Angeles.

Vellucci, Sherry Lynn. 1994. Bibliographic relationships among musical bibliographic entities: A conceptual analysis of music represented in a library catalog with a taxonomy of the relationships discovered. DLS dissertation, Columbia University.

Yee, Martha M. 1993. Moving image works and manifestations. PhD dissertation, University of California, Los Angeles.

PART II: HOW TO CREATE, APPLY, AND USE METADATA

From Cataloging to Metadata: Dublin Core Records for the Library Catalog

Anita S. Coleman

SUMMARY. The Dublin Core is an international standard for describing and cataloging all kinds of information resources: books, articles, videos, and World Wide Web (web) resources. Sixteen Dublin Core (DC) elements and the steps for cataloging web resources using these elements and minimal controlled values are discussed, general guidelines for metadata creation are highlighted, a worksheet is provided to create

Anita S. Coleman is Assistant Professor, School of Information Resources and Library Science, University of Arizona at Tucson, Tucson, AZ 85719 (E-mail: asc@u.arizona.edu).

[Haworth co-indexing entry note]: "From Cataloging to Metadata: Dublin Core Records for the Library Catalog." Coleman, Anita S. Co-published simultaneously in *Cataloging & Classification Quarterly* (The Haworth Information Press, an imprint of The Haworth Press, Inc.) Vol. 40, No. 3/4, 2005, pp. 153-181; and: *Metadata: A Cataloger's Primer* (ed: Richard P. Smiraglia) The Haworth Information Press, an imprint of The Haworth Press, Inc., 2005, pp. 153-181. Single or multiple copies of this article are available for a fee from The Haworth Document Delivery Service [1-800-HAWORTH, 9:00 a.m. - 5:00 p.m. (EST). E-mail address: docdelivery@haworthpress.com].

Available online at http://www.haworthpress.com/web/CCQ

doi:10.1300/J104v40n03_08

the DC metadata records for the library catalog, and sample resource descriptions in DC are included.

KEYWORDS. Dublin Core, cataloging, resource description

INTRODUCTION

Professional positions like Metadata Architect and Metadata Librarian are increasingly becoming common in both business settings and in libraries. Some libraries are even replacing job titles such as Cataloger with them. Metadata creation and cataloging are both activities that involve the description of information resources in order to facilitate their information discovery and retrieval in tools such as library catalogs. However, as more and more information, especially electronic, continues to be produced and proliferated, new and simpler standards for resource description became necessary to accomplish the goal of universal bibliographical control and information access.

Library catalogs use the *Anglo-American Cataloging Rules, Second Edition Revised* (AACR2R) to describe resources in a standard way; these descriptions are encoded in the Machine Readable Cataloging (MARC) format. Bibliographic utilities like OCLC and RLIN are first checked before the library cataloger creates a bibliographic record for the resource. If the bibliographic description already exists, the record is modified or adapted and exported into the Online Public Access Catalog (OPAC) of the library. Some libraries, rather than using OCLC and an integrated library automation system to hold their OPAC, may use a proprietary database using SQL or other technologies. DC emerged as a simpler alternate to MARC to describe electronic resources and is now used widely to describe all types of resources, including books.

WHAT IS DUBLIN CORE?

DC stands for Dublin Core, a standard from the National Information Standards Organization (NISO) and the International Organization for Standardization (ISO). Originally, there were 15 DC elements that could be used for creating resource descriptions. Last year DC was extended with a 16th element, Audience. When only the original 15 DC elements are used in metadata creation, the level of DC use is called Simple; this can be considered equivalent to minimal level cataloging. When the 16th element, refinements to the original 15, such as qualifiers and encoding schemes (for example, the vocabulary term and name of the vocabulary from which it is derived), are used, the level of DC use is called Qualified; think of this as full level cataloging. This article provides directions for *use* of a level of DC that is Qualified and yet very simple and straightforward to practice. I do so because (1) simple DC does not help in the goal of information discovery, (2) not all born-digital resources, i.e., electronic resources, have a print equivalent or share the characteristics of books, serials, videos, computer files, and other information resources traditionally organized in the library, and thus require more complex descriptions than simple, (3) for digital resources to be included in the library catalog integrating new metadata standards such as DC with older standards such as MARC and *AACR2R*, or more complete standards such as EAD, is necessary. A barrier to electronic resource cataloging is that many library professionals and information specialists continue to believe that cataloging web resources is a waste of time; it is better to make web pages (essentially webliographies or lists) because many of the web resources are too ephemeral to be included in the library catalog. However, new tools such as URL link checkers make the maintenance of metadata for web resources much simpler. It is more efficient to have users start with the library catalog as a single gateway to the universe of knowledge, no matter the format or type of information sought. The usage of DC refinements and principles advocated in this article is both integrative and time saving. It will save the time of the library cataloger and the user because it recognizes the lessons learned by the library, archival, and museum cataloging communities and tries to incorporate them into DC metadata creation.

DC elements of description may be encoded as text in XML, HTML meta tags, or RDF. I will not describe here the encoding of DC records or the use of bibliographic utilities like OCLC or general document interchange standards such as XML or other library standards such as MARC to encode DC. The sixteen DC elements are:

Title

Creator

Subject

Description

Publisher

Contributor

Date

Type

Format

Identifier

Source

Language

Relation

Coverage

Rights

Audience

Each of these elements is described further. Some general guidelines about metadata creation that can be drawn from the rich history of libraries in descriptive and subject cataloging, and museums and archival description are first presented.

BRIDGING THE CATALOGING AND METADATA CREATION GAP

Library cataloging has always been considered costly and prone to budget cuts and criticisms. Even as early as the late 1800s American libraries were concerned about the unit cost of cataloging, i.e., how much did it cost to catalog a book? Providing resource descriptions for information access is thus a costly business and little by little libraries have relinquished new forms of materials to others. DC was envisioned as a simple way to get novices–people who are new to cataloging information resources for discovery–as a way to help solve this problem. This has influenced the language used by the DC standard greatly. Thus, cataloging is synonymous for the activity of metadata description. Resource descriptions are synonymous for DC records. Instead of language such as tags, fields, and subfields (words used in the MARC standard), DC uses elements. It is also for this reason that DC has 16 elements while the library MARC has 999 tags, which can be considered the top level fields of description (not that all resources require 999 tags; most use only about 5 to 10 tags of description). While it certainly is easier to create 15 elements as opposed to 'tags and fields and subfields' it is also less easy to uniquely identify information resources. The best of cataloging practices can however be captured in two simple guidelines for metadata creation using DC. These are:

> Guideline 1: Resource description should be **as complete as possible**. If you are unable to describe based on your examination of the resource, first, try to supply the data. For example, if there is no title, make up a title. Leave the element blank only as a last resort. When no information is completed for an element it is essentially meaningless. See also the DC Dumb-down Principle and corollary described below.

> Guideline 2: Resource description should be **consistent**. Human nature tends to be more inconsistent than consistent. However, the research evidence indicates that principles of consistency and uniformity are used in cataloging and classification to help both the humans doing the work to avoid cognitive overload, lessen judgment, and also aid users with better information retrieval. There are many techniques for ensuring consistency and the simplest is to use words from a pre-determined and authoritative list whenever possible for controlled values.

In addition, there are general principles of metadata creation as per the DC standard. These are:

> Guideline 3: All of the DC elements are optional, repeatable, and modifiable by qualifiers. All elements are optional, which means that any of the DC elements may be omitted. All elements are repeatable; this means that if there is more than one person who created the resource, and you can use the Creator element as many times as you need to record the names of multiple creators. Similarly, all other elements (Title, Subject, etc.) may be repeated as many times as needed. DC elements are often modifiable by qualifiers, which means that elements have qualifiers. These include element refinements or encoding schemes that refine the original DC elements further with the use of controlled vocabularies. DC qualifiers are optional, too. Refinement qualifiers may be vocabulary terms from registered lists such as standard library tools like the *Library of Congress Subject Headings* and *Dewey Decimal*

Classification; these two may be used to qualify the subject element. There are other vocabularies that may be used. The name of the vocabulary used is the encoding scheme qualifier.

HOW TO CREATE DC METADATA

This section provides an element-by-element description of how to create DC metadata for an electronic (web) information resource; all 16 elements are described in detail and each element includes the following categories of instruction and information: **Name**, **Label**, **Definition**, **Comments**, **Chief Source of Information**, **Controlled Values**, **Inputting Guidelines**, and **Notes**. **Name** is the name given to the element in the DC standard. **Label** refers to the label you will see in an integrated library system or a bibliographic utility such as OCLC for entering this information. Often, the Label will be the same as the element name, but sometimes it may be different. **Definition** is the definition given in the DC standard. **Comments** also come for the DC as appropriate. **Chief source of information** is instruction that is modeled after the technical reading of the item for cataloging practices of the *Anglo American Cataloging Rules, Second Edition, Revised (AACR2R). AACR2R* helps the cataloger by providing a list of the places and components in the resource being cataloged that may be consulted for information about the element being described; this is known as technical reading of an item. In other words, the process of technical reading provides specific guidance to the sources of information, the exact places in the resource from which the metadata for each element may be selected. **Controlled values** is also modeled after *AACR2R* and MARC to some extent and allows the metadata creator to know if the element uses a list of controlled values, a classification, or controlled vocabulary. These values may be made enforceable by the software or humanly selected from a given list or through consultation of an external list/source such as registries. Controlled values help make meaning clearer and consistent. They do so by keeping the form of element values, the metadata content for each element describing the resource, the same across multiple resources. Precision, increased relevance of results retrieved in response to a query, is improved in subject information retrieval by the use of controlled values and vocabularies. **Inputting guidelines** provide special directions that must be followed to enter the resource description. These illustrate the general principles of DC metadata creation. **Metadata Creator Notes** discuss how much of the cataloger's (metadata creator) judgment is involved in creating the metadata for each element. Metadata creation is often subjective rather than objective. Without clear rules and standards, two different catalogers may describe the same resource quite differently. The term subjective is used to indicate that a particular element can be described based on the personal judgment of the resource cataloger and objective is used to denote objectivity, when the data or content is found on the resource or may be identified in a similar manner by all resource metadata creators and catalogers. Appendix 1 contains a form that can be used to practice DC metadata creation and Appendix 2 contains samples of DC metadata for web information resources.

Element: Title

Name: Title.
Label: Title.
Definition: A name given to the resource.
Comment: Typically, a Title will be a name by which the resource is formally known.
Chief Source of Information: Take title from the actual information resource; if none found on resource take from the browser title and if nothing is there, use other sources as appropriate or supply the title.
Controlled Values: No.
Inputting Guidelines: Enter the title information as found in the resource. Use capitalization and punctuation as found in resource.
Metadata Creator Notes: Generally, there should be no individual judgment involved as the metadata creator is merely transcribing the title, when the resource has a clearly presented title. Many electronic resources, however, may not have a title clearly visible or the title may be generic for the whole and not the specific part being cataloged. In these cases, creating the metadata for the title, where the cataloger must create or supply title, can become subjective. Follow the guidance prescribed in the Chief source of information and generally take title from the actual information resource whenever possible.

Element: Creator

Name: Creator.
Label: Creator.

Definition: An entity primarily responsible for making the content of the resource.
Comments: Examples of a Creator include a person, an organization, or a service. Typically, the name of a Creator should be used to indicate the entity.
Chief Source of Information: Take Creator from the actual information resource; if none found on resource, take from the browser title including parts of the resource, or use other sources as appropriate.
Controlled Values: No.
Inputting Guidelines: Enter the Creator as found in the resource. Use capitalization and punctuation as found in resource. If Creator is an organization, enter the name of the organization.
Metadata Creator Notes: Objective. Cataloging the creator becomes a subjective activity should the creator not be listed in the resource; while it is possible through extra research to find out this information, generally this would take too much time and hence, most cataloging is only done based on actual examination of the resource. If creator cannot be readily determined from this, leave this element blank. Many electronic resources do not have the creator easily identifiable.

Element: Subject

Name: Subject.
Label: Subject.
Definition: The topic of the content of the resource.
Comment: Typically, a Subject will be expressed as keywords, key phrases, or classification codes that describe a topic of the resource. Recommended best practice is to select a value from a controlled vocabulary or formal classification scheme.
Chief Source of Information: Determine Subject from the actual information resource.
Controlled Values: Optional. Use *Library of Congress Subject Headings* (LCSH) or keywords found on the resource.
Inputting Guidelines: Input subject from *LCSH* or from resource as Keywords.
Metadata Creator Notes: Objective when the terms are found on the resource. Subjective, if cataloger supplied. Most often will be cataloger supplied.

Element: Description

Name: Description.
Label: Description.
Definition: An account of the content of the resource.
Comment: Description may include but is not limited to: an abstract, table of contents, reference to a graphical representation of content, or a free-text account of the content.
Chief Source of Information: Take information from abstract or table of contents of the actual information resource to include in this element; if no abstract or table of contents is found on resource, write a small description in your own words.
Controlled Values: No.
Inputting Guidelines: Provide abstract, table of contents, or description of the resource.
Metadata Creator Notes: Objective if taken from resource. The information in this element may be subjective if it is a summary provided by the cataloger.

Element: Publisher

Name: Publisher.
Label: Publisher.
Definition: An entity responsible for making the resource available.
Comment: Examples of a Publisher include a person, an organisation, or a service. Typically, the name of a Publisher should be used to indicate the entity.
Chief Source of Information: Take the name of the publisher from the actual information resource; if none is found on resource take from the browser title including parts of the resource, or use other sources as appropriate.
Controlled Values: No.
Inputting Guidelines: Enter the Publisher as found in the resource. Use capitalization and punctuation as found in resource. If Publisher is an organization, enter the name of the organization.
Metadata Creator Notes: Objective. May become subjective. It is often difficult to find the name of the publisher for electronic resources. For example, consider the homepage. Who is the publisher? We generally consider the organization or individual who is hosting the web page

to be the publisher. Thus, the publisher for this author's home page is the University of Arizona.

Element: Contributor

Name: Contributor.
Label: Contributor.
Definition: An entity responsible for making contributions to the content of the resource.
Comment: Examples of a Contributor include a person, an organization, or a service. Typically, the name of a Contributor should be used to indicate the entity.
Chief Source of Information: Take Contributor from the actual information resource; if none found on resource take from the browser title including parts of the resource, or use other sources as appropriate.
Controlled Values: No.
Inputting Guidelines: Enter the Contributor as found in the resource. Use capitalization and punctuation as found in resource. Contributors play different roles and you can indicate the role by using parenthesis following the name. Thus, some roles are Editor, Translator, Illustrator. Record these as follows: Smith, Michael (Editor).
Metadata Creator Notes: Objective. There are a great many more roles that Contributors can fall into. But, to keep the activity of metadata creation simple and save time, the above three above are sufficient.

Element: Date

Name: Date.
Label: Date.
Definition: A date associated with an event in the life cycle of the resource.
Comment: Typically, Date will be associated with the creation or availability of the resource. Recommended best practice for encoding the date value is defined in a profile of ISO 8601 [W3CDTF] and follows the YYYY-MM-DD format.
Chief Source of Information: Take Date from the actual information resource; if none found on resource take from the browser title including parts of the resource, or use other sources as appropriate.
Controlled Values: No. However, the format–the way in which date is to be reported–and exactly what type of date it is are strictly specified. See next page.

Inputting Guidelines: Follow the YYYY-MM-DD format and choose from list what type of date is being recorded, whether the date is the date the resource was created or modified. If no date is available, leave blank; if multiple dates are found, enter the most recent only and indicate type. Enter 00-00 for month and date when it is not found on the resource easily. Dates can be entered for the following:

Created: date the resource was created
Valid: date or range of dates a resource is valid
Available: date when the resource became or will become available
Issued: date the resource was published
Modified: date the resource was changed
Accepted: date the resource was accepted (for example, theses have acceptance dates)
Submitted: date resource was submitted

Metadata Creator Notes: Objective. Keep cataloging simple and only specify one or two dates, when found, based on your local user needs.

Element: Type

Name: Resource Type.
Label: Type.
Definition: The nature or genre of the content of the resource.
Comment: Type includes terms describing general categories, functions, genres, or aggregation levels for content. Recommended best practice is to select a value from a controlled vocabulary (for example, the list of DCMI Type Vocabulary [DCMI]). To describe the physical or digital manifestation of the resource, use the Element: Format.
Chief Source of Information: Determine Type from the actual information resource and the definition for each type as given below.
Controlled Values: Yes. There is a list of ten (10) types used from the DCMI Type vocabulary. Type is also called form or genre, sometimes. Definitions of the values, the vocabulary to be used, for the ten (10) DCMI types are:

Collection: A collection is an aggregation of items. The term collection means that the resource is described as a group; its parts may be separately described and navigated.

Dataset: A dataset is information encoded in a defined structure (for example, lists, tables, and databases), intended to be useful for direct machine processing.

Event: An event is a non-persistent, time-based occurrence. Metadata for an event provides descriptive information that is the basis for discovery of the purpose, location, duration, responsible agents, and links to related events and resources. The resource of type event may not be retrievable if the described instantiation has expired or is yet to occur. Examples–exhibition, web-cast, conference, workshop, open-day, performance, battle, trial, wedding, tea-party, conflagration.

Image: An image is a primarily symbolic visual representation other than text. For example–images and photographs of physical objects, paintings, prints, drawings, other images and graphics, animations and moving pictures, film, diagrams, maps, musical notation. Note that image may include both electronic and physical representations.

Interactive Resource: An interactive resource is a resource which requires interaction from the user to be understood, executed, or experienced. For example–forms on web pages, applets, multimedia learning objects, chat services, virtual reality.

Service: A service is a system that provides one or more functions of value to the end-user. Examples include: a photocopying service, a banking service, an authentication service, interlibrary loans, a Z39.50 or Web server.

Software: Software is a computer program in source or compiled form, which may be available for installation non-transiently on another machine. For software, which exists only to create an interactive environment, use interactive instead.

Sound: A sound is a resource whose content is primarily intended to be rendered as audio. For example–a music playback file format, an audio compact disc, and recorded speech or sound.

Text: A text is a resource whose content is primarily words for reading. For example–books, letters, dissertations, poems, newspapers, articles, archives of mailing lists. Note that facsimiles or images of texts are still considered to be of the genre text.

Physical Object: An inanimate, three-dimensional object or substance. For example, a computer, the great pyramid, a sculpture. Note that digital representations of, or surrogates for, these things should use Image, Text, or one of the other types.

Inputting Guidelines: You may select as many types from the ten (10) DCMI types defined above that can be found in the resource.

Metadata Creator Notes: Objective.

Element: Format

Name: Format.
Label: Format.
Definition: The physical or digital manifestation of the resource.
Comment: Typically, Format may include the media-type or dimensions of the resource. Format may be used to determine the software, hardware, or other equipment needed to display or operate the resource. Examples of dimensions include size and duration. Recommended best practice is to select a value from a controlled vocabulary (for example, the list of Internet Media Types [IMT] defining computer media formats).
Chief Source of Information: Determine Format from the actual information resource.
Controlled Values: Yes. Choose from values given below. Like Type (form) a resource that exhibits more than one Format may be described as many times as needed. Values for formats are usually taken from IMT. Here is a partial list of IMT types; ebook is not from IMT. Use the term Other if your resource falls outside the list given here and you're unable to select from the IMT list.

text/html

text/xml

text/rtf

application/ms-word

application/ms-excel

application/ms-publisher

application/pdf

multipart/mixed

audio/mpeg

ebook

video/mpeg

video/quicktime

Other

Inputting Guidelines: Select one or more of the formats.
Metadata Creator Notes: Objective.

Element: Identifier

Name: Resource Identifier.
Label: Identifier.
Definition: An unambiguous reference to the resource within a given context.
Comment: Recommended best practice is to identify the resource by means of a string or number conforming to a formal identification system. Example formal identification systems include the Uniform Resource Identifier (URI) (including the Uniform Resource Locator (URL)), the Digital Object Identifier (DOI), and the International Standard Book Number (ISBN).
Chief Source of Information: Take URL from the Location of the actual information resource as seen in the web browser Address bar.
Controlled Values: No. But, the format of the URL is specified (http:// . . .).
Inputting Guidelines: Give full URL starting with http://
Metadata Creator Notes: Objective.

Element: Source

Name: Source.
Label: Source.
Definition: A reference to a resource from which the present resource is derived.
Comment: The present resource may be derived from the Source resource in whole or in part. Recommended best practice is to reference the resource by means of a string or number conforming to a formal identification system.
Chief Source of Information: Take the original Source Title and URL from the actual information resource, browser title, and/or browser location (address bar).
Controlled Values: No.
Inputting Guidelines: Enter the title followed by a comma and the URL. If no title or URL found or the original source is a print or other format, describe in own words. Many electronic resources are born-dig-

ital and have no print or other digital counterpart. Hence, Source may often be left blank.
Metadata Creator Notes: Objective.

Element: Language

Name: Language.
Label: Language.
Definition: A language of the intellectual content of the resource.
Comment: Recommended best practice is to use RFC 3066 [RFC3066], which, in conjunction with ISO 639 [ISO639], defines two- and three-letter primary language tags with optional subtags. Examples include "en" or "eng" for English, "akk" for Akkadian, and "en-GB" for English used in the United Kingdom.
Chief Source of Information: Determine language from the actual information resource.
Controlled Values: No.
Inputting Guidelines: Select the language of the resource.
Metadata Creator Notes: Objective. Note that many learning resources are available in versions other than English; therefore, record the language to match the object being cataloged. Do not use the Language element to record version information. Use Relation *HasVersion* (described below).

Element: Relation

Name: Relation.
Label: Relation.
Definition: A reference to a related resource.
Comment: Recommended best practice is to reference the resource by means of a string or number conforming to a formal identification system.
Chief Source of Information: Determine from the actual information resource(s).
Controlled Values: No. The following refinements, each of which are defined, may be used:

IsVersionOf	is version, edition, or historical state of the second resource
HasVersion	contains version, edition, or historical state of the second resource

IsReplacedBy	is supplanted, displaced, or superseded by the referenced source
Replaces	supplants, displaces, or supercedes the referenced resource
IsRequiredBy	is required by second resource for functioning, delivery, content, etc.
Requires	requires second resource for functioning, delivery, content, etc.
IsPartOf	is contained in another resource
HasPart	contains part of another resource
IsReferencedBy	is referenced by second resource
References	references second resource
IsFormatOf	is format or mechanically reproduced representation of second resource
HasFormat	has format or mechanically reproduced representation of second
ConformsTo	resource conforms to an educational, accessibility or other standard

Inputting Guidelines: Select the appropriate relationship(s) between two or more resources. A resource may have multiple relationships. Add Title and URL.
Metadata Creator Notes: Objective.

Element: Coverage

Name: Coverage.
Label: Coverage.
Definition: The extent or scope of the content of the resource.
Comment: Coverage will typically include geographical and historical coverage in terms of ***spatial location***, a place name, feature name, or geographic coordinates such as Paris, Pima River, ***temporal period***, a period label such as *Ming*, *Jurassic*, *Renaissance*, date, or date range, and/or **jurisdiction**, such as a named administrative entity. Recommended best practice is to select a value from a controlled vocabulary. For example, the *Thesaurus of Geographic Names* and, where appropriate, use named places or time periods in preference to numeric identifiers such as sets of coordinates or date ranges.
Chief Source of Information: Determine from the actual information resource(s).

Controlled Values: No.
Inputting Guidelines: Select the appropriate spatial, temporal, jurisdiction coverage of the resource and use the words in the resources or your own to describe.
Metadata Creator Notes: Objective. For some types of literary materials, this might be subjective.

Element: Rights

Name: Rights Management.
Label: Rights.
Definition: Information about rights held in and over the resource.
Comment: Typically, a Rights element will contain a rights management statement for the resource, or reference a service providing such information. Rights information often encompasses Intellectual Property Rights (IPR), Copyright, and various Property Rights. If the Rights element is absent, no assumptions can be made about the status of these and other rights with respect to the resource.
Chief Source of Information: Take from the actual information resource, and if unavailable, look for a rights management or copyright statement page.
Controlled Values: Yes. See list below and select as appropriate.

Accessible freely

License restrictions apply

Restrictions apply

Subscription needed

Public domain

Inputting Guidelines: Enter from list above as many as needed. If a separate page is given with rights information, include the URL. Example: Restrictions apply. URL:___
Metadata Creator Notes: Objective.

Element: Audience

Name: Audience.
Label: Audience.

Definition: Intended user for the resource.
Chief Source of Information: Determine from the actual information resource; if none found on resource use your best judgment.
Controlled Values: Yes. Use one or more from the list of values for educational level given below:

Elementary

Middle School

High School

Undergraduate Level

Graduate Level

Professional

General Education

Inputting Guidelines: Look for this information on the main resource page; if none is found, browse the resource and select one or more of the values from above.
Metadata Creator Notes: Subjective, if not found explicitly stated in resource.

CONCLUSION

The traditional library catalog, over the last 100 years, has evolved to fulfill the following functions:

- Finding
- Identifying
- Locating
- Selecting
- Collocating

The first objective of the library catalog is to help the user find, identify, and locate materials when the author, title, or subject is known. The second objective of the catalog is to bring like materials together (collocation) and aid in selection. In digital libraries, the information discovery function (finding and locating) continues to be given the most importance. Thus, in the development of the DC metadata standard by the DCMI, initial emphasis has been in getting minimal bibliographic control over electronic resources. Recently, phrases such as the life of the catalog record or lifecycle of the metadata record point to the fact that resource metadata creation can be an ongoing process. That is, metadata for electronic records are more similar to serials catalog records, which require constant maintenance, changes, and updates as serials evolve throughout their life. I have tried to bridge the cataloging and metadata creation gap by outlining some important ways in which DC metadata can be created in harmony with and harnessing the lessons learned by the library cataloging community.

WORKS CITED

Anglo-American Cataloging Rules, Second Edition, 1988 Revision. Chicago: American Library Association, 1988.

Caplan, Priscilla. "Cataloging Internet Resources." The Public-Access Computer Systems Review 4, no. 2 (1993): 61-66. <http://info.lib.uh.edu/pr/v4/n2/caplan.4n2> Accessed: Sept. 10, 2003.

Coleman, Anita. 2003. *Knowledge Structures Toolbox*. <http://radio.weblogs.com/0109575/stories/2003/01/17/toolbox.html> Accessed: Sept. 10, 2003.

This document is updated regularly and provides a list of digital libraries and tools useful for metadata creation. It also points to resources such as the Metadata Resources page maintained by IFLA.

DCMI Bibliography. 2003. Corey A. Harper and Eric Sharfe <http://dublincore.org/usageguide/bibliography.shtml> DCMI Type Vocabulary. <http://dublincore.org/documents/dcmi-terms/#H5> Accessed: Dec. 3, 2003.

This WWW document is a small controlled vocabulary for the DC element Type. It lists the names of the vocabulary terms used for this element and provides a brief definition. These controlled vocabulary terms have all been approved by the DCMI Usage Board. A new vocabulary term, Physical Object was added in the last year.

Hillmann, Diane. 2003. *Using Dublin Core*. <http://dublincore.org/documents/usageguide> Accessed: Sept. 10, 2003.

This is the most recent (published August 26, 2003), newly revised, official guide to using the DC elements, available freely via the WWW. The previous version of this document was published in 2001. The new version provides more examples for the elements. It also streamlines the distinctions between using DC in one of two levels: simple and qualified. The Bibliography covers the years 1994 through mid-2003 and lists more than 100 entries and is arranged by year. Diane Hillman is the author of the base document titled Using Dublin Core. But, in the tradition of WWW resources, which seldom have one creator, others have contributed sections. The whole document is available by following hyperlinks in the Table of Contents.

The title and creators of the section and direct URLs for each of the sections are as follows:

Introduction–Diane Hillman
Syntax, Storage and Maintenance Issues–Diane Hillman
Element Content and Controlled Vocabularies–Diane Hillmann
<http://dublincore.org/documents/usageguide>
The Elements–Diane Hillman
<http://dublincore.org/documents/usageguide/elements.shtml>
Dublin Core Qualifiers–Diane Hillmann
<http://dublincore.org/usageguide/qualifiers.shtml>
Glossary–Mary S. Woodley, Gail Clement, and Peter Winn
<http://dublincore.org/usageguide/glossary.shtml>

IEEE LTSC. 2002. *Draft Standard for Learning Object Metadata.* <http://ltsc.ieee.org/doc/wg12/LOM_1484_12_1_v1_Final_Draft.pdf> Accessed: Sept. 10, 2003.

This document is an Adobe PDF file (needs the Adobe Acrobat reader). The Learning Technologies Standards Committee has been working on Learning Object metadata for a long time and it is now a fully approved IEEE standard. A joint memorandum was signed in 2001 by IEEE and Dublin Core agreeing to work together on the development of the educational elements of the metadata.

OCLC. 2003. *Cataloging Electronic Resources: OCLC-MARC Coding Guidelines.* <http://www.oclc.org/support/documentation/worldcat/cataloging/electronicresources/> Accessed: Sept. 10, 2003.

This document provides detailed help on the definition of electronic resources, how to determine form and type and on 'integrating resources.' It is a good background document to read although it is a guide for using MARC in electronic resources cataloging.

Olson, Nancy. Editor. Cataloging Internet Resources. <http://www.oclc.org/support/documentation/worldcat/cataloging/internetguide/> Accessed: Sept. 10, 2003.

Request to catalog an internet resource: UCSD Library bibliographers only. 2003. <http://tpot.ucsd.edu/Cataloging/coldev.html> Accessed: Sept. 10, 2003.

This online form is part of the University of San Diego's TPOT, Technical Processing Online Tools website, which has been serving the libraries since 1994. This site shows how electronic government documents and other genres of electronic resources are fast becoming standard items for description in the library catalog. The related websites cataloging practice section is an especially good one to read. Common bibliographic relationships among web documents are described.

Web Resources on "Cataloging Internet Resources"–the following two guides were written in the 1990s. They are thus not about cataloging using DC but, they are excellent guides, although outdated, for cataloging electronic resources using MARC/AACR2R.

APPENDIX 1. DC Metadata Creation Form

Name of Metadata Creator:____

Date of Metadata Creation:____

Title:____

Identifier (URL): ____

Description: [Use Abstract to provide your own brief summary of the resource; use quotation marks if summary is taken directly from resource. Use TableOfContents to include the sections/components.]

Abstract:

TableofContents:

Subject: [Use *Library of Congress Subject Headings* or just enter Keywords.]

1.______________________ 2.______________________
3.______________________ 4.______________________

Keyword: [Use keywords to express additional ideas and concepts to describe the resource not already expressed in the *Title*, *Description*, *Coverage*, or *Subject Fields*. Use keywords from the resource itself and not from a controlled vocabulary.]

1.______________________ 2.______________________
3.______________________ 4.______________________

Coverage: [Use geographical terms to indicate spatial coverage and time periods or years to indicate temporal.]

Temporal: **Spatial:**

Date: [Enter date in YYYY-MM-DD format. Enter the last date found or estimated for one or more of the following as is possible. Leave month and day blank if it is not found on resource, and leave date blank if it is not possible to easily determine from resource.]

Created: Issued:
Valid: Modified:
Available: Accepted:
Submitted:

Creator [First Author]: ____________________

Creator [Second Author]: ____________________

Creator [Third Author]: ____________________

Contributor: [Enter additional contributors, if any, as follows:]

Editor(s): ____

Translator(s): ____

Illustrator(s): ____

Publisher: [Enter the publisher name.] ________________________

APPENDIX 1 (continued)

Rights: [Search the resource for an explicit copyright statement and/or information about cost or license and select from list below. Add notes and URL as necessary.]

Accessible freely
Copyrighted
Copyright unknown
Copyright and cost restrictions unknown
Cost unknown
License restrictions apply
Restrictions apply
Subscription needed
Public domain

Type: [Select ONLY ONE categorical Type (form or genre) of the resource.]

Collection
Dataset
Event
Image
Interactive Resource
Service
Software
Sound
Text

Format: [Use this to indicate the media-type, the physical manifestation of the resource and select as many as are applicable.]

Application/ms-word
Application/ms-excel
Application/ms-publisher
Application/pdf
Audio/mpeg
Ebook
Image/gif
Image/jpg
Image/png
Multipart/mixed
Text/html
Text/xml
Text/rtf
Video/mpeg
Video/quicktime
Other

Language: [Select one or more from list; add other languages as needed.]

English
French
German
Spanish

Relation: [Select from list and add Title and Identifier (URL), when available.]

IsVersionOf
HasVersion
IsReplacedBy
Replaces
IsRequiredBy
Requires
IsPartOf
HasPart
IsReferencedBy
References
IsFormatOf
HasFormat
ConformsTo

Source: [Enter Title and URL or description.]

Audience: [Select the educational level of the audience for the resource from list.]

Elementary School
Middle School
High School
Undergraduate Level
Graduate Level
Professional
General Education

APPENDIX 2. Sample Resource Descriptions

Resource # 1: Resource is a database of educational standards described as Service

Name of Metadata Creator: Anita Coleman

Date of Metadata Creation: 2003-09-03

Title: McRel: Online Compendium of Standards and Benchmarks: the 4th edition of content knowledge in Language Arts, Mathematics, and Science

Identifier (URL): http://www.mcrel.org/compendium/kSkillsIntro.asp

Description: [Use Abstract to provide your own brief summary of the resource; use quotation marks if summary is taken directly from resource. Use TableOfContents to include the sections/components.]

Abstract: "As part of the ongoing effort to provide the best of current information related to standards, we have undertaken a significant update of the standards database. As the 4th edition for each subject area is completed, it will be added to those available from this page. By the end of 2003, geography and economics will be placed on line. By the end of 2004, the balance of the social studies (behavioral studies, civics, and history) in Content Knowledge will also be revised to include the following features and additions: Browsable Topics, Knowledge skill/statements, Revised vocabulary terms, and Pre-kindergarten benchmarks."

TableofContents:__________

Subject: [Use *Library of Congress Subject Headings* or just enter Keywords.]

1. Language arts–Standards
2. Mathematics–Standards
3. Science–Standards
4. Education–Standards

Keyword: [Use keywords to express additional ideas and concepts to describe the resource not already expressed in the *Title, Description*, or *Subject Fields*. Use keywords from the resource itself and not from a controlled vocabulary.]

1. __________ 2. __________

Coverage: [Use geographical terms to indicate spatial coverage and time periods or years to indicate temporal.]

Temporal: Nineteen nineties **Spatial:** United States

Date: [Enter date in YYYY-MM-DD format. Enter the last date found or estimated for one or more of the following as is possible. Leave month and day blank if it is not found on resource, and leave date blank if it is not possible to easily determine from resource.]

Created:
Valid: 2003-12-03
Available:
Issued:
Modified:
Accepted:
Submitted:

Creator [First Author]: __________

Creator [Second Author]: __________

Creator [Third Author]: __________

APPENDIX 2 (continued)

Contributor: [Enter additional contributors, if any, as follows.]

Editor(s): ______________________________

Translator(s): ______________________________

Illustrator(s): ______________________________

Publisher: [Enter the publisher name.] Mid-continent Research for Education and Learning, http://www.mcrel.org/

Rights: [Search the resource for an explicit copyright statement and/or information about cost or license and select from list below. Add notes and URL as necessary.]

Accessible freely
Copyrighted
Copyright unknown
Copyright and cost restrictions unknown
Cost Unknown
License restrictions apply
Restrictions apply
Subscription needed
√Public domain

Type: [Select ONLY ONE categorical Type (form or genre) of the resource.]

Collection
Dataset
Event
Image
Interactive Resource
√Service
Software
Sound
Text

Format: [Use this to indicate the media-type, the physical manifestation of the resource and select as many as are applicable.]

Application/ms-word
Application/ms-excel
Application/ms-publisher
Application/pdf
Audio/mpeg
Ebook
Image/gif
Image/jpg
Image/png
Multipart/mixed
√Text/html
Text/xml
Text/rtf
Video/mpeg
Video/quicktime
Other

Language: [Select one or more from list; add other languages as needed.]

√English
French
German
Spanish

Relation: [Select from list and add Title and Identifier (URL), when available.]

√IsVersionOf
HasVersion
IsReplacedBy
Replaces
IsRequiredBy
Requires
IsPartOf
HasPart

Content Knowledge, 3rd ed,
http://www.mcrel.org/standards-benchmarks/

IsReferencedBy
References
IsFormatOf
HasFormat
ConformsTo

Source: [Enter Title and URL or description.]

Audience: [Select the educational level of the audience for the resource from list.]

√Elementary Graduate Level

√Middle School Professional

√High School General Education

Undergraduate Level

Resource # 2: Resource is a 'mathematical problem' described as Text

Name of Metadata Creator: Anita Coleman

Date of Metadata Creation: 2003-08-03

Title: Problems: Mathematics

Identifier (URL): http://www.student-automotive.com/problems/mathematics.html

Description: [Use Abstract to provide your own brief summary of the resource; use quotation marks if summary is taken directly from resource. Use TableOfContents to include the sections/components.]

Abstract: The objectives of this webpage on mathematical problems are two fold: for pre-university students to be able to use mathematics in solving automotive problems, and for them to be able to understand the importance of mathematics for professional preparation in automotive engineering.

TableofContents: ______

Subject: [Use *Library of Congress Subject Headings* or just enter Keywords.]

1. Torque
2. ______
3. ______
4. ______

Keyword: [Use keywords to express additional ideas and concepts to describe the resource not already expressed in the *Title*, *Description*, or *Subject Fields*. Use keywords from the resource itself and not from a controlled vocabulary.]

1. Mathematical modeling for the automotive industry 2. Engine model
3. Vehicle dynamics 4. Damped oscillations 5. Model of the motion of a car

Coverage: [Use geographical terms to indicate spatial coverage and time periods or years to indicate temporal.]

Temporal: **Spatial:**

APPENDIX 2 (continued)

Date: [Enter date in YYYY-MM-DD format. Enter the last date found or estimated for one or more of the following as is possible. Leave month and day blank if it is not found on resource, and leave date blank if it is not possible to easily determine from resource.]

Created:
Valid: 2003-12-00
Available:
Issued:
Modified:
Accepted:
Submitted:

Creator [First Author]: Fonteijne, Robert J.

Creator [Second Author]: ______________

Creator [Third Author]: ______________

Contributor: [Enter additional contributors, if any, as follows:]

Editor(s): ______________

Translator(s): ______________

Illustrator(s): ______________

Publisher: [Enter the publisher name.] Fonteijne, Robert N.

Rights: [Search the resource for an explicit copyright statement and/or information about cost or license and select from list below. Add notes and URL as necessary.]

Accessible freely
Copyrighted
Copyright unknown
Copyright and cost restrictions unknown
Cost Unknown
License restrictions apply
Restrictions apply
Subscription needed
√Public domain

Type: [Select ONLY ONE categorical Type (form or genre) of the resource.]

Collection
Dataset
Event
Image
Interactive Resource
Service
Software
Sound
√Text

Format: [Use this to indicate the media-type, the physical manifestation of the resource and select as many as are applicable.]

Application/ms-word
Application/ms-excel
Application/ms-publisher
Application/pdf
Audio/mpeg
Ebook
Image/gif
Image/jpg
Image/png
Multipart/mixed
√Text/html
Text/xml
Text/rtf
Video/mpeg
Video/quicktime
Other

Language: [Select one or more from list; add other languages as needed.]

√English
French
German
Spanish

Relation: [Select from list and add Title and Identifier (URL), when available.]

IsVersionOf
HasVersion
IsReplacedBy
Replaces
IsRequiredBy
Requires
√IsPartOf http://www.student-automotive.com/
HasPart
IsReferencedBy
References
IsFormatOf
HasFormat
ConformsTo

Source: [Enter Title and URL or description.]

Audience: [Select the educational level of the audience for the resource from list.]

Elementary
Middle School
High School
Undergraduate Level
Graduate Level
√Professional
√General Education

Resource # 3: Resource is a Tutorial

Name of Metadata Creator: Anita Coleman

Date of Metadata Creation: 2008-03-03

Title: PowerPoint Tutorials: Electric Teacher

Identifier (URL): http://www.electricteacher.com/tutorial3.htm

Description: [Use Abstract to provide your own brief summary of the resource; use quotation marks if summary is taken directly from resource. Use TableOfContents to include the sections/components.]

Abstract: This tutorial describes how to do several common tasks in PowerPoint with detailed directions and screenshots. Table of contents: Starting Presentations, Common Features, Working with Text, Working with Graphics, and Finishing Up.

TableofContents: ______________________________

APPENDIX 2 (continued)

Subject: [Use *Library of Congress Subject Headings* or just enter Keywords.]

1.____Microsoft PowerPoint____ 2.Computer software–Study and Teaching
3.________________ 4.________________

Keyword: [Use keywords to express additional ideas and concepts to describe the resource not already expressed in the *Title*, *Description*, or *Subject Fields*. Use keywords from the resource itself and not from a controlled vocabulary.]

1.________________ 2.________________

Coverage: [Use geographical terms to indicate spatial coverage and time periods or years to indicate temporal.]

Temporal: **Spatial:**

Date: [Enter date in YYYY-MM-DD format. Enter the last date found or estimated for one or more of the following as is possible. Leave month and day blank if it is not found on resource, and leave date blank if it is not possible to easily determine from resource.]

Created:
Valid:
Available:
Issued:
Modified:
Accepted:
Submitted:

Creator [First Author]: ____Chamberlain, Cathy____

Creator [Second Author]: ________________

Creator [Third Author]: ________________

Contributor: [Enter additional contributors, if any, as follows:]

Editor(s): ________________

Translator(s): ________________

Illustrator(s): ________________

Publisher: [Enter the publisher name.] ____Electric Teacher____

Rights: [Search the resource for an explicit copyright statement and/or information about cost or license and select from list below. Add notes and URL as necessary.]

√**Accessible freely**
√**Copyrighted**
Copyright unknown
Copyright and cost restrictions unknown
Cost Unknown
License restrictions apply
Restrictions apply
Subscription needed
√**Public domain**

Type: [Select ONLY ONE categorical Type (form or genre) of the resource.]

Collection
Dataset
Event
Image
Interactive Resource
Service
Software
Sound
√**Text**

Format: [Use this to indicate the media-type, the physical manifestation of the resource and select as many as are applicable.]

Application/ms-word
Application/ms-excel
Application/ms-publisher
Application/pdf
Audio/mpeg
Ebook
Image/gif
Image/jpg
Image/png
Multipart/mixed
√Text/html
Text/xml
Text/rtf
Video/mpeg
Video/quicktime
Other

Language: [Select one or more from list; add other languages as needed.]

√English
French
German
Spanish

Relation: [Select from list and add Title and Identifier (URL), when available.]

IsVersionOf
HasVersion
IsReplacedBy
Replaces
IsRequiredBy
Requires
√IsPartOf http://www.electricteacher.com/
HasPart
IsReferencedBy
References
IsFormatOf
HasFormat
ConformsTo

Source: [Enter Title and URL or description.]

Audience: [Select the educational level of the audience for the resource from list.]

Elementary
Middle School
High School
Undergraduate Level

Graduate Level
Professional
√General Education

Metadata Standards for Archival Control: An Introduction to EAD and EAC

Alexander C. Thurman

SUMMARY. This article provides a concise guide to the structure and use of the Encoded Archival Description (EAD) and Encoded Archival Context (EAC) metadata standards. After a brief outline of archival description, the finding aid, and the objectives behind EAD, the structure of EAD is examined in detail. Discussion of all of the important elements in the EAD document-type definition (DTD) will be supplemented with examples of actual finding aids and their encoding, with attention to the common necessity of "reengineering" existing finding aids. The current status of EAD implementation and some issues affecting the widespread adoption of EAD are considered. A close look at the emerging EAC standard closes the article, providing key element definitions from the EAC Tag Library (Beta version, Feb. 2004), and examples of EAC records–including early implementations such as the University College London's LEADERS project. *[Article copies available for a fee from The Haworth Document Delivery Service: 1-800-HAWORTH. E-mail address: <docdelivery@haworthpress.com> Website: <http://www.HaworthPress.com> © 2005 by The Haworth Press, Inc. All rights reserved.]*

Alexander C. Thurman is Cataloger, Columbia University Libraries, 102 Butler Library, 535 West 114th Street, New York, NY 10027 (E-mail: at2186@columbia.edu).

[Haworth co-indexing entry note]: "Metadata Standards for Archival Control: An Introduction to EAD and EAC." Thurman, Alexander C. Co-published simultaneously in *Cataloging & Classification Quarterly* (The Haworth Information Press, an imprint of The Haworth Press, Inc.) Vol. 40, No. 3/4, 2005, pp. 183-212; and: *Metadata: A Cataloger's Primer* (ed: Richard P. Smiraglia) The Haworth Information Press, an imprint of The Haworth Press, Inc., 2005, pp. 183-212. Single or multiple copies of this article are available for a fee from The Haworth Document Delivery Service [1-800-HAWORTH, 9:00 a.m. - 5:00 p.m. (EST). E-mail address: docdelivery@haworthpress.com].

Available online at http://www.haworthpress.com/web/CCQ

doi:10.1300/J104v40n03_09

KEYWORDS. Archival description, authority control, collection, EAD, EAC, finding aid, fonds, provenance

ARCHIVAL CONTROL

The goal of cataloging is to provide maximum access to organized information. Archival materials–the unique, unpublished by-products of the everyday activities of organizations, families, or individuals–are valuable information resources that have been difficult to integrate into the rapidly consolidating bibliographic universe. The formal introduction of Encoded Archival Description (EAD) Version 1.0 in 1998 provided archivists with a powerful tool for overcoming this difficulty. EAD enables the encoding of archival finding aids into records that are platform-independent, machine-readable, and fully searchable, helping to standardize archival descriptive practices while increasing our progress toward union access to archival materials. The related new metadata scheme Encoded Archival Context (EAC) goes further, allowing archivists to encode information about the creators and context of creation of archival materials, and to make that information available to users as an independent resource separate from individual finding aids. This article presents an overview of the role of these metadata standards in the achievement of archival control, featuring a concise guide to the structure and use of EAD (Version 2002) and an introduction to the emerging EAC standard.

The structure of archival entities is hierarchical, proceeding from the most to the least comprehensive level. The names given to the various levels vary, particularly between American and Anglo-Canadian practices. The term *collection*, as used in an American archival context, usually refers to a group of materials associated with an individual, a family, or a corporate body, which may have been generated either "organically" (as a by-product of the everyday life/operations of the person or family or corporate body) or "artificially" (i.e., regardless of provenance). The term *fonds*, more commonly used in Anglo-Canadian practice, has a narrower denotation than "collection" in that it refers exclusively to organically generated records and documents. The evidential and research value of the interrelated materials within fonds is strongly tied to their provenance, the context of their common origins. The fundamental archival principle of "respect du fonds" mandates that archival materials be arranged and described with careful attention to their original function and order.

Archival description is also hierarchical, beginning with information pertaining to an entire whole (whether a collection, fonds, series, or other unit) and following with descriptions of the subordinate levels within the whole. Unlike bibliographic description, which usually focuses on an individual manifestation of a published work, an archival description typically involves a complex group of interrelated unique materials whose shared provenance (or lack thereof, in an "artificial" collection) and hierarchical arrangement must be articulated. A MARC record is an effective "surrogate" with which to describe and provide access to a bibliographic item. Collection-level MARC records for archival materials also continue to be useful for providing limited access to these materials in library catalogs. But the main tool for archival description is the *finding aid*, which allows for a much more detailed presentation of an archival entity's context and hierarchical arrangement.

The term *finding aid* can be loosely applied to a wide range of formats, including card indices, calendars, guides, inventories, shelf and container lists, and registers. The more specific denotation of the term used in current archival practice is summed up in the following definition (Pearce-Moses 2004):

> [A] finding aid is a single document that places the materials in context by consolidating information about acquisition and processing; provenance, including administrative history or biographical note; scope of the collection, including size, subjects, media; organization and arrangement; and an inventory of the series and the folders.

Beyond these general shared characteristics, finding aids vary greatly, both due to the differences in the described archival entities themselves and as a result of differing practices between archival repositories and/or national archival traditions. (See Appendix 1 for an invented sample print finding aid.) Until very recently, there was no authoritative content standard governing the creation of finding aids. The most relevant standards had been the American archival cataloging manual *Archives, Personal Papers, and Manuscripts* (*APPM*) (Hensen 1989), the Canadian *Rules for Archival Description* (*RAD*) (Canadian Committee 2003), and the *General International Standard for Archival Description* (*ISAD(G)*) (International Council 2000). The CUSTARD project (Canadian-U.S. Task Force on ARchival Description) worked to synthesize these standards into "a robust data content standard for the description of archival standards based on a harmonization of *APPM* and *RAD* within the framework of *ISAD(G)*" (Statement of Principles 2003).

The result was *Describing Archives: A Content Standard* (*DACS*) (Society 2004), which now replaces *APPM* in the United States as the content standard for the creation of catalog records and finding aids for archival materials.

EAD BACKGROUND

As late as the early 1990s, finding aids for archival materials existed mainly in paper copies held by the repositories of those materials. To be sure, preliminary efforts at providing union access to archival materials were long underway: the Library of Congress's print *National Union Catalog of Manuscript Collections* [NUCMC] began to appear in 1962; Chadwyck-Healy released their *National Inventory of Documentary Sources in the United States* on microfiche in 1983; and the USMARC Archival and Manuscripts Control (MARC AMC) format was released by LC in 1984, allowing the introduction of collection-level MARC records for archival materials into library catalogs (my principal source for this account of EAD's prehistory is (Ruth 2001)). But neither the NUCMC nor MARC AMC records could provide access to all the descriptive information available in finding aids, while the microfiche format remained non-machine-readable and not searchable.

In the early 1990s, remote access to and keyword searching of finding aids became possible through the appearance of the Internet and of Gopher technology (using ASCII text files). The World Wide Web and HTML (HyperText Markup Language) subsequently enabled a more sophisticated display of online finding aids along with the additional navigational advantages made possible by hyperlinks. But because HTML is an SGML (Standard Generalized Markup Language) "document type definition" intended only for displaying hypertext or hypermedia on the Web, it cannot capture the underlying intellectual structure represented in a finding aid. HTML elements determine such things as the font size or line breaks of a document; they cannot encode the difference, for example, between information describing the provenance of an archival fonds from information about its scope and content, or the difference between a personal name and a corporate name. But such distinctions are critical for search and retrieval and indexing. A finding aid encoded only in HTML is in that regard "flat," or retrievable only via keyword searching, which is notoriously inefficient.

EAD is the result of an effort begun in 1993 at the library of the University of California, Berkeley, led by Daniel Pitti, to develop a nonproprietary standard for encoding finding aids that would overcome these limitations of HTML. Pitti's objectives for the new standard included:

- Accurate representation of archival principles and practice, including hierarchical arrangement
- Support for element-specific indexing and retrieval
- Support for intelligent access to and navigation of archival materials
- Improved communication and sharing of collection information between repositories

The approach Pitti and his team chose was to create a new document type definition (DTD) in SGML for encoding finding aids. SGML is an international standard metalanguage that can be used to define the rules for the structure of any kind of document. Within an SGML document type definition, a specific set of markup tags is defined to encode the different parts of a document of a given sort, such as an archival finding aid. In order to create a new DTD for finding aids that would be maximally useful to archivists–as flexible as need be yet structured enough to encourage consistency in archival practice–Pitti gathered a wide variety of sample finding aids from many different repositories and set about constructing a DTD that would best accommodate them.

In 1995 the Berkeley team submitted their resulting FINDAID DTD for wider review. In late 1998, after considerable refinement (including a name change to Encoded Archival Description) based on feedback from the wider archival community to numerous trial versions, Version 1.0 of the EAD DTD was released. Version 1.0 was the first iteration of EAD to be compliant with the new XML (Extensible Markup Language) standard. (XML is a simplified version of SGML intended for use on the Web that is considerably easier for programmers and software developers.) The latest version of the EAD DTD, updated to maintain compatibility with the 2000 edition of *ISAD(G)*, is EAD Version 2002.

EAD STRUCTURE

The EAD DTD is an XML file that defines a set of tags and structural rules for encoding archival finding aids. Archivists using EAD to encode a finding aid will, in practice, most likely not be working directly with the DTD file, but instead will be consulting the *Encoded Archival Description Tag Library* (currently Version 2002) and the *Encoded Archival Description Application Guidelines* (1999). The Tag Library lists all the defined EAD elements along with their coding tags and explains and provides examples of their use.

Each element has a full name, such as EAD Header, along with a machine-readable tag name that appears between angle brackets in lowercase, e.g., <eadheader>. Many elements can be refined with particular attributes, which appear within the same set of angle brackets as the tag name, along with the attribute(s)' given value. For example, the element Archival Description, whose tag is <archdesc>, can be refined with the attribute [level] set to the value "collection," appearing as:

<archdesc level ="collection">

This signifies that the hierarchical level of the archival materials being described is a "collection," but the value could be changed to "fonds," "series," "file," etc., as necessary. Other important attributes include [label] and [encodinganalog]. The [label] attribute is used to supply a display label for an element when a heading element <head> is not available. The optional attribute [encodinganalog] can be used to provide a comparable element from a different encoding system, such as MARC; its use may enable archivists to derive collection-level MARC records from finding aids automatically.

EAD is a hierarchical scheme in which elements are nested within one another. (This structure can be seen in Appendix 2, which shows the encoded version of the sample finding aid from Appendix 1.) Some elements can contain text directly, while other elements are intended to help structure the finding aid into sections and cannot take text directly but instead must contain other elements inside them–these structural elements are called "wrapper elements." The outermost wrapper element, used to introduce an encoded archival finding aid, is Encoded Archival Description <ead>. The level below <ead> has three high-level sections, also wrapper elements: EAD Header <eadheader>, Front Matter <frontmatter>, and Archival Description <archdesc> (see Figure 1). The <eadheader> and <frontmatter> wrapper elements open sections that include information about the finding aid itself, while <archdesc> contains the actual description of the archival materials in question. The EAD Header is a required element used to capture metadata about the creation and publication of the finding aid document itself; its consistent use enables more efficient search and retrieval in a machine-readable environment. It must contain the sub-elements <eadid> and <filedesc>, and may also contain the optional sub-elements <profiledesc> and <revisiondesc> (see Figure 2).

FIGURE 1

<ead> high-level wrapper elements		
Tags	*element names*	*information content*
<eadheader>	EAD Header	creation and use of the finding aid itself
<frontmatter>	Front Matter	title page, prefatory material [*optional*]
<archdesc>	Archival Description	content, context, and extent of body of archival material

FIGURE 2

<eadheader> elements		
Tags	*element names*	*information content*
<eadid>	EAD Identifier	unique identification code for the finding aid
<filedesc>	File Description	creation of finding aid (i.e., author, title, publisher)
<profiledesc>	Profile Description	encoding of finding aid (i.e., agent, date, language)
<revisiondesc>	Revision Description	changes to the encoded finding aid

Front Matter is an optional wrapper element that can be used to generate a title page and/or other prefatory text about the finding aid itself, rather than information about the archival materials. Much of this title page information may be repeated from the <eadheader>, but using <frontmatter> allows archivists some leeway for local practices regarding sequence and display. Since the same flexibility can be achieved by using stylesheets to extract and display the relevant information from the <eadheader>, <frontmatter> is often omitted.

Archival Description <archdesc> is the wrapper element for the core of the EAD finding aid, the description of a body of archival materials. The <archdesc> element has a required attribute, [level], for which a value is set to identify the level of archival materials involved, for example, "collection." The description is hierarchical, so in this example the description would begin with information that pertains to the entire "collection." This description of the whole "collection" is then inherited by each of the parts (e.g., "series") outlined within the Description of Subordinate Components <dsc> sub-element. These "series" may then have their own more specific descriptions, and may further contain their own parts (e.g., "subseries"), and so forth.

Figure 3 lists the top-level elements within <archdesc>, along with brief descriptions adapted from the Tag Library. The DTD mandates

FIGURE 3

<archdesc> elements		
Tags	*element names*	*information content*
<did>	Descriptive Identification	core identifying elements, including origination and physical description and location
<accessrestrict>	Conditions Governing Access	availability of physical access to material
<accruals>	Accruals	anticipated additions to material
<acqinfo>	Acquisition Information	immediate source of material
<altformavail>	Alternative Form Available	copies of material in additional formats
<appraisal>	Appraisal Information	process of determining archival value of material
<arrangement>	Arrangement	internal structure and ordering of material
<bibliography>	Bibliography	citations to works related to material
<bioghist>	Biography or History	creator (individual, family, or corporate body) of materials, to provide context
<controlaccess>	Controlled Access Headings	personal, corporate, and geographic name headings, and subject headings
<custodhist>	Custodial History	chain of intellectual ownership and physical possession
<descgrp>	Description Group	[generic wrapper for grouping other elements]
<fileplan>	File Plan	classification scheme(s) used by material's creator(s)
<index>	Index	list of key terms, subjects, entities–may include links
<odd>	Other Descriptive Data	[last resort for miscellaneous data not fitting other elements]
<originalsloc>	Location of Originals	existence, location, and availability of originals when materials described are copies
<otherfindingaid>	Other Finding Aid	alternative guides to the material
<phystech>	Physical Characteristics and Technical Requirements	physical or technical needs affecting storage, preservation, and use of material
<prefercite>	Preferred Citation	Wording for citing material
<processinfo>	Processing Information	preparation of material for research use
<relatedmaterial>	Related Material	material not included in collection that may be of interest
<scopecontent>	Scope and Content	range and topical coverage of material
<separatedmaterial>	Separated Material	material of common provenance that has been physically separated
<userestrict>	Conditions Governing Use	conditions affecting use of material after access has been granted
<dsc>	Description of Subordinate Components	[wrapper element containing hierarchical structure of material]

that the summary of important information contained in the Descriptive Identification <did> wrapper element appear as the first section in <archdesc>. The <dsc> element logically belongs at the end of the <archdesc> element sequence, as it contains all lower levels of the hierarchy. The order of all other top-level elements within <archdesc> is flexible, and determined by archivists locally–ideally with a focus upon prioritizing information most valuable to users. It is important to note that unless a given sequence is proscribed by the EAD DTD (such as the <did> in <archref> appearing before the <dsc>), the order in which the information in an encoded finding aid is displayed will be determined by local preferences, as embodied in stylesheets.

The Descriptive Identification <did> element is used in the <archdesc> to group together key information about the entire body of material being described. The <did> and its sub-elements can also be used within a Component <c> to describe a particular subset of material. The <did> that leads off the <archdesc> provides an important high-level orientation to users, and in finding aids the information coded in the <did> will usually be given a heading (in a <head> sub-element) like "Collection Overview" or "Descriptive Summary." The <did> elements are shown in Figure 4.

Important information presented to users in the <did> includes: in <origination>, the name(s) of the "creator(s)" of the materials being described; in <unittitle>, <unitid>, and <unitdate>, the materials' title,

FIGURE 4

<did> elements		
Tags	*element names*	*information content*
<abstract>	Abstract	brief summary of material for quick user reference
<container>	Container	identifies number of the unit (carton, box, folder) where material is held
<origination>	Origination	individuals or organizations responsible for the creation or assembly of material
<physdesc>	Physical Description	extent, dimensions, genre, form
<physloc>	Physical Location	storage location, i.e., shelf, stack, or room number
<repository>	Repository	institution or agency responsible for intellectual access to material
<unitdate>	Date of the Unit	Creation dates of material
<unitid>	ID of the Unit	unique identifier for material, i.e., accession or classification number
<unittitle>	Title of the Unit	name of material

unique identifier number, and dates of creation; in <repository>, the name of the institution responsible for intellectual access to the material and for the content of the finding aid; and in <physdesc>, the extent, dimensions and form of the materials. Archivists can also include in the <did> a brief summary of the materials in the <abstract> sub-element, to help users quickly assess the materials' relevance to their research.

The description begun with the brief high-level summary in the <did> is typically followed by other high-level <archdesc> elements presenting a more detailed picture about the contents and context of the archival materials in question. These elements can be provided with headings according to local preferences using <head>, and the information itself is presented in prose form within Paragraph <p> elements, which can in turn contain many linking, formatting, and controlled access elements. Most useful for providing context information about the creator(s) of the materials is the Biography or History <bioghist> element, which contains a concise essay about the life of an individual or family or about the history of a corporate body. (The new Encoded Archival Context metadata scheme will allow archivists to share such information across multiple finding aids, as discussed below.) Equally important for users is the Scope and Content <scopecontent> statement, a prose overview of the topical content of the materials often highlighting the significant individuals and organizations represented therein. The <arrangement> element can be used either inside <scopecontent> or as a distinct parallel section of its own for a description of the internal structure of the materials.

To provide maximum access to the materials through authority-controlled searching, the Controlled Access Headings <controlaccess> wrapper element allows the use of terms analogous to those used in MARC 1XX, 6XX, and 7XX fields. Sub-elements within <controlaccess> include <persname>, <corpname>, <genreform>, <geogname>, <subject>, and <title>, which can be used along with [source] attributes specifying the controlled vocabulary being used, i.e., "naf" or "lcsh."

Several of the remaining high-level <archdesc> elements (namely <accessrestrict>, <accruals>, <acqinfo>, <altformavail>, <appraisal>, <custodhist>, <prefercite>, <processinfo>, and <userestrict>) focus on the administrative background, processing history, and use policies of the described archival materials. In EAD Version 1.0 these elements were originally clustered together under the now officially "deprecated" element Administrative Information <admininfo>. Since these elements may appear at multiple hierarchical levels within a finding aid, they were "unbundled" in EAD Version 2002 to reduce tagging overhead at the Component level. However, to allow archivists to continue to group these and/or other related elements in finding aids as necessary, EAD Version 2002 includes a new generic wrapper element called Description Group <descgrp>. Through the use of a <head> element inside <descgrp>, many finding aids still contain a section labeled "Administrative Information," or something similar.

The final key element in <archdesc> is the Description of Subordinate Components <dsc>, where information is encoded that pertains only to specific parts of the body of materials being described. The <dsc> has a required [type] attribute that identifies the form of presentation of the subordinate components. The most commonly used [type] value is "combined," indicating that the component description will be followed directly by an itemization of the contents of the component. If the archivist prefers to provide an overview of all the component series and subseries first, then the [type] value to use would be "analyticover," followed by a second <dsc> listing the contents in which the [type] value would be "in-depth." This latter method requires some component information to be encoded twice (once in each of the <dsc> elements) and is therefore less elegant. Moreover, a similar overview of component series can be provided in an <arrangement> element (either within or parallel to <scopecontent>) before opening the <dsc>. In the sample finding aid represented in Appendix 1 and 2, a brief series overview is provided in <arrangement>, and the <dsc> [type] value used is "combined."

In the <dsc> each subordinate part is designated with a Component <c> wrapper element that must contain a <did>. It is recommended that each <c> component be given a [level] attribute (i.e., "series," "subseries," "file," etc.). Since components often appear within other components, it is helpful to use numbered components to clarify the hierarchical relationship between the components. For example, a <c01 level="series"> might contain one or more <c02 level="subseries"> component(s), which in turn contain one or more <c03 level="file"> component(s), and so on. This recursive structure of smaller and smaller components could reach the level of a single item. All the <archdesc> elements available to describe the entire body of materials can also be used within <dsc> to provide information about the content, context, and extent of a specific component of the materials. But as all the information provided about the collection as a whole is inherited by each subordinate component, a component will typically contain only new information, such as in component-specific <scopecontent> notes or elements like <container> or <unittitle>. The <container> element can include a [type] attribute to specify whether the component represents a "box," "folder," or other kind of container. The <table> element and its sub-elements can be used to display container lists or other information in tabular form.

To provide finding aids with the full access and navigation benefits of hypermedia and hypertext, EAD features several linking elements. Internal links within the finding aid can be made using Reference <ref> (which can contain text to describe the referenced object) and Pointer <ptr> (which cannot contain descriptive text). Links to separately described archival materials are possible using Archival Reference <archref>, as are links to published works through Bibliographic Reference <bibref>, and links to external electronic objects with External Reference <extref>. The Digital Archival Object <dao> element allows finding aids to include links to electronic representations of the materials being described. Other elements are available to create multidirectional links and to create groups of links. Although the details of the practical interaction of EAD and EAC information in software applications is still under development, the existence of this robust set of linking elements in EAD will no doubt facilitate the sharing of archival context information promised by EAC.

EAC BACKGROUND

Provenance is the central principle of archival control. Archival materials are the records generated by the everyday activities of individuals, families, and corporate bodies. Therefore, contextual information about the lives, activities, and functions of these creators–and of the relationships existing between creators, functions, and records–is essential for the understanding and use of the materials. *ISAD(G)* and EAD's <bioghist> element allow archivists to supply such contextual information about the creators of archival materials within finding aids, i.e., descriptions of individual archival entities. But there are compelling reasons to separate and formalize the collection and maintenance of this type of information, which Daniel Pitti neatly terms "creator description." In a recent article, Pitti (2004) makes a strong argument for the potential value of separately maintained creator description via EAC; the following four paragraphs summarize this argument.

The first obvious reason is authority control, the need to establish preferred name headings for the individuals, families, and corporate bodies responsible for creating archival materials in order to help collocate dispersed materials sharing the same creator(s), enhancing access. The *International Standard Archival Authority Record for Corporate Bodies, Persons, and Families* (*ISAAR (CPF)*) (International Council 1996) was developed to provide an archival authority control standard to supplement *ISAD(G)*; Encoded Archival Context (EAC) is intended to complement EAD in the same way. The benefits of separately captured and maintained standardized creator descriptions encompass much more than just authority control, however.

Creator description entails expensive and time-consuming biographical and/or historical research, which is now routinely duplicated when materials sharing the same provenance are dispersed. If several different archival repositories happen to contain archival materials created by William Faulkner, for example, then at present each of these repositories must research and prepare creator descriptions for Faulkner. If a single creator description was created in a shared authority file, following an established standard, and collaboratively modified as appropriate, it could be shared to the economic benefit of all these repositories as well as any repository that acquires Faulkner materials in the future.

Moreover, the contextual importance of creator description extends beyond the relationships between creators (individuals, families, corporate bodies) and the archival records they have created. Also significant are the relationships between different creators, and between creators and the functions and activities that are recorded. Through the emergence of the Internet and of hypermedia tools, this web of relationships can be expressed more fully than ever before–and much more efficiently (and economically) if creator description information is captured and maintained separately from the description of the archival records in finding aids.

A last main point Pitti makes is that archival collections constitute the core of primary sources that inform biographical and historical research, so archivists are uniquely well placed (and bear a professional responsibility) to establish authoritative creator descriptions that trace the complex web of relationships between creators, activities, and records. The result of this applied expertise by archivists would be the establishment of a collaborative international biographical and historical resource of unprecedented scope. This new resource could import existing information, such as the contents of the Library of Congress's vast National Authority File (NAF), while adding much greater depth of creator description via newly created EAC records.

The work to develop the new encoding standard that would come to be known as Encoded Archival Context began in earnest when an international group of archivists and information scientists met for that purpose at the University of Toronto in 2001. From this meeting came a document called the "Toronto Tenets: Principles and Criteria for a Model for Archival Context Information" (Toronto Archival Context 2001). A working group was formed, and at a subsequent meeting in the same year at the University of Virginia, the first draft of the new XML DTD for Encoded Archival Context was put together. Now the *Encoded Archival Context Tag Library (Beta August 2004 Working Draft)* has been made available on the EAC web site hosted by the Institute for Advanced Studies at the University of Virginia. This draft is still in revision and therefore not authoritative, but it is sufficiently far along to allow an overview of the structure of EAC.

EAC STRUCTURE

EAC documents feature a nesting structure similar to that of EAD. The outermost element is Encoded Archival Context <eac>, identifying the document as an archival authority record. The <eac> element must be accompanied by a [type] attribute indicating whether the subject of the authority record is a corporate body ("corpname"), person ("persname"), or family ("famname"). For example, an EAC record for a person would begin:

<eac type="persname">

There are two main sections in <eac>: the EAC Header <eacheader>, containing information about the creation, maintenance, and control of the authority record itself; and the Context Description <condesc>, containing the actual creator description information (see Figure 5).

The <eacheader> has a required [status] attribute designating whether the description is a "draft," "edited" (i.e., approved), or "deleted." Within <eacheader> are two required sub-elements and four optional sub-elements. The required sub-elements are: the EAC Identifier <eacid>, which provides a unique identifier number or code for the EAC record; and the Maintenance History <mainhist>, which contains the name, date, and description of any actions/updates involving the record. The optional sub-elements are Language Declaration <langdecl>, Rules Declaration <ruledecl>, Source Declaration <sourcedecl>, and Authority Declaration <authdecl> (see Figure 6).

The <condesc> is a wrapper element containing groups of elements that comprise the creator description, including the entity's name, biog-

FIGURE 5

<eac> high-level wrapper elements		
Tags	*element names*	*information content*
<eacheader>	EAC Header	creation, maintenance, and control of the authority record itself
<condesc>	Context Description	description of the creating entity, including name(s) and references to related creators, resources, and/or functions

FIGURE 6

<eacheader> elements		
Tags	*element names*	*information content*
<eacid>	EAC Identifier	unique identification number or code for the authority record
<mainhist>	Maintenance History	actions or maintenance events involving the record
<languagedecl>	Language Declaration	predominant language(s) used in description
<ruledecl>	Rules Declaration	content standard(s) used in description
<sourcedecl>	Source Declaration	sources used for description
<authdecl>	Authority Declaration	authorized controlled vocabularies or thesauri used in description

raphy/history, and significant relations to other entities, resources, or functions. The one required sub-element within <condesc> is Identity <identity>, which is used to establish authorized and alternative name forms for the entity. The attribute [authorized] is used within <identity> to designate a particular name heading as the privileged form for indexing or display purposes. Other attributes are available for complex cases where different name forms are authorized in different languages or situations. The optional Description <desc> element can contain biographical or historical context information about the entity in prose and/or list form (see Figure 7).

Three optional elements are available in <condesc> for documenting relationships involving the entity being described. EAC Relations <eacrels> is an element grouping references to descriptions of individuals, families, or corporate bodies related to the entity. The [reltype] attribute in <eacrels> can specify certain hierarchical, temporal, familial, and other types of relationships between entities, using a closed list of values (superior, subordinate, earlier, later, associative, parent, child, identity, other).

FIGURE 7

<condesc> elements		
Tags	*element names*	*information content*
<identity>	Identity	authorized and alternative name headings used by entity
<desc>	Description	formal or informal description of the entity
<eacrels>	EAC Relations	one or more relations between the entity and another corporate body, person, or family
<resourcerels>	Resource Relations	one or more relations between the entity and a resource
<funactrels>	Function or Activity Relations	one or more controlled function or activity terms related to the entity

Resource Relations <resourcerels> contains references to other related records or resources. The nature of the resource is first identified with one of the following three sub-elements: Archival Unit <archunit>; Bibliographic Description <bibunit>; or, Museum Description <musunit>. The [reltype] attribute can then be used with a closed list of values (origination, destruction, control, causa, subject, other) to identify the type of relation. Lastly, for references to descriptions of related functions or activities, there is the Function or Activity Relations <funactrels> element. The designers of EAC have deferred the detailed typing of functions and activities until more standardization has been accomplished in their description.

Appendix 3 is a sample EAC record for user display (modeled on the examples available on the official EAC Working group Web site hosted by the University of Virginia's Institute of Advanced Studies in the Humanities (IATH)) (Encoded Archival Context 2004). Appendix 4 shows the same record in encoded form. Note that the section headings present in the display version are not represented in the encoded version; they would likely be generated by a stylesheet.

EAD/EAC IMPLEMENTATION

Archivists and institutions interested in providing online access to their archival holdings and considering EAD implementation usually face the challenge of deciding how to convert their existing finding aids into XML. These legacy finding aids can exist in many different forms, including paper only, word processing files, spreadsheets, HTML files, or SGML files that predate the development of EAD and XML. Numerous programs have been written to help migrate information in practically any of these formats into EAD, some from commercial services and others freely available on the Web sites of the institutions responsible for them. The use of institutional or consortial templates and stylesheets and the availability of commercial and free XML-editing software has greatly streamlined the process of migrating finding aids into EAD or creating new finding aids directly in EAD.

However, choosing large-scale outsourcing or mechanical conversion methods in order to expedite the effort or lower costs can defer issues about the adequacy of the archival descriptions contained in the older finding aids for meeting users' needs. The evaluation of legacy finding aids in preparation for conversion into EAD often beneficially forces archivists to reassess the usefulness of their existing finding aid designs, a process Dennis Meissner (1997) called "reengineering." Putting poorly organized legacy archival descriptions online hastily in order to increase access in the short term may prove a costly missed opportunity. Thoughtfully applied EAD can greatly magnify the accessibility and usefulness of a repository's older finding aids. With respect to the ongoing creation of new finding aids, EAD has already sparked a movement toward standardization of archival descriptive practices that should greatly benefit users.

EAD has attracted a great deal of attention from archivists in the United States and around the world, and implementation of EAD is increasingly widespread. The "EAD Help Pages" Web site maintained by the EAD Round Table (2004) of the Society of American Archivists features a list of "EAD Sites Annotated," which includes over sixty individual institutions (mainly university libraries, historical archives, and a few museums) from the U.S., U.K., Australia, Portugal, and the Netherlands, as well as nineteen "cooperative projects." Notable among these latter consortial approaches to EAD implementation are the American Heritage Virtual Archive Project (2000) (a collaboration between UC Berkeley, Stanford, Duke, and Virginia), the Online Archive of California (OAC) (California Digital Library 2004), and the MALVINE (Manuscripts and Letters Via Integrated Networks in Europe 2003) Project.

The development of EAC is not yet complete, and it has so far been implemented only experimentally. The first prominent test implementation of EAC shows great promise for its potential future uses in combination with EAD and other standards. The University College London's LEADERS (Linking EAD to Electronically Retrievable Project Sources 2004) Project is attempting to develop "an online environment which integrates EAD encoded finding aids and EAC authority records with TEI encoded transcripts and digitised images of archival material." (TEI, the Text Encoding Initiative, is an XML DTD designed to enable the encoding of electronic texts.) The LEADERS "demonstrator application" presents a split-screen display that can simultaneously display or toggle between a digitized image of an archival resource, such as a handwritten letter, a searchable transcript of the letter (TEI), and columns describing the context of the letter (EAD) and of its creator (EAC). In a relatively short time, the development of EAD and now EAC has driven the evolution of archival control from paper finding aids (accessible only in person or through the mail) to the extraordinary "environment" of easy access, complex information retrieval, and rich presentation of archival context represented by the LEADERS project.

WORKS CITED

American Heritage Project. 2000. Berkeley: Univ. of California, available at http://sunsite.berkeley.edu/amher/ (accessed 17 September, 2004).

California Digital Library. 2004. *Online Archive of California*. Oakland: Univ. of California, available at http://www.oac.cdlib.org/ (accessed 17 September, 2004).

Canadian Committee on Archival Description. 2003. *Rules for archival description*, available at http://www.cdncouncilarchives.ca/archdesrules.html (accessed 17 September, 2004).

EAD Round Table. 2004. *EAD help pages*. Chicago: Society of American Archivists, available at http://www.iath.virginia.edu/ead/ (accessed 17 September, 2004).

Encoded archival context tag library, Beta August 2004. 2004. Charlottesville: Ad Hoc Encoded Archival Context Working Group, available at http://www.iath.virginia.edu/eac/ (accessed 17 September, 2004).

Encoded archival description: Application guidelines for version 1.0. 1999. Chicago, Society of American Archivists, available at http://www.loc.gov/ead/ag/aghome.html (accessed 17 September, 2004).

Encoded archival description tag library, version 2002. Chicago: Society of American Archivists, available at http://www.loc.gov/ead/tglib/index.html (accessed 17 September, 2004).

Hensen, Steven L. 1989. *Archives, personal papers, and manuscripts: A cataloging manual for archival repositories, historical societies, and manuscript libraries*, 2nd ed. Chicago: Society of American Archivists.

International Council on Archives. 1996. *ISAAR (cpf): International standard archival authority record for corporate bodies, persons, and families*. Ottawa: ICA, available at http://www.ica.org/biblio/isaar_eng.html (accessed 17 September, 2004).

International Council on Archives. 2000. *ISAD(G): General international standard archival description*, 2nd ed. Ottawa: ICAD, available at http://www.ica.org/biblio/cds/isad_g_2e.pdf (accessed 17 September, 2004).

LEADERS: Linking EAD to Electronically Available Sources. 2004. London: School of Library, Archive and Information Studies, University College London, available at http://www.ucl.ac.uk/leaders-project/ (accessed 17 September, 2004).

MALVINE Consortium. 2003. *MALVINE manuscripts and letters via integrated networks in Europe*, available at http://www.malvine.org/ (accessed 17 September, 2004).

Meissner, Dennis. 1997. First things first: Reengineering finding aids for implementation of EAD. *American archivist* 60: 372-387.

Pearce-Moses, Richard. 2004. *A glossary of archival and records terminology*, s.v. "Finding aid" (Chicago: Society of American Archivists, 2004), available at http://www.archivists.org/glossary (accessed 17 September, 2004).

Pitti, Daniel V. 2004. Creator description: Encoded archival context. *Cataloging & classification quarterly* 38n3/4.

Ruth, Janice E. 2001. "The development and structure of the Encoded Archival Description (EAD) document type definition." In *Encoded archival description on the internet*, Daniel V. Pitti, Wendy M. Duff, eds. Binghamton, NY: The Haworth Information Press, pp. 27-59.

Society of American Archivists. 2004. *Describing archives: A content standard.* Chicago: The Society.

"Statement of Principles for the CUSTARD Project." 2003. available at http://www.archivists.org/news/custardproject.asp (accessed 17 September, 2004).

Toronto Archival Context Meeting. 2001. Toronto tenets: Principles and criteria for a model for archival context information, available at http://www.library.yale.edu/eac/torontotenets.htm (accessed 17 September 2004).

APPENDIX 1. Guide to the Basham Kelly Papers, 1936-1988

Descriptive Summary

Creator:	Kelly, Basham, 1914-1990.
Title:	Basham Kelly papers, 1936-1988 (bulk 1949-1984).
Size:	11 linear ft. (25 boxes)
Coll. No.:	MS-F24
Repository:	Bluegrass State University. Rodgers Library. University Archives.
Abstract:	The Basham Kelly papers, 1936-1988, include manuscripts of Kelly's books and articles, personal correspondence with many noted Kentucky writers and musicians, official correspondence from his tenure as chair of the Dept. of English at Bluegrass State University (1949-1984), course material, lecture notes, photographs, audiotapes and videotapes.

Administrative Information

Provenance
The Basham Kelly papers were donated by Mary Lilly Kelly to the University Archives, Bluegrass State University, in 1991.

Access
The collection is open for research use, with the exception of the correspondence files in Series 1, Box 10, which are restricted until 2030.

Publication Rights
For permission to publish, contact the Curator of the University Archives.

Preferred Citation
[Item, folder title, box number], Basham Kelly papers, University Archives, Rodgers Library, Bluegrass State University.

Processing Information
The collection was processed at the University Archives in 1992 by Judith Morgan. The finding aid was prepared by Diana Elizabeth in 1992.

Biographical Note

Dr. Basham Kelly, who served as the Chair of the Department of English at Bluegrass State University from 1949 until his retirement in 1984, was born in Bullitt County, Kentucky, in 1914. He married Mary Lilly, of Georgetown, Kentucky, in 1938. He received his B.A. from Western Kentucky University, his M.A. from the University of Kentucky, and Ph.D. from the University of Iowa. Before joining the faculty of Bluegrass State University, he taught at Stephen F. Austin College and Oklahoma City University.

An influential literary scholar and folklorist, Dr. Kelly was a central figure in Kentucky literary and arts circles for decades, cultivating long-lasting correspondences with numerous novelists, poets, and musicians, including prominent Kentuckians such as Robert Penn Warren, Jesse Stuart, Harriette Arnow, Hollis Summers, Bradley Kincaid, and Bill Monroe.

Dr. Kelly authored four books: *Melville's Politics* (1947); *Shakespeare in Nineteenth-Century America* (1960); *Fugitive Traces: Robert Penn Warren and Contemporary Fiction* (1966); and *Mountain Music: A Guide to Kentucky Folk Arts* (1980). He edited *Tall Tales of Madison County* (1983), and was a frequent contributor to the *Register of the Kentucky Historical Society.*

Collection Scope and Content

The Basham Kelly Papers range in date from 1936 to 1968, with the bulk of the material dating from Kelly's tenure as Chair of the Dept. of English at Bluegrass State University (1949-1984). The collection includes: personal correspondence with family, friends, and many notable Kentucky writers and musicians; official English Dept. correspondence; course material, lecture notes, and conference papers; typescript drafts and published editions of all of Kelly's books and articles; six audiotapes and four videotapes of radio and television interviews, lectures and commencement addresses; and 27 photographs of Kelly and his friends and acquaintances.

The collection is a valuable primary source for research on Kentucky's literary and folk music scenes, as it includes lively correspondence from the writers Robert Penn Warren, Jesse Stuart, Harriette Arnow, and Hollis Summers, and the musicians Bradley Kincaid (the "Kentucky Mountain Boy"), and Bill Monroe, the bluegrass pioneer.

The collection is arranged in four series: Personal Correspondence (10 boxes); Official Correspondence, Course Material, Lectures (9 boxes); Manuscripts of Publications (4 boxes); and Photographs, Audiotapes, and Videotapes (2 boxes).

Index Terms

This collection is indexed under the following headings in the online catalog of the Rodgers Library.

Kelly, Basham, 1914-1990.
Warren, Robert Penn, 1905-
Stuart, Jesse, 1906-1984.
Arnow, Harriette Louisa Simpson, 1908-
Summers, Hollis Spurgeon, 1916-
Kincaid, Bradley.
Monroe, Bill, 1911-
Bluegrass State University–Faculty.
Bluegrass State University–Dept. of English and American Literature.
American literature–Kentucky–History and criticism.
Folk literature, American–Kentucky.
Folk music–Kentucky.
Folklorists–Kentucky.

Description of Series/Container List

Series 1–Personal Correspondence, 1936-1988
4 linear ft. (10 boxes)

Consists of autograph and typed letters written to Kelly, along with some copies of letters by Kelly. Includes substantial correspondence from Robert Penn Warren, Jesse Stuart, Harriette Arnow, Hollis Summers, Bradley Kincaid, Bill Monroe, and others.

Arranged alphabetically by correspondent. Letters by Kelly are filed with letters from correspondents under correspondents' names.

Access to the correspondence files in Series 1, Box 10, is restricted until 2030.

Box 1 A-D
Box 2 E-G
[*Boxes 3-10 omitted from sample*]

APPENDIX 1 (continued)

Series 2–Official Correspondence, Course Material, Lectures, 1949-1984

Subseries 1–Official Correspondence
2 linear ft. (5 boxes)

Consists of official correspondence written by and to Kelly in his role as Chair of the English Dept. at Bluegrass State University.

Arranged alphabetically by correspondent or topic.

Box 11 A-G
Box 12 H-J
[*Boxes 13-15 omitted from sample*]

Subseries 2–Course Material, Lectures
1.5 linear ft. (4 boxes)

Syllabi, assignments, handouts, and lecture notes from Kelly's courses on literature and folklore at Bluegrass State University.

Arranged chronologically.
[*Remaining series/container list omitted from finding aid sample*]

APPENDIX 2. Sample Encoded EAD Record

```
<?xmlversion="1.0" encoding="ISO-8859-1"?>
<!DOCTYPE ead PUBLIC "+//ISBN 1-931666-00-8//DTD ead.dtd (Encoded Archival
 Description (EAD) Version 2002)//EN" "../shared/ead/ead.dtd>

<ead>
    <eadheader audience="internal" countryencoding="iso3166-1"
    dateencoding="iso8601" langencoding="iso639-2b" repositoryencoding="iso15511">
        <eadid countrycode="us" mainagencycode="xx-x" publicid="-//us::xx-x//TEXT
        us::xx-x::f24.sgm//EN">Basham Kelly papers</eadid>
        <filedesc>
            <titlestmt>
                <titleproper>Guide to the Basham Kelly papers, 1936-1988</titleproper>
                <author>Collection processed by Judith Morgan, finding aid prepared by
                Diana Elizabeth</author>
            </titlestmt>
            <publicationstmt>
                <publisher>University Archives, Rodgers Library, Bluegrass State
                University.</publisher>
                <date>&copy; 1992</date>
            </publicationstmt>
        </filedesc>
        <profiledesc>
            <creation>Finding aid encoded by Richard Cooper,
            <date>2004.</date></creation>
            <langusage>Finding aid is written in
```

```
        <language>English</language></langusage>
        <descrules>APPM used for description; AACR2r used for descriptive headings;
        LCSH used for subject headings.</descrules>
    </profiledesc>
</eadheader>
<frontmatter>
    <titlepage>
        <titleproper>Guide to the Basham Kelly Papers.</titleproper>
        <num>MS-F24</num>
        <publisher>University Archives<lb>Rodgers Library<lb>Bluegrass State University
            <lb>Danville, Kentucky</publisher>
        <list type="deflist">
            <defitem>
                <label> Processed by:</label>
                <item>Judith Morgan</item>
            </defitem>
            <defitem>
                <label> Finding aid prepared by:</label>
                <item>Diana Elizabeth</item>
            </defitem>
            <defitem>
                <label> Encoded by:</label>
                <item>Richard Cooper</item>
            </defitem>
        </list>
        <p>&copy 1992 Bluegrass University. All rights reserved.</p>
    </titlepage>
</frontmatter>
<archdesc level="collection" relatedencoding="MARC">
    <did>
        <head>Descriptive Summary</head>
        <origination label="Creator"><persname encodinganalog="100">Kelly,
        Basham, 1914-1990</persname></origination>
        <unittitle label="Title" encodinganalog="245">Basham Kelly papers, <unitdate
        type="inclusive" normal="1936/1988" encodinganalog="260">1936-1988
        </unitdate><unitdate type="bulk" normal="1949/1984">1949-
        1984</unitdate></unittitle>
        <physdesc label="Size" encodinganalog="300"><extent>11 linear ft. (25
        boxes)</extent></physdesc>
        <unitid countrycode="us" repositorycode="xx-x" type="classification"
        label="Collection No.">MS-F24</unitid>
        <repository label="Repository"><corpname>Bluegrass State University.
        Rodgers Library. University Archives.</corpname></repository>
        <abstract label="Abstract">The Basham Kelly papers, 1936-1988, include
        manuscripts of Kelly's books and articles, personal correspondence with many
        noted Kentucky writers and musicians, official correspondence from his tenure
        as chair of the Dept. of English at Bluegrass State University (1949-1984),
        course material, lecture notes, photographs, and audiotapes and
        videotapes.</abstract>
    </did>
    <descgrp>
        <head>Administrative Information</head>
        <acqinfo encodinganalog="541">
            <head>Provenance</head>
            <p> The Basham Kelly papers were donated by Mary Lilly Kelly to the
            University Archives, Bluegrass State University, in 1991.</p>
```

APPENDIX 2 (continued)

```
        </acqinfo>
        <accessrestrict encodinganalog="506">
            <head>Access</head>
            <p> The collection is open for research use, with the exception of the
            correspondence files in Series 1, Box 7, which are restricted until 2030.</p>
        </accessrestrict>
        <userestrict encodinganalog="540">
            <head>Publication Rights</head>
            <p> For permission to publish, contact the Curator of the University
            Archives.</p>
        </userestrict>
        <prefercite encodinganalog="524">
            <head>Preferred Citation</head>
            <p>[Item, folder title, box number], Basham Kelly papers, University
            Archives, Rodgers Library, Bluegrass State University.</p>
        </prefercite>
        <processinfo encodinganalog="583">
            <head>Processing Information</head>
            <p> The collection was processed at the University Archives in 1992 by
            Judith Morgan. The finding aid was prepared by Diana Elizabeth in 1992.</p>
        </processinfo>
    </descgrp>
    <bioghist encodinganalog="545">
        <head>Biographical Note</head>
        <p> Dr. Basham Kelly, who served as the Chair of the Department of English at
        Bluegrass State University from 1949 until his retirement in 1984, was born in
        Bullitt County, Kentucky in 1914. He married Mary Lilly, of Georgetown,
        Kentucky, in 1938. He received his B.A. from Western Kentucky University, his
        M.A. from the University of Kentucky, and Ph.D. from the University of Iowa.
        Before joining the faculty of Bluegrass State University, he taught at Stephen F.
        Austin College and Oklahoma City University.</p>
        <p>An influential literary scholar and folklorist, Dr. Kelly was a central figure
        in Kentucky literary and arts circles for decades, cultivating long-lasting
        correspondences with numerous novelists, poets, and musicians, including
        prominent Kentuckians such as Robert Penn Warren, Jesse Stuart, Harriette
        Arnow, Hollis Summers, Bradley Kincaid, and Bill Monroe.</p>
        <p>Dr. Kelly authored four books: Melville's Politics (1947); Shakespeare in
        Nineteenth-Century America (1960); Fugitive Traces: Robert Penn Warren and
        Contemporary Fiction (1966); and Mountain Music: A Guide to Kentucky Folk
        Arts (1980). He edited Tall Tales of Madison County (1983), and was a frequent
        contributor to the Register of the Kentucky Historical Society.</p>
    </bioghist>
    <scopecontent encodinganalog="520">
        <head>Collection Scope and Content</head>
        <p> The Basham Kelly Papers range in date from 1936 to 1968, with the bulk of
        the material dating from Kelly's tenure as Chair of the Dept. of English at
        Bluegrass State University (1949-1984). The collection includes: personal
        correspondence with family, friends, and many notable Kentucky writers and
        musicians (10 boxes); official English Dept. correspondence (6 boxes); course
        material, lecture notes, and conference papers (3 boxes); typescript drafts and
        published editions of all of Kelly's books and articles (4 boxes); six audiotapes
        and four videotapes of radio and television interviews, lectures and
        commencement addresses (1 box); and 27 photographs of Kelly and his friends
        and acquaintances (1 box).</p>
```

```xml
        <p>The collection is a valuable primary source for research on Kentucky's
        literary and folk music scenes, as it contains interesting correspondence from
        writers such as Robert Penn Warren, Jesse Stuart, Harriette Arnow, and Hollis
        Summers, and musicians including Bradley Kincaid (the "Kentucky Mountain
        Boy"), and Bill Monroe, the bluegrass pioneer. </p>
        <arrangement>
            <p> The collection is arranged in four series: Personal Correspondence;
            Official Correspondence, Course Material, Lectures; Manuscripts of
            Publications; and Photographs, Audiotapes, and Videotapes.</p>
        </arrangement>
    </scopecontent>
    <controlaccess>
        <head>Index Terms</head>
        <p> This collection is indexed under the following headings in the online
        catalog of the Rodgers Library.</p>
        <persname encodinganalog="600">Kelly, Basham, 1914-1990.</persname>
        <persname encodinganalog="600">Warren, Robert Penn, 1905- </persname>
        <persname encodinganalog="600">Stuart, Jesse, 1906-1984. </persname>
        <persname encodinganalog="600">Arnow, Harriette Louisa Simpson, 1908-
        </persname>
        <persname encodinganalog="600">Summers, Hollis Spurgeon, 1916- </persname>
        <persname encodinganalog="600">Kincaid, Bradley. </persname>
        <persname encodinganalog="600">Monroe, Bill, 1911- </persname>
        <corpname encodinganalog="610">Bluegrass State University–Faculty.</corpname>
        <corpname encodinganalog="610">Bluegrass State University–Dept. of
        English and American Literature. </corpname>
        <subject encodinganalog="650">American literature–Kentucky–History and
        criticism.</subject>
        <subject encodinganalog="650">Folk literature, American–
        Kentucky.</subject>
        <subject encodinganalog="650">Folk music – Kentucky.</subject>
        <subject encodinganalog="650">Folklorists – Kentucky.</subject>
    </controlaccess>
    <dsc type="combined">
        <head>Description of Series/Container List</head>
        <c01 level="series">
            <head>Series 1</head>
            <did>
                <unittitle>Personal Correspondence<unitdate type="inclusive"
                normal="1936/1988">1936-1988</unitdate></unittitle>
                <physdesc><extent>4 linear ft. (10 boxes)</extent></physdesc>
            </did>
            <scopecontent>
                <p>Consists of autograph and typed letters written to Kelly, along
                with some copies of letters by Kelly. Includes substantial correspondence from
                Robert Penn Warren, Jesse Stuart, Harriette Arnow, Hollis Summers,
                Bradley Kincaid, Bill Monroe, and others.</p>
                <arrangement>
                    <p>Arranged alphabetically by correspondent. Letters by Kelly are
                    filed with letters from correspondents under correspondents' names.</p>
                </arrangement>
            </scopecontent>
            <accessrestrict>
```

APPENDIX 2 (continued)

```
        <p>Access to the correspondence files in Series 1, Box 10, is restricted
        until 2030.</p>
    </accessrestrict>
    <c02 level="file">
        <did>
            <container label="Box" type="box">1</container>
            <unittitle>A-D</unittitle>
        </did>
    </c02>
    <c02 level="file">
        <did>
            <container label="Box" type="box">2</container>
            <unittitle>E-G</unittitle>
        </did>
    </c02> . . . [remaining Series 1 boxes omitted from sample]
</c01>
<c01 level="series">
    <head>Series 2</head>
    <did>
        <unittitle>Official Correspondence, Course Material, Lectures, <unitdate
        type="inclusive" normal="1949/1984">1949-1984</unitdate></unittitle>
    </did>
    <c02 level="subseries">
        <head>Subseries 1</head>
        <did>
            <unittitle>Official Correspondence</unittitle>
            <physdesc><extent>2 linear ft. (5 boxes)</extent></physdesc>
        </did>
        <scopecontent>
            <p>Consists of official correspondence written by and to Kelly in his
            role as Chair of the English Dept. at Bluegrass State University.</p>
            <arrangement>
                <p>Arranged alphabetically by correspondent or topic.</p>
            </arrangement>
        </scopecontent>
        <c03 level="file">
            <did>
                <container label="Box" type="box">11</container>
                <unittitle>A-G</unittitle>
            </did>
        </c03>
        <c03 level="file">
            <did>
                <container label="Box" type="box">12</container>
                <unittitle>H-J</unittitle>
            </did>
        </c03>
    </c02>
    <c02 level="subseries">
        <head>Subseries 2</head>
        <did>
            <unittitle>Course Material, Lectures </unittitle>
            <physdesc><extent>1.5 linear ft. (4 boxes)</extent></physdesc>
```

```
                </did>
                <scopecontent>
                    <p>Consists of official correspondence written by and to Kelly in his
                    role as Chair of the English Dept. at Bluegrass State University.</p>
                    <arrangement>
                        <p>Arranged alphabetically by correspondent or topic.</p>
                    </arrangement>
                </scopecontent>
                <c03> [contents of Series 2, Subseries 2 omitted from sample]
                </c03>
            </c02>
        </c01>[contents of Series 3-4 omitted from sample]
    </dsc>
  </archdesc>
</ead>
```

APPENDIX 3. Sample EAC Record

Entity Description

Identity

Used

Bluegrass State University [1 September 1919-]

Not used

BSU [1 September 1919-]

Description

The school that later became Bluegrass State University was founded by John Jefferson Rodgers in 1883 as the Danmont Agricultural Institute. By 1919 the curriculum had expanded beyond technical instruction to include arts and sciences, and the name was changed to Bluegrass State University.

Related Entities

Previously known as
Danmont Agricultural Institute [1883-1919]

Founder
Rodgers, John Jefferson, 1829-1911

APPENDIX 3 (continued)

Related Resources

Bibliographic Source
Bluegrass State University. *Bluegrass State University, 1883-1983: A Centennial Celebration.* Danmont, Ky: Bluegrass State University Press, 1983.

Record Control Information

Record type: corporate name
Editorial status: draft
Language encoding standard: iso639-2b
Script encoding standard: iso15924
Date encoding standard: iso8601
Country encoding standard: iso3166-1
Owner encoding standard: iso15511
Record identifier: US:: BSUKY::Bluegrass State University::A1
Maintenance history:

Event: Record created
Date: 22 April 2003
Name: Richard Cooper

Event: Record updated
Date: May 12, 2003
Name: Richard Cooper

Language/Script of description: English in Latin Script

APPENDIX 4. Sample Encoded EAC Record

```
<eac type="corpname">
    <eacheader status="draft" langencoding="iso639-2b"
    scriptencoding="iso15924" dateencoding="iso8601"
    countryencoding="iso3166-1" ownerencoding="iso15511">
        <eacid countrycode="US"
        ownercode="BSUKY">US::BSUKY::Bluegrass State University::A1</eacid>
        <mainhist>
            <mainevent maintype="create">
                <name>Richard Cooper</name>
                <maindate calendar="gregorian" normal="20030422">22 April 2003</maindate>
            </mainevent>
            <mainevent maintype="update">
                <name>Richard Cooper</name>
                <maindate calendar="gregorian" normal="20030512">12 May 2003</maindate>
            </mainevent>
        </mainhist>
        <languagedecl>
            <language languagecode="eng" scriptcode="latn">English in Latin script</language>
        </languagedecl>
        <sourcedecl>
            <source id="s1">http://www.bsuky.edu/</source>
        </sourcedecl>
    </eacheader>
    <condesc>
        <identity>
            <corphead authorized="BSUKY">
                <part>Bluegrass State University. </part>
                <usedate scope="begin-end" form="openspan"
                era="ce" calendar="gregorian" normal="19190901/">1
                September 1919–</usedate>
            </corphead>
            <corphead>
                <part>BSU.</part>
            </corphead>
        </identity>
        <desc>
            <bioghist>
                <p>The school that later became Bluegrass State University was founded by John
                Jefferson Rodgers in 1883 as the Danmont Agricultural Institute. By 1919 the
                curriculum had expanded beyond technical instruction to include arts and sciences,
                and the name was changed to Bluegrass State University.</p>
            </bioghist>
        </desc>
        <eacrels>
            <eacrel reltype="earlier" type="Previous">
                <corpname> Danmont Agricultural Institute. 1883-1919 </corpname>
            </eacrel>
            <eacrel reltype="associative" type="Founder">
                <persname>Rodgers, John Jefferson. 1829-1911.</persname>
            </eacrel>
        </eacrels>
        <resourcerels>
            <resourcerel type="Primary" reltype="subject">
```

APPENDIX 4 (continued)


```
        <bibunit>
            <name type="author">Bluegrass State University.</name>
            <title render="italic">Bluegrass State University, 1883-1983:
            A Centennial Celebration. </title>
            <imprint><publisher>Bluegrass State University Press, </publisher>
            <date era="ce" calendar="gregorian">1983.</date>
            </imprint>
        </bibunit>
      </resourcerel>
    </resourcerels>
  </condesc>
</eac>
```

Introduction to XML

Patrick Yott

SUMMARY. This chapter begins with a brief history of markup technologies and an examination of two of the most commonly encountered markup languages: HTML and XML. The basic structural components of an XML document are described, and the rules for creating "well-formed" documents are discussed. The concept of data modeling and document "validity" will be demonstrated using a simple DTD (Document Type Definition), and several markup examples will follow. The notions of XML as a data interchange system and XSLT as a transformation and display language will be examined. *[Article copies available for a fee from The Haworth Document Delivery Service: 1-800-HAWORTH. E-mail address: <docdelivery@haworthpress.com> Website: <http://www.HaworthPress.com> © 2005 by The Haworth Press, Inc. All rights reserved.]*

KEYWORDS. Markup languages, XML, data modeling, document validity, DTD (Document Type Definition)

A BRIEF HISTORY OF MARKUP LANGUAGES

The past 35 years have seen a movement from specific encoding of electronic documents to generic encoding of electronic documents. In specific encoding an electronic document contains control codes that

---

Patrick Yott is Head, Digital Services, Brown University Library, Box A, Rockefeller Library, Brown University, Providence, RI 02912 (E-mail: Patrick_Yott@brown.edu).

[Haworth co-indexing entry note]: "Introduction to XML." Yott, Patrick. Co-published simultaneously in *Cataloging & Classification Quarterly* (The Haworth Information Press, an imprint of The Haworth Press, Inc.) Vol. 40, No. 3/4, 2005, pp. 213-235; and: *Metadata: A Cataloger's Primer* (ed: Richard P. Smiraglia) The Haworth Information Press, an imprint of The Haworth Press, Inc., 2005, pp. 213-235. Single or multiple copies of this article are available for a fee from The Haworth Document Delivery Service [1-800-HAWORTH, 9:00 a.m. - 5:00 p.m. (EST). E-mail address: docdelivery@haworthpress.com].

Available online at http://www.haworthpress.com/web/CCQ

doi:10.1300/J104v40n03_10

would dictate how the document was to be formatted. These codes were generally specific to one hardware or software configuration and would not work if one moved from, for example, Waterloo script on a mainframe to WordPerfect on a DOS machine. Generic encoding, which many trace back to Tunnicliffe's 1967 presentation on separating content from format (Goldfarb 1990, 567), focuses on describing the structural and semantic content of a document, and leaves formatting instructions to external documents and tools thus allowing content to be shared between computing environments.

By 1969, engineers at IBM had taken Tunnicliffe's ideas and produced a language called Generalized Markup Language, or GML. In 1986, the International Standards Organization (ISO) adopted an advanced version of GML, the Standard Generalized Markup Language (SGML) as an ISO standard. SGML was a meta-language–a set of rules and principles with which one could create content specific tag sets, such as the Text Encoding Initiative (TEI), the Encoded Archival Description (EAD), and in 1991, the Hypertext Markup Language (HTML).

In 1996, faced with the successful implementation of HTML across the World Wide Web, and a simultaneous dissatisfaction with the limitations of the finite HTML tag set and its focus on presentation (see below), the World Wide Web Consortium adopted XML as a specification. XML fits the middle ground between SGML and HTML. Like SGML it is a meta-language and has led to the rapid development of content specific markup languages, including X versions of the TEI, EAD, and HTML languages. Because it is less complex (and leads to more easily processed documents) than SGML, a wide variety of open-source and commercial XML applications have quickly followed its introduction.

From the perspective of the librarian or information manager, the widespread development of XML technologies has had profound effects. Where MARC once ruled as the primary metadata format used by librarians and library systems, librarians are routinely encountering XML based metadata standards, such as the TEI (full text databases), EAD (manuscript and archival finding aids), METS (complex digital object structures), and MODS/Dublin Core (alternative descriptive cataloging systems).

XML, HTML, WHAT'S THE DIFFERENCE?

Before we go any further, we must eliminate the most common of misconceptions–XML is not HTML on steroids (University of Virginia n.d.). The most fundamental difference between HTML and XML is that XML is a set of rules that are used to create markup languages while HTML is itself a markup language. XML is a meta-language. While one can correctly state that she is marking up a document in HTML, it would be technically inaccurate to state that she is marking up a document in XML. It would be better to state that she is marking up a document in the TEI or EAD markup language, both of which are implementations of XML.

HTML is a remarkably simple markup language. It was this simplicity that allowed the World Wide Web to grow at the bewildering rate that it has. Quickly learned and easily implemented (there is a wide variety of HTML editors available), HTML contains a finite set of tags that are used to instruct browsers how to display information and how to link between documents, images, and other objects present on the web.

So what then is XML?

> On one level, XML is a protocol for containing and managing information. On another level, it's a family of technologies that can do everything from formatting documents to filtering data. And on the highest level, it's a philosophy for information handling that seeks maximum usefulness and flexibility for data by refining it to its purest and most structured form. (Ray 2001, 2)

It is, in essence, a methodology for creating self-describing documents.

Looking at this difference in less abstract terms, one would use HTML to describe the appearance of a document and would use an XML language to describe the structure of a document. For example, suppose you were cataloging a collection of musical recordings and wanted to move beyond MARC to handle this task. For this example, and throughout this article, we'll look at creating a non-MARC catalog record for Fripp and Eno's groundbreaking recording: *No pussyfooting* (EG, 1973). Let's look at how this could be done with HTML and a portion of an implementation of XML.

slash_2-238845.html

```
<html>
<body>
<h2 align="center">No Pussyfooting</h2>
<strong> Fripp and Eno </strong><br>
```

```
<strong>EG (2)</strong><br>
<strong>1973</strong><br>
<strong>39:38</strong><br>
<strong>Experimental</strong>
<p>
<h4>Credits</h4>
<ul>
<li>Brian Eno (Synthesizer, Keyboards, Vocals. . .)
<li>Robert Fripp (Guitar, Producer. . .)
</ul>
</body>
</html>
```

slash_2-238845.xml (portion)

```
<?xml version="1.0" encoding="UTF-8"?>
<!DOCTYPE recording SYSTEM "c:\xmlfiles\dtds\music.dtd">
<recording ID="CD1" condition="fine">
<albuminfo>
<title>No Pussyfooting</title>
<creator>Fripp and Eno</creator>
<label catno="2">EG</label>
<genre>Experimental</genre>
<year>1973</year>
<credits>
<credit>
<creator>Brian Eno</creator>
<role>Synthesizer</role>
<role>Keyboards</role>
<role>Vocals</role>
</credit>
</credits>
<time>39:38</time>
</albuminfo>
</recording>
```

Both of these documents contain identical information, but differ greatly in the utility of that information. If we were principally concerned with display, the HTML example would work very well, and one might ultimately want to display the XML content in such a manner. But if we wanted, for example, to identify specific catalog records by searching for a given label, the XML-based representation would be more effective. In the HTML example, the record label is visually identifiable but is not encoded in a way that would permit efficient machine processing.

RULES FOR WELL-FORMEDNESS

When working with documents encoded using an XML-based markup language we must be concerned with both the shape of the document (its well-formedness) and the syntax of the language used (its validity). We'll deal with validity in a later section. Before we can do anything with a document based on an XML markup language, that document must be well-formed. There are four basic tenets of well-formedness: (1) every opening tag must be matched with a corresponding closing tag; (2) tags must nest cleanly; (3) values assigned to attributes must be placed within quotation marks; and (4) every document must have a root element. Let's take a quick look at each of these basic rules.

Opening and Closing Tags

Look at our HTML example above. In the list of performers each performer is encoded as a list item (the <li> element in HTML), and are encoded with the open (<li>) tag but without the close (</li>) tag. Since HTML is derived from SGML and since SGML allows for tag minimization (the lack of closing tags), this is not a problem, and web browsers have been developed to allow for the resulting ambiguity. In an XML-based markup language (such as XHTML), we would have to both open and close our list item tags, like this: <li>Ritchie, Brian (Guitar Bass)</li>. We have now removed any ambiguity as to where one list item ends and another begins.

Case counts. In an XML-based markup language <Name> is a different element from <name>. While they may look confusingly similar to human eyes, any software that can process an XML-based structure can easily differentiate the two. In HTML <h2> and <H2> are considered synonymous, so you can open a node with <h2> and close it with </H2> without generating an error. Not so in XML–these two tags are considered to be completely unrelated.

For elements that don't contain any data or other elements (empty elements), these tags can close themselves either by opening and immediately closing or by closing within their opening tag.

Nesting Tags

It is important that when you open a tag within a previously opened tag, that you close the inner tag pair before closing the outer pair. While Netscape browsers used to consider improperly nested tags an error (they no longer do), HTML will render when a document is so encoded. In a document based on XML markup rules, any document that violates this practice will fail to parse and will generate an error.

Attributes and Values

Attributes are used to refine an element. In our XML example above, we refine each performer node (that area bounded by a tag pair) by indicating; in an attribute, what the role of each performer was in this recording. The value assigned to each role attribute must be enclosed within matching quotation marks (either single/single or double/double). Not to continually pick on HTML, but in HTML while this is considered good practice, you are not required to so enclose your values.

The Root Element

Every well-formed XML document contains a root element. The root element opens and closes the document and can only occur once in the document.

TESTING FOR WELL-FORMEDNESS

The rules for well-formedness ensure that any simple XML-enabled tool, such as an up-to-date web browser, can read your document. In fact, "reading" your XML document in a browser is often the simplest and quickest test for well-formedness. If the document is well-formed, it will *parse*, and can be displayed.

When a web browser parses a document, it does so in complete ignorance of the semantic and syntactic rules the lay behind the tags it encounters. We call this type of parser a non-validating parser. Because the browser is limited to checking that the fundamental rules of any XML document are followed, it is a very useful tool when encoding a document that doesn't follow any specific document model (more on this soon . . .). Notice the plus and minus signs to the left of your tags (see Figure 1). These allow you to expand and collapse any node within

FIGURE 1. A Well-Formed XML Document Viewed in Internet Explorer

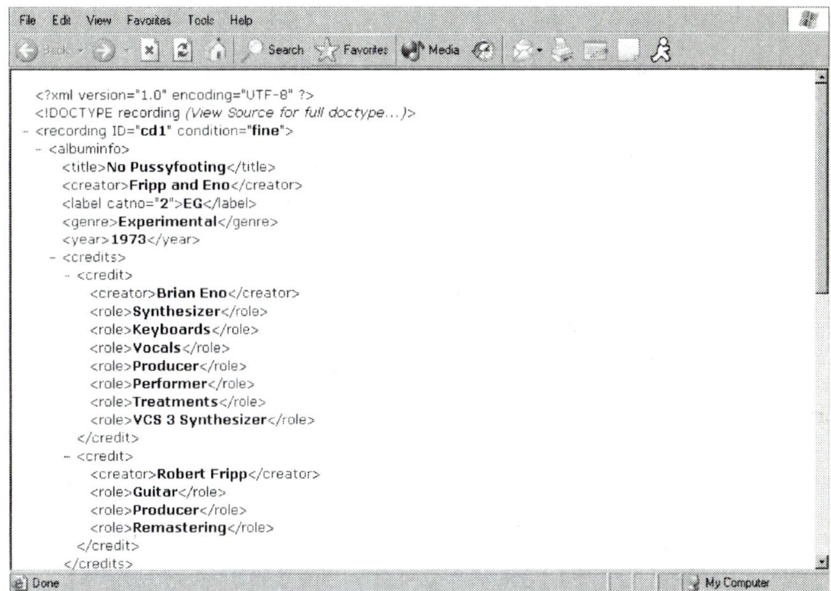

```
<?xml version="1.0" encoding="UTF-8" ?>
<!DOCTYPE recording (View Source for full doctype...)>
- <recording ID="cd1" condition="fine">
  - <albuminfo>
      <title>No Pussyfooting</title>
      <creator>Fripp and Eno</creator>
      <label catno="2">EG</label>
      <genre>Experimental</genre>
      <year>1973</year>
    - <credits>
      - <credit>
          <creator>Brian Eno</creator>
          <role>Synthesizer</role>
          <role>Keyboards</role>
          <role>Vocals</role>
          <role>Producer</role>
          <role>Performer</role>
          <role>Treatments</role>
          <role>VCS 3 Synthesizer</role>
        </credit>
      - <credit>
          <creator>Robert Fripp</creator>
          <role>Guitar</role>
          <role>Producer</role>
          <role>Remastering</role>
        </credit>
      </credits>
```

your document, and are a very useful way of exploring a document's structure.

If a document is not well-formed, a non-validating parser will stop processing (displaying if you are using a web browser) the document when it encounters its first well-formedness error. It generally provides an error message alerting you to the nature of the violation (see Figure 2). For example, the following example displays the Internet Explorer error message we generate if we attempt to close a creator tag with a credit tag, like this:

```
<creator>Brian Eno</credit>
```

DOCUMENT MODELING AND DOCUMENT VALIDITY

The rules described above are obviously ignorant of content considerations–they only insure that a document adheres to a minimal syntactical cleanliness. In order to have documents that maintain a predictable structure and that can be shared between various organizations and sys-

FIGURE 2. A Non-Well-Formed XML Document Viewed in Internet Explorer

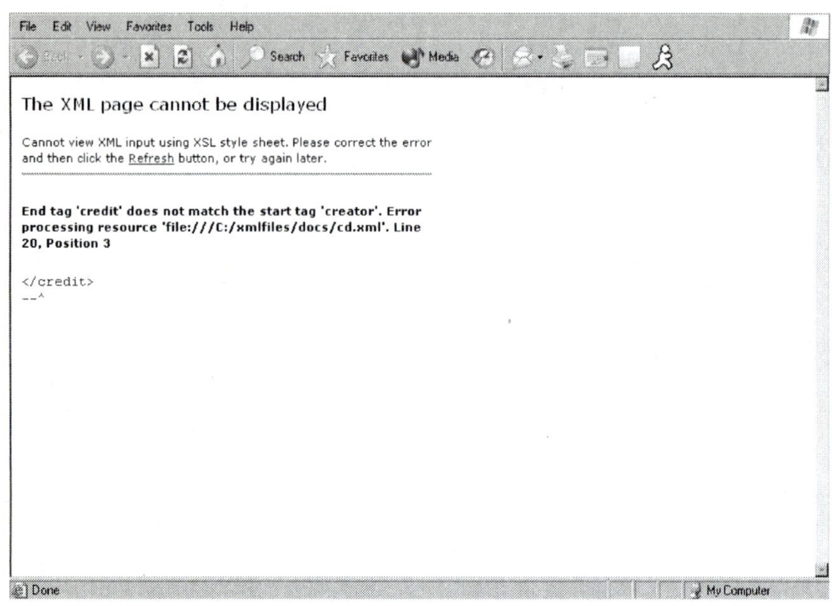

tems, a content model needs to be established and standardized. Documents that conform to this content model are said to be valid.

Content models have traditionally been recorded in documents called Document Type Definitions (DTDs), a document modeling technology dating back to the advent of GML and SGML. A newer technology, the XML Schema, encodes a document model as an XML document and offers more specific data modeling options than the DTD. For the purposes of this introduction we'll explore the DTD as a document modeling language.

Found within a DTD (or schema) are the grammar and vocabulary for encoding a given type of document–the DTD lists all the elements that are permissible, the order and/or places where those elements can exist within your document and any specific nesting rules. Your document is said to be valid when it adheres to these rules. If you use an element that is not listed in the DTD, or use a listed element in an unacceptable way, your document will not validate. Only when members of a community agree to encode their documents according to a specific content model does it becomes possible to share content. (A registry of published

DTDs and schema is available from xml.org at http://www.xml.org/xml/registry.jsp.) The following DTD was used to create the XML record seen earlier.

```
<!-- Sample DTD for encoding musical recordings -->
<!-- Patrick M. Yott, July 2004 -->

<!ELEMENT recording (albuminfo, tracklist)>
        <!ATTLIST recording
                ID ID #REQUIRED
                condition (mint | fine | good | poor) #REQUIRED
        >
<!ELEMENT albuminfo (title, creator*, label, genre+, year, credits, time)>
<!ELEMENT creator (#PCDATA)>
<!ELEMENT credit (creator, role+)>
<!ELEMENT credits (credit+)>
<!ELEMENT label (#PCDATA)>
        <!ATTLIST label
                catno CDATA #IMPLIED
        >
<!ELEMENT genre (#PCDATA)>
<!ELEMENT year (#PCDATA)>
<!ELEMENT role (#PCDATA)>
<!ELEMENT time (#PCDATA)>
<!ELEMENT title (#PCDATA)>
<!ELEMENT track (title, credits, time)>
        <!ATTLIST track
                sequence CDATA #REQUIRED
        >
<!ELEMENT tracklist (track+)>
```

In looking at this DTD, you should notice that the structure is deceptively simple–it consists of a series of element and attribute declarations. This is the vocabulary for your document. Within each declaration are the rules for constructing that element or attribute. This is the grammar for your document. Let's look at these in more detail.

Declaring an Element

Elements are declared with this basic syntax:

```
<!ELEMENT name content-model>
```

The name of an element represents a tag that you are permitted to use in your XML document. The content model dictates what that element can contain in your document. There are five general content models that are used with elements: empty, parsed character data (#PCDATA), element, mixed, and all. Let's look at each of these in turn.

Empty

An empty content model specifies that there can be nothing between the opening and closing of the element in your document. In fact, elements designed as empty elements generally "self-close" when used, such as <hr/> or <br/>. An empty element may contain attributes.

Parsed Character Data

PCDATA content models specify that you can include text between the open and close of the tag set (referred to as a node), but that you cannot include any other tags. These are declared as:

```
<!ELEMENT title (#PCDATA)>
```

Element

Element data models signify that the element can contain other elements, and they specify the order and quantity of these nested elements. For example, the declaration:

```
<!ELEMENT recording (albuminfo, tracklist)>
```

specifies that any recording node in your document must include an album info node followed by a tracklist node.

The order in which elements are listed in this content model specifies the order in which they must be used in your document. The comma equates to "followed by," so in the example above, albuminfo must be followed by tracklist and both occur within recording. If two elements in a content model are separated by a vertical bar (|), this specifies that you can use one or the other but not both.

Aside for the order of elements in the content model, the DTD also specifies the quantity of each element. It does this by affixing a symbol (*, +, ?) to the element name.

*	0 or more occurrences of this element are permitted.
+	1 or more occurrences of this element are permitted.
?	0 or 1 occurrences of this element are permitted.
no symbol	1 occurrence of this element is mandatory.

Thus, the element declaration:

```
<!ELEMENT track (title, credits, time)>
```

specifies that if you have a track node, it must contain one title node, followed by one credits node, followed by one time node. Notice that this declaration doesn't provide any information about when and where you can use a track node. You have to examine all the other element declarations in the DTD to determine where this element is acceptable. In this case, you'll find it listed within the tracklist element's content model, which is itself found within the recording content model.

Mixed

A mixed content data model allows for both PCDATA as well as elements to be included within a given element node. The same rules that govern order and quantity for element data models apply to the mixed data model. Although our DTD doesn't contain any mixed content models, the general structure would look like this:

```
<!ELEMENT p (#PCDATA | i | br)*>
```

This declares that you can use an element named p (the paragraph tag) and it can contain a mix of character data, italic tags (<i>), and line break tags (<br>).

All

The all data model specifies that there is no restriction whatsoever on what a particular element can contain, and as such is not very useful since there is really no point in declaring an element if it doesn't have any structural/content restrictions.

Declaring an Attribute

The attributes for any given element are declared using this basic syntax:

```
<!ATTLIST element_name
        attribute_name  attribute_type  attribute_behavior
>
```

In our DTD, the label element can take one attribute, the catno (catalog number) attribute. This is modeled in the DTD as:

```
<!ATTLIST label
        catno CDATA #IMPLIED
>
```

You can list multiple attributes for any given element. Our DTD defines two attributes for the recording element using this syntax:

```
<!ATTLIST recording
        ID ID #REQUIRED
        condition (mint | fine | good | poor) #REQUIRED
>
```

Note that the first attribute is named ID and is of type ID. There are several types of attributes available in a DTD. The type determines what type of content can be assigned as a value to a given attribute. The three most commonly used types of attribute are character data (CDATA), an enumerated list of values, or a specific (tokenized) constraint, such as uniqueness.

CDATA

A CDATA attribute type signifies that the value can be any text string. The label element can have an attribute and value of catno="2-23845", for example. CDATA types allow us to use any text string as a value, including numbers. In our DTD this is controlled by:

```
<!ATTLIST label
        catno CDATA #IMPLIED
>
```

Enumerated List

The recording element accepts an attribute called condition (in addition to the ID attribute), but instead of letting the encoder enter any value, restricts valid values to a standardized list. This attribute is controlled like this:

```
<!ATTLIST recording
        ID ID #REQUIRED
        condition (mint | fine | good | poor) #REQUIRED
>
```

If the individual encoding a document enters a value other than mint, fine, good, or poor, the document may be well-formed (assuming she has followed good form throughout), but it will not be valid.

Tokenized Attributes

A tokenized attribute has some sort of constraint placed upon it. There are seven types of constraints, but for now we'll look at the ID and IDREF/IDREFS tokenized attribute types.

The ID data type is one of the more useful tokenized attributes because its value must be unique. No two elements can have the same value assigned to an ID type attribute. This ID is useful anytime you want to "reach" into your document to retrieve a specific piece of information. For instance, if you have a bunch of albums in your database, it might be a good idea to give them an ID attribute so that each album can be referenced uniquely. The recording element in our DTD has an attribute of type ID:

```
<!ATTLIST recording id  ID #REQUIRED>
```

In this line, the name of the attribute is id (in lower case) and the type is ID (which is always in upper case).

The IDREF data type is used to reference an ID data type that has been specified at some other point in the document. (The only difference between IDREF and IDREFS is that IDREFS point to/refer to more than one specified ID. In an IDREFS data type, a whitespace character separates each referenced ID.)

In addition to assigning a type to an attribute (thus limiting the types of data that can be assigned to it), the DTD also provides behavioral guidance on the use of the Attribute. The two most commonly encountered behaviors are #REQUIRED and #IMPLIED.

Required

When an attribute is declared with the #REQUIRED behavior, you are required to use that attribute. Failure to include that attribute whenever you use the element it is assigned to will cause the document to fail a validity test. So, the attribute declaration:

```
<!ATTLIST recording
        ID ID #REQUIRED
>
```

informs us that we are required to use an attribute called ID (which is of type ID) whenever we open a recording node.

Implied

An implied attribute indicates that you can decide whether or not to include this attribute in your document. This declaration from our DTD:

```
<!ATTLIST label
        catno CDATA #IMPLIED
>
```

informs us that we can choose to include (or not to include) the catno attribute when we use the label element. Thus, a document will be valid with or without this attribute assigned to the label element. However, if we do choose to include this attribute, it must have unique values, as it is of type ID.

TESTING FOR DOCUMENT VALIDITY

As we saw earlier, a document must be well-formed before it can be processed by any XML software. A second, more rigorous test involves checking an encoding against a document model (DTD or schema) to make sure all elements and attributes are used appropriately. To do so, we need a validating parser. There are several validating parsers available (for reviews and links to XML software, check out the XML Cover Pages at http://xml.coverpages.org/). In the following examples, we will perform validity tests using the xmlint parser from Microsoft which we have bundled into the NoteTab Light text editor. (The NoteTab Light software used in this article can be downloaded from http://notetab.com. The clips and batch files, along with installation notes, can be downloaded from http://dl.lib.brown.edu/staff/yott/software/xmltool.html.)

We'll be stepping through the encoding of this document in a bit, but let's assume we have the following document to validate (see Figure 3). For the sake of this example, we have encoded the condition as "excellent," which is a violation of the content model for the condition attribute. The DTD we examined earlier only accepts one of four possible values (mint, fine, good, or poor), so while this remains well-formed, it is no longer valid.

If we attempt to validate the document, we get the error message shown in Figure 4.

If we correct the error by replacing the condition value with "fine," and attempt to validate the document again, we receive the name of the validated document with no errors reported (see Figure 5). This informs us that the document is now both well-formed and valid.

FIGURE 3. An XML Document in NoteTab Light

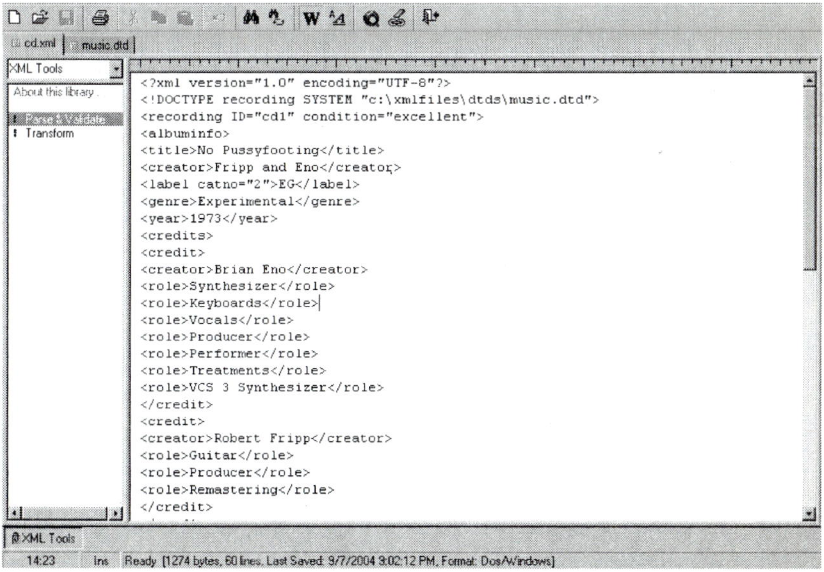

```
<?xml version="1.0" encoding="UTF-8"?>
<!DOCTYPE recording SYSTEM "c:\xmlfiles\dtds\music.dtd">
<recording ID="cd1" condition="excellent">
<albuminfo>
<title>No Pussyfooting</title>
<creator>Fripp and Eno</creator>
<label catno="2">EG</label>
<genre>Experimental</genre>
<year>1973</year>
<credits>
<credit>
<creator>Brian Eno</creator>
<role>Synthesizer</role>
<role>Keyboards</role>
<role>Vocals</role>
<role>Producer</role>
<role>Performer</role>
<role>Treatments</role>
<role>VCS 3 Synthesizer</role>
</credit>
<credit>
<creator>Robert Fripp</creator>
<role>Guitar</role>
<role>Producer</role>
<role>Remastering</role>
</credit>
```

FIGURE 4. Error Message Generated by xmlint

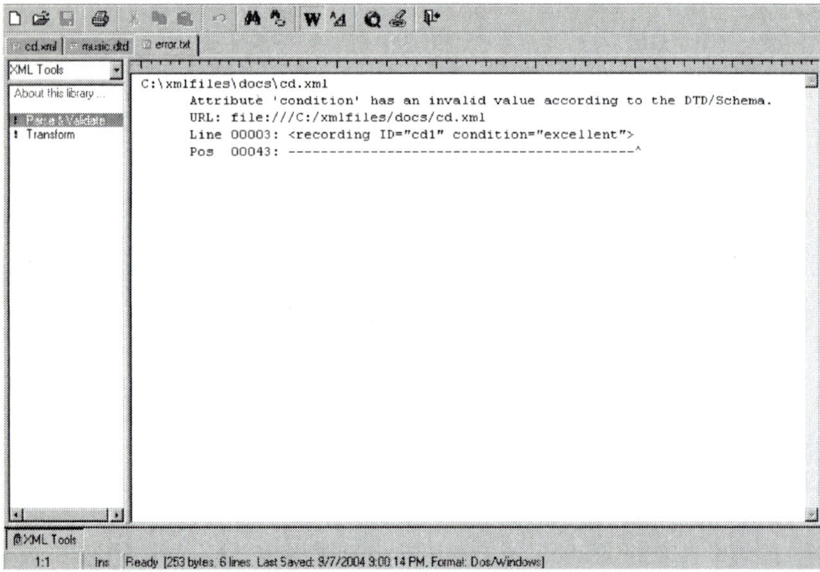

FIGURE 5. xmlint Message from Successful Validation

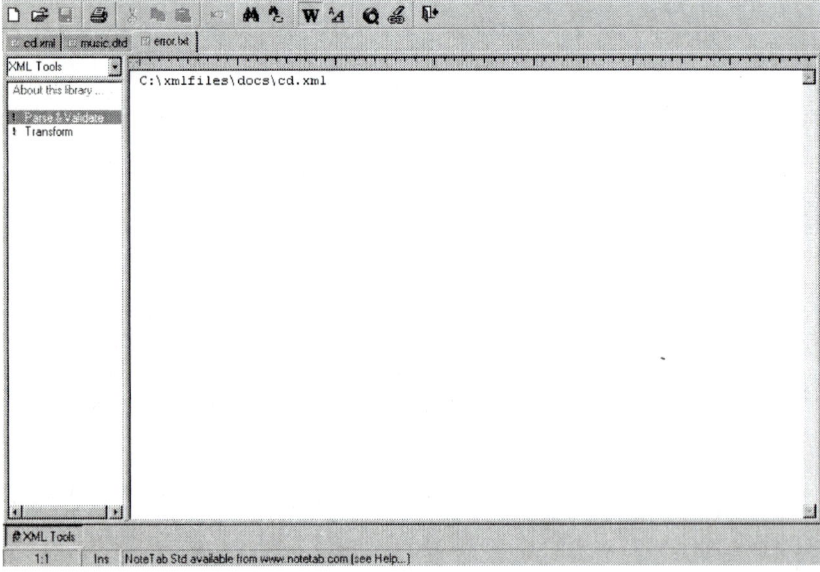

CREATING AN XML DOCUMENT

In this section, we'll step through the creation of an XML document using the DTD explored earlier.

Encode the Prologue

The Prologue exists at the top of your document, and contains very important information that will be used by your operating system and any XML aware applications you use to further process or analyze this document. The prologue begins with a *processing instruction* that tells your operating system that the document is an XML document followed by information identifying the *root element* and the DTD that governs the document.

```
<?xml version="1.0" encoding="UTF-8"?>
<!DOCTYPE recording SYSTEM "c:\dtds\music.dtd">
```

The Root Element

In our prologue, we indicated that *recording* was the root element of our document. If you examine the DTD, you will notice that recording is the only element that doesn't exist within any other element and can only occur once. Usually, but not always, you'll find the root element listed at the top of the DTD, but the placement of any element within the DTD is purely arbitrary.

```
<?xml version="1.0" encoding="UTF-8"?>
<!DOCTYPE recording SYSTEM "c:\dtds\music.dtd">
<recording>
</recording>
```

Our recording node is not correct. Why? Look back at the DTD; the recording element has two required attributes–the ID attribute, which is of type ID, and the condition attribute, which must have a value from the specified list. So a correctly encoded root element would look like this:

```
<?xml version="1.0" encoding="UTF-8"?>
<!DOCTYPE recording SYSTEM "c:\dtds\music.dtd">
<recording ID="cd1" condition="fine">
</recording>
```

Note that while you indicated all needed attributes when you open a tag, you don't list them when you close it. This is important–if you close a node and list the attributes within the closing tag your document will not be well-formed.

When you try to parse this, you get a new error message stating that the recording element cannot be empty. Look at the DTD and examine the content model for this element. Note that it specifies two elements must be placed within the recording node. Both albuminfo and tracklist must occur, once, and in that order.

```
<?xml version="1.0" encoding="UTF-8"?>
<!DOCTYPE recording SYSTEM "c:\xmlfiles\dtds\music.dtd">
<recording ID="cd1" condition="fine">
<albuminfo>
</albuminfo>
<tracklist>
</tracklist>
</recording>
```

When you try to validate the document now, you receive a similar error message regarding the albuminfo element. Look again at the DTD–what is the content model for albuminfo? Follow this process for each element you place within the albuminfo node. Below is an abbreviated encoding, skipping some of the creators for brevity.

```
<?xml version="1.0" encoding="UTF-8"?>
<!DOCTYPE recording SYSTEM "c:\xmlfiles\dtds\music.dtd">
<recording ID="cd1" condition="fine">
<albuminfo>
<title>No Pussyfooting</title>
<creator>Fripp and Eno</creator>
<label catno="2">EG</label>
<genre>Experimental</genre>
<genre>Electronic</genre>
<year>1973</year>
<credits>
<credit>
<creator>Brian Eno</creator>
<role>Synthesizer</role>
<role>Keyboards</role>
```

```
<role>Vocals</role>
<role>Producer</role>
<role>Performer</role>
<role>Treatments</role>
<role>VCS 3 Synthesizer</role>
</credit>
<credit>
<creator>Robert Fripp</creator>
<role>Guitar</role>
<role>Producer</role>
<role>Remastering</role>
</credit>
</credits>
<time>39:38</time>
</albuminfo>
<tracklist>
</tracklist>
</recording>
```

The last section of the document to encode is the tracklist node. Looking at the DTD, we notice that the content model of tracklist specifies that it includes a minimum of one track element, and only the track element can exist within it. Next, examine its content model. Each track that you include in the tracklist node contains a title node, a credits node, and a time node. Each of these nodes can only occur once, and in the order specified.

Once the tracks are encoded (there are only two tracks on this particular CD), the complete XML document looks like this:

```
<?xml version="1.0" encoding="UTF-8"?>
<!DOCTYPE recording SYSTEM "c:\xmlfiles\dtds\music.dtd">
<recording ID="cd1" condition="fine">
<albuminfo>
<title>No Pussyfooting</title>
<creator>Fripp and Eno</creator>
<label catno="2">EG</label>
<genre>Experimental</genre>
<year>1973</year>
<credits>
```

```
<credit>
<creator>Brian Eno</creator>
<role>Synthesizer</role>
<role>Keyboards</role>
<role>Vocals</role>
<role>Producer</role>
<role>Performer</role>
<role>Treatments</role>
<role>VCS 3 Synthesizer</role>
</credit>
<credit>
<creator>Robert Fripp</creator>
<role>Guitar</role>
<role>Producer</role>
<role>Remastering</role>
</credit>
</credits>
<time>39:38</time>
</albuminfo>
<tracklist>
<track sequence="1">
<title>The Heavenly Music Corporation</title>
<credits>
<credit>
<creator>Brian Eno</creator>
<role>Composer</role>
</credit>
<credit>
<creator>Robert Fripp</creator>
<role>Composer</role>
</credit>
</credits>
<time>20:55</time>
</track>
<track sequence="2">
<title>Swastika Girls</title>
<credits>
```

```
<credit>
<creator>Brian Eno</creator>
<role>Composer</role>
</credit>
<credit>
<creator>Robert Fripp</creator>
<role>Composer</role>
</credit>
</credits>
<time>18:43</time>
</track>
</tracklist>
</recording>
```

MY XML IS WELL-FORMED AND VALID, NOW WHAT?

One of the primary advantages XML holds over HTML is that it allows you to create whatever elements and tags you need to achieve a particular goal. One of the primary complications of XML when contrasted to HTML is that it allows you to create whatever elements and tags you need to achieve a particular goal. While this flexibility can be restrained by standardizing your encoding according to a DTD or schema, there remains the potential for endless variation.

Because of this, web browsers are unable to do anything more than to check for well-formedness and display the hierarchical outline of your document. (These abilities should not be minimized!) They understand only one set of tags–HTML, so if you plan on using your XML documents in a web application, they will, at some point in the process, have to be converted to HTML. This is where XSLT comes in.

XSLT (Extensible Stylesheet Language for Transformation) is an XML-based technology that allows you to take a source document (as long as it is well-formed), and by applying a set of template-based rules, create, amongst other possibilities, a new XML or HTML file. While the particulars of the XSLT syntax are beyond the scope of this article, the basic processing model of an XSLT stylesheet is to look for a node in the source document (or tree), and then establishing what to output when that node is found. Using our CD document, for example, we would look for the <title> node within an <albuminfo> node, and when we find one, output its contents between <h2> tags, and look for the <title> node within the <track> node and output it between <font color="blue"> tags. In so doing, we work with the structural knowledge embedded in the source document (referred to as the source tree) and apply presentational rules that permit browsers to display the selected data.

There are a variety of ways you can handle these sorts of transformations. You can send the entire XML document to the user's browser with an embedded stylesheet reference. Recent versions of the major browsers have built-in transformation engines (such as msxml in the Internet Explorer browser), and these browsers can perform the transformations on the client workstation and display only the acceptable result of the transformation. Alternatively, you can process the XSLT instructions on the server (via a servlet or CGI call) and return not the source document, but the results of the transformation. Some prefer to use XML as their storage medium, and run the XSLT transformations as part of publishing their documents to the web site, so that the user never encounters pure XML, but only the results of an a-priori processing.

Putting this all together, we can visualize the overall XML environment (greatly simplified, of course) in this manner:

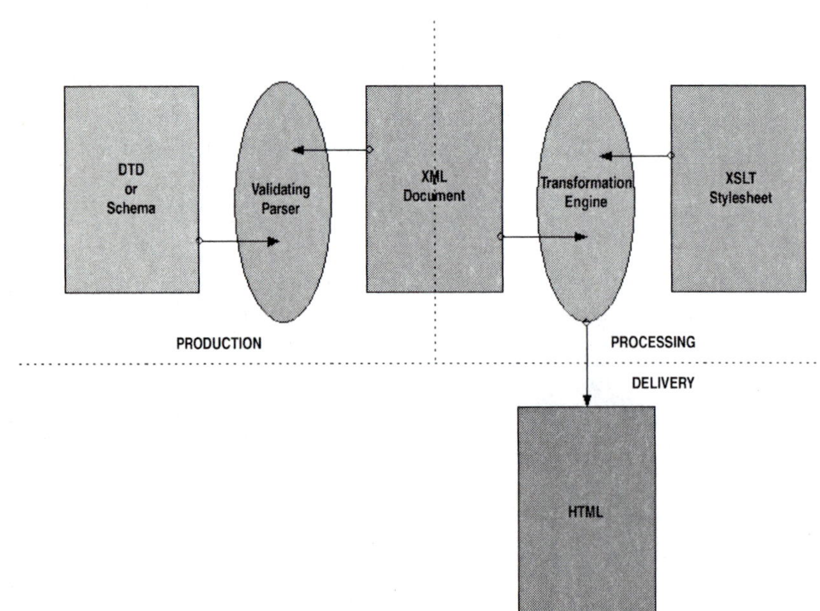

WORKS CITED

Goldfarb, Charles F. 1990. *The SGML handbook*. Oxford: Clarendon Press.
Ray, Erik T. 2001. *Learning XML*. Sebastopol, CA: O'Reilly.
University of Virginia Electronic Text Center. *XML for fun and profit*. http://etext.lib.virginia.edu/helpsheets/xml-basic.html.

METS: The Metadata Encoding and Transmission Standard

Linda Cantara

SUMMARY. The Metadata Encoding and Transmission Standard (METS) is a data communication standard for encoding descriptive, administrative, and structural metadata regarding objects within a digital library, expressed using the XML Schema Language of the World Wide Web Consortium. An initiative of the Digital Library Federation, METS is under development by an international editorial board and is maintained in the Network Development and MARC Standards Office of the Library of Congress. Designed in conformance with the Open Archival Information System (OAIS) Reference Model, a METS document encapsulates digital objects and metadata as Information Packages for transmitting and/or exchanging digital objects to and from digital repositories, disseminating digital objects via the Web, and archiving digital objects for long-term preservation and access. This paper represents an introduction to the METS standard and, through illustrated examples, how to build a METS document. *[Article copies available for a fee from The Haworth Document Delivery Service: 1-800-HAWORTH. E-mail address: <docdelivery@haworthpress.com> Website: <http://www.HaworthPress.com> © 2005 by The Haworth Press, Inc. All rights reserved.]*

Linda Cantara is Metadata Librarian, Kelvin Smith Library, 11055 Euclid Avenue, Case Western Reserve University, Cleveland, OH 44106 (E-mail: linda.cantara@case.edu).

[Haworth co-indexing entry note]: "METS: The Metadata Encoding and Transmission Standard." Cantara, Linda. Co-published simultaneously in *Cataloging & Classification Quarterly* (The Haworth Information Press, an imprint of The Haworth Press, Inc.) Vol. 40, No. 3/4, 2005, pp. 237-253; and: *Metadata: A Cataloger's Primer* (ed: Richard P. Smiraglia) The Haworth Information Press, an imprint of The Haworth Press, Inc., 2005, pp. 237-253. Single or multiple copies of this article are available for a fee from The Haworth Document Delivery Service [1-800-HAWORTH, 9:00 a.m. - 5:00 p.m. (EST). E-mail address: docdelivery@haworthpress.com].

Available online at http://www.haworthpress.com/web/CCQ

doi:10.1300/J104v40n03_11

KEYWORDS. Metadata, XML (Document Markup Language), digital libraries–administration, digital preservation

The Metadata Encoding and Transmission Standard (METS) is a data communication standard for encoding descriptive, administrative, and structural metadata regarding objects within a digital library, expressed using the Extensible Markup Language Schema (XSD) of the World Wide Web Consortium (see METS Home Page, and W3C XML Schema Web Site). An initiative of the Digital Library Federation (DLF), METS is under development by an international editorial board and is maintained in the Network Development and MARC Standards Office of the Library of Congress.

METS is a direct successor to the Making of America II (MOA2) Project, a multi-institutional library effort to create a standard for encoding descriptive, administrative, and structural metadata inside a digital library object. (Participants included the University of California at Berkeley, Cornell University, New York Public Library, The Pennsylvania State University, and Stanford University. For more information on MOA2, see *The Making of America II White Paper*, 1998 and *The Making of America II Home Page*, 2001.) The primary goal of the project was to develop a standard that would promote interoperability, scalability, and digital preservation of digital library objects. MOA2 designed an XML Document Type Definition (DTD) for encoding the required metadata and in February 2001, the Digital Library Federation sponsored a workshop to build on and extend the MOA2 DTD (see Structural, Technical, and Administrative Metadata Standards 2000; and McDonough et al. 2001). Around the same time, the International Organization for Standardization (ISO) and the Consultative Committee for Space Data Systems (CCSDS) of the National Aeronautics and Space Administration (NASA) issued the first draft of its *Reference Model for an Open Archival Information System* (OAIS), "a framework for understanding and applying concepts needed for long-term digital information preservation." Although it does not specify implementation procedures, OAIS defines a model for archiving digital (and nondigital) objects and describes the composition of three types of "information packages" for a digital repository: submission information packages for transmission and/or exchange of digital objects to and from a digital repository (SIP), archival information packages to archive digital objects for long-term preservation and access (AIP), and dissemination information packages to publish digital objects via the web to end users

(DIP) (see also Sawyer et al. 2002). METS can be used to create any or all of these information packages.

The following sections introduce the different components of a METS document and illustrate how to construct one using examples from a METS document for a digitized monograph. The files include master images in tiff format; the full text of the book, encoded in Extensible Markup Language (XML) using the Text Encoding Initiative (TEI) Document Type Definition (DTD); an Extensible Stylesheet Language Transformations (XSLT) stylesheet for rendering the text in HTML for online display; and a Cascading Stylesheet (CSS) for defining how the HTML version should be displayed (see Text Encoding Initiative Consortium 1999 and *W3C Cascading* 2004).

HOW TO BUILD A METS DOCUMENT

There are seven possible sections of a METS document:

- METS Header (metsHdr)
- Descriptive Metadata Section (dmdSec)
- Administrative Metadata Section (amdSec)
- File Group Section (fileSec)
- Structural Map (structMap)
- Structural Map Linking Section (structLink)
- Behavior Section (behaviorSec)

Although the only mandatory section is the Structural Map, the following discussion will address each of these sections in the order they appear in a METS document.

Root Element

A well-formed XML document must have exactly one *root* element, that is, an element that includes all the other elements but which is not itself included in any other element. The root element of a METS document is <mets> which has five optional attributes. ID (XML Identifier) and OBJID (Object Identifier) identify the specific METS document under construction. The TYPE attribute indicates the type of object documented–e.g., book, journal, oral history collection–while the LABEL attribute provides the actual title of the object. If a registered profile (more about METS profiles later) was used to create the METS document, this information is encoded in the PROFILE attribute.

XML Schema allows the encoder to use elements and attributes from one or more XML Schemas in a single XML document instance. To differentiate the source of elements with the same name (e.g., title, date, creator, etc.) from two or more different schemas, XML Namespace Declarations (xmlns) are included as attributes of the root element and each namespace is identified by a URI (Uniform Resource Identifier). As illustrated in Figure 1, included are namespaces for the XML Schema Recommendation, the METS Schema, the XLink Recommendation, and the Metadata Object Description (MODS) Schema, which is used in the Descriptive Metadata Section of this METS document. In addition, the location of the XML Schemas used in the METS document must be provided using the xsi:schemaLocation attribute. Element names in the document include their corresponding namespace prefixes (e.g., mets:div, mods:title, xlink:href).

METS Header

Modeled after the Text Encoding Initiative (TEI) Header (although much less complex) (TEI Consortium 2002), the optional METS Header documents the creation and maintenance of the METS document itself (see Figure 2). It can include one or more of the following attributes: ID (XML Identifier), CREATEDATE (the day and time the METS document was created), LASTMODDATE (the day and time the METS document was last modified), and RECORDSTATUS (a text string documenting the status of the METS document, primarily for

FIGURE 1. METS Root Element

```
<mets:mets xmlns:xsi="http://www.w3.org/2001/XMLSchema-instance"
     xmlns:mets="http://www.loc.gov/METS/"
     xmlns:xlink="http://www.w3.org/TR/xlink"
     xmlns:mods="http://www.loc.gov/MODS"
     xsi:schemaLocation="http://loc.gov/METS
               http://www.loc.gov/standards/mets/mets.xsd
               http://www.loc.gov/standards/mods/mods.xsd"
     ID="beelos00" OBJID="digbk" TYPE="book" LABEL="The Loss of the S.S. Titanic">
```

FIGURE 2. METS Header

```
<mets:metsHdr CREATEDATE="2004-07-30T15:10:00"LASTMODDATE="2004-08-04T16:39:00"
RECORDSTATUS="demo">
        <mets:agent ROLE="CREATOR" TYPE="INDIVIDUAL">
            <mets:name>Linda Cantara</mets:name>
        </mets:agent>
        <mets:agent ROLE="DISSEMINATOR" TYPE="ORGANIZATION">
            <mets:name>Kelvin Smith Library</mets:name>
        </mets:agent>
        <mets:agent ROLE="IPOWNER" TYPE="ORGANIZATION">
            <mets:name>Case Western Reserve University</mets:name>
        </mets:agent>
    </mets:metsHdr>
```

internal processing purposes). The <metsHdr> element may include one or both sub-elements <agent> and <altRecordID>.

The <agent> (METS agent) element documents the personnel responsible for the METS document, with attributes ROLE (with enumerated values CREATOR, EDITOR, ARCHIVIST, PRESERVATION, DISSEMINATOR, CUSTODIAN, IPOWNER, and OTHER) and TYPE (with enumerated values INDIVIDUAL and ORGANIZATION). The sub-element <name> records the name of the person or institution with a role in creating and providing access to the METS document, while the sub-element <note> may contain a text string providing further information. The <altRecordID> (Alternate Record Identifier) element allows for documentation of alternative ID values for the METS document in addition to the primary ID stored in the OBJID attribute in the root <mets> element. It has two attributes, ID and TYPE.

Descriptive Metadata

The Descriptive Metadata Section (dmdSec) comprises one or more descriptive metadata sets which either are linked via ID/IDREF attributes to divisions and files documented elsewhere in the METS document or which exist outside the METS document. An ID attribute is required for each <dmdSec> since the value of this ID may be referenced by other sections of the METS document using the DMDID attribute. If the metadata exists outside the METS document, a Metadata Reference (<mdRef>) sub-element is used to point to the source of the metadata (see Figure 3). Attributes for the <mdRef> element may include LOCTYPE (Location Type), MDTYPE (Metadata Type), MIMETYPE, LABEL, XPTR (XPointer), and various XLink attributes. The value of MDTYPE must be one of the following enumerated values: MODS (Metadata Object Description Schema), EAD (Encoded Archival Description), DC (Dublin Core), VRA (Visual Resources Association Core), TEIHDR (Text Encoding Initiative Header), DDI (Data Documentation Initiative), FGDC (Federal Geographic Data Committee), and OTHER. If the value OTHER is selected, an additional attribute on the <metsRef> element, OTHERTYPE, must be used to designate the applicable metadata standard. The XPTR attribute is used to point to a specific location in the referenced file.

Descriptive metadata included in the METS document itself must be encoded in XML and nested inside an xmlData (XML Data) element within the mdWrap (Metadata Wrapper) sub-element (see Figure 4). In addition to the required ID attribute (which is referenced from other sections of the METS document through DMDID attribute values), the <mdWrap> element may include optional MIMETYPE and LABEL attributes. If the metadata is not encoded in XML, it must be Base64 encoded and nested inside a binData (Binary Data) element. (Base64 "is a data encoding scheme whereby binary-encoded data is converted to printable ASCII characters." See "Base64," *Wikipedia: the Free Encyclopedia*, <http://en.wikipedia.org/wiki/Base64> (last revised 30 July 2004).) Although there are no restrictions concerning which descriptive metadata standards can be used (thus, the OTHER value enumerated for the MDTYPE attribute), to promote interoperability the METS Editorial

FIGURE 3. Descriptive Metadata: mdRef

```
<mets:dmdSec ID="beelos00d">
  <mets:mdRef LOCTYPE="URN"
        MDTYPE="TEIHDR"
        xlink:type="simple"
        xlink:href="http://path/beelos00.xml"
        XPTR="//teiHeader"/>
</mets:dmdSec>
```

Board has endorsed a finite list of "extension schemas" for descriptive metadata encoded in a METS document. Currently, these include Simple Dublin Core (DC), Metadata Object Description Schema (MODS), MARC 21 XML Schema (MARCXML), and IEEE Learning Object Metadata (LOM). Other metadata standards based on XML Schemas may also be embedded in the METS document but standards based on Document Type Definitions (DTDs), like the TEI Header or Encoded Archival Description (EAD), must be referenced outside the METS document.

Administrative Metadata

The optional Administrative Metadata Section (<amdSec>) is a wrapper for sub-elements which document information regarding a file's creation, format, and use characteristics (<techMD>); intellectual property rights and licensing information (<rightsMD>); descriptive and administrative metadata regarding the analog source from which the digital library object derives (<sourceMD>); and digital provenance information, such as master/derivative file relationships, migration/transformation information, and other administrative decisions and actions affecting the digital library object (<digiprovMD>). Like the content of the <dmdSec> element, the content of the <amdSec> element

FIGURE 4. Descriptive Metadata: mdWrap

```
<mets:dmdSec ID="beelos00d">
 <mets:mdWrap MDTYPE="MODS">
  <mets:xmlData>
   <mods:mods version="3.0">
    <mods:titleInfo xlink:type="simple">
     <mods:nonSort>The </mods:nonSort>
     <mods:title>loss of the SS. Titanic</mods:title>
     <mods:subTitle>its story and its lessons</mods:subTitle>
    </mods:titleInfo>
    <!-- rest of MODS descriptive metadata here -->
     </mods:mods>
  </mets:xmlData>
 </mets:mdWrap>
</mets:dmdSec>
```

and its sub-elements can either point to metadata existing outside the METS document using the <mdRef> element, or if the metadata is encoded in XML it can be included in the METS document using the <mdWrap> element. Metadata schemas for administrative metadata currently endorsed by the METS Editorial Board include Text Metadata Schema; the Library of Congress's Audio Technical Metadata Extension Schema (AUDIOMD), Video Technical Metadata Extension Schema (VIDEOMD), Digital Production and Provenance Metadata Extension Schema (DIGIPROVMD), Image Technical Metadata Extension Schema (IMAGEMD), and Rights Metadata Extension Schema (RIGHTSMD); NISO Metadata for Images in XML Schema (MIX); Schema for Rights Declaration (METSRights); and Open Digital Rights Language (ODRL). The <amdSec> element can be repeated as many times as needed to document all of the files and divisions of the digital object. Each <amdSec> element–as well as each <techMD>, <rightsMD>, <sourceMD>, and <digiprovMD> element–must include an ID value which can be referenced by other sections of the METS document via the ADMID value.

File Section

The File Section (<fileSec>) provides an inventory of all the files included in the digital library object (see Figure 5). The <fileSec> element has a single (optional) ID attribute. Groups of related files are wrapped in a File Group (<fileGrp>) sub-element; thus, a <fileSec> element may contain multiple <fileGrp> elements, one for each type of file (see Figure 6). Each <fileGrp> element includes one or more <file> elements which must include an ID attribute value and may include one or more of the following optional attributes: MIMETYPE, SEQ, SIZE (in kilobytes), CREATED (the date the file was created), CHECKSUM, CHECKSUMTYPE (the type of checksum included in the CHECKSUM attribute), OWNERID (an identifier assigned to the file by its owner), ADMID, DMDID, and USE (a string indicating the intended use of the file). (For a definition of "checksum" see "Checksum," *Wikipedia, the Free Encyclopedia*, <http://en.wikipedia.org/wiki/Checksum> (last modified 19 July 2004).)

Another optional attribute on the <file> element is GROUPID. The value of this attribute establishes a correspondence between files in different file groups and is useful for associating a master file in one file group with derivative files in other file groups.

FIGURE 5. File Section


```
<mets:fileSec>
  <mets:fileGrp ID="xml">
    <mets:file ID="beelos00x" MIMETYPE="text/xml" SIZE="296" USE="encoded
      text" DMDID="beelos00d" ADMID="beelos00a1" GROUPID="xml">
      <mets:FLocat LOCTYPE="URN" xlink:type="simple"
        xlink:href="http://path/beelos00.xml"/>
    </mets:file>
    <mets:file ID="beelos00s" MIMETYPE="text/xml" SIZE="5" USE="transform XML
      to HTML" GROUPID="xml">
      <mets:FLocat LOCTYPE="URN" xlink:type="simple"
      xlink:href="http://path/brittlebks.xsl"/>
    </mets:file>
  </mets:fileGrp>
    <mets:fileGrp ID="css">
    <mets:file ID="beelos00c" MIMETYPE="text/css" SIZE="5"  USE="definition
      of HTML display" GROUPID="css">
      <mets:FLocat LOCTYPE="URN" xlink:type="simple"
        xlink:href="http://path/brittlebks.css"/>
    </mets:file>
  </mets:fileGrp>
  <mets:fileGrp ID="tif" USE="master digital images" ADMID="beelos00a2">
    <!-- first 12 images here -->
    <mets:file ID="t9_0013" MIMETYPE="image/tif" SEQ="13" SIZE="10645"/>
    <mets:file ID="t9_0014" MIMETYPE="image/tif" SEQ="14" SIZE="10645"/>
    <mets:file ID="t9_0015" MIMETYPE="image/tif" SEQ="15" SIZE="10645"/>
    <mets:file ID="t9_0016" MIMETYPE="image/tif" SEQ="16" SIZE="10645"/>
    <mets:file ID="t9_0017" MIMETYPE="image/tif" SEQ="17" SIZE="10645"/>
    <mets:file ID="t9_0018" MIMETYPE="image/tif" SEQ="18" SIZE="10645"/>
    <mets:file ID="t9_0019" MIMETYPE="image/tif" SEQ="19" SIZE="10645"/>
    <mets:file ID="t9_0020" MIMETYPE="image/tif" SEQ="20" SIZE="10645"/>
    <mets:file ID="t9_0021" MIMETYPE="image/tif" SEQ="21" SIZE="10645"/>
    <mets:file ID="t9_0022" MIMETYPE="image/tif" SEQ="22" SIZE="10645"/>
    <mets:file ID="t9_0023" MIMETYPE="image/tif" SEQ="23" SIZE="10645"/>
    <mets:file ID="t9_0024" MIMETYPE="image/tif" SEQ="24" SIZE="10645"/>
    <mets:file ID="t9_0026" MIMETYPE="image/tif" SEQ="26" SIZE="10645"/>
    <mets:file ID="t9_0027" MIMETYPE="image/tif" SEQ="27" SIZE="10645"/>
    <mets:file ID="t9_0028" MIMETYPE="image/tif" SEQ="28" SIZE="10645"/>
    <mets:file ID="t9_0029" MIMETYPE="image/tif" SEQ="29" SIZE="10645"/>
    <mets:file ID="t9_0025" MIMETYPE="image/tif" SEQ="25" SIZE="10645"/>
    <!-- remaining images here -->
  </mets:fileGrp>
</mets:fileSec>
```

FIGURE 6. File Element GROUPID

```
<mets:fileSec>
  <mets:fileGrp ID="tif" USE="master">
    <mets:file ID="image1a" MIMETYPE="image/tif" SEQ="1" GROUPID="A"/>
    <mets:file ID="image2a" MIMETYPE="image/tif" SEQ="2" GROUPID="B"/>
  </mets:fileGrp>
  <mets:fileGrp ID="jpeg" USE="display">
    <mets:file ID="image1b" MIMETYPE="image/jpeg" SEQ="1" GROUPID="A"/>
    <mets:file ID="image2b" MIMETYPE="image/jpeg" SEQ="2" GROUPID="B"/>
  </mets:fileGrp>
  <mets:fileGrp ID="png" USE="thumbnail">
    <mets:file ID="image1c" MIMETYPE="image/png" SEQ="1" GROUPID="A"/>
    <mets:file ID="image2c" MIMETYPE="image/png" SEQ="2" GROUPID="B"/>
  </mets:fileGrp>
</mets:fileSec>
```

A link to an actual file may be included in one of two ways. If the content is external to the METS document, a File Location (<FLocat>) element is used to point to the file. The <FLocat> element is an empty element but must include a LOCTYPE attribute with a value selected from URN, URL, PURL, HANDLE, DOI, and OTHER. (If the value is OTHER, the location type must be indicated in an OTHERLOCTYPE attribute.) It may also include one or more xlink attributes, including a mandatory xlink:href attribute which points to the file. Other optional attributes include ID and USE. Alternatively, the content of the file may be embedded in the METS document itself using the File Content (<FContent>) element. The content file must either be Base64 encoded and included in a <binData> sub-element, or must be encoded in XML and included in an <xmlData> sub-element. The <FContent> element may also include optional ID and USE attributes.

Structural Map

The Structural Map, often referred to as "the heart of a METS document," comprises a series of nested division (<div>) elements and is the only mandatory section of a METS document. It outlines the hierarchical structure of a digital object, facilitates navigation of the resource, and may point to parts of the descriptive and administrative metadata from different places in the structural hierarchy, enabling cross-linking of information between different parts of the METS document. The <structMap> element may include one or more attributes: ID (XML Identifier), LABEL (a text string describing the structMap), and TYPE. The TYPE attribute may have one of two values. TYPE="PHYSICAL" describes the physical organization of the original work (e.g., a book with pages) while TYPE="LOGICAL" describes the intellectual organization of the original work (e.g., a book with a table of contents, preface, chapters, index). If appropriate, a METS document may include both a physical and a logical structural map.

Each <div> element nested in a <structMap> element may contain one or more of the following attributes: ID (XML Identifier), TYPE (the structural type of the division, such as book, chapter, page, etc.), LABEL (the name of the division), ORDER (an integer designating the sequential position of the division in relation to the entire digital object), ORDERLABEL (an alphanumeric string designating the sequence of the division in the terminology of the digital object), DMDID (one or more references to the unique identifiers of descriptive metadata sections applicable to the division), and ADMID (one or more references to the unique identifiers of administrative metadata sections applicable to the division).

Elements that may nest within a <div> element include <mptr> (METS Pointer) and <fptr> (File Pointer). The <mptr> element is used to point to a separate METS document rather than to an internal file or file group. For example, a METS document for a collection of digitized books might have the physical structMap found in Figure 7. Here, the xlink:href attribute values point to the METS documents for every book in the collection. A similar application of the <mptr> element could be applied to a METS document for an electronic journal, with separate <mptr> elements pointing to the METS documents for every volume of the journal which in turn could include <mptr> elements pointing to the METS documents for every issue of the volume.

The <fptr> element either points directly to the file content of the division using the FILEID attribute, or provides more complex linking of file content and the document division through the sub-elements <area> (area), <seq> (sequence), and <par> (parallel files). The <area> element links a division to a specific location in a content file identified by the FILEID attribute value, and specifies the beginning and ending points in the file corresponding to the division by means of the BEGIN and END attribute values. In Figure 8, the BETYPE attribute indicates that

FIGURE 7. Physical StructMap with <mptr> Elements

```
<mets:structMap TYPE="PHYSICAL">
  <mets:div ID="ksldigbks" TYPE="digital book collection" LABEL="DIGITAL
    CASE E-BOOK COLLECTION">
    <mets:div ID="bk1" TYPE="book">
      <mets:mptr LOCTYPE="URL" xlink:href="http://path/bk1-mets.xml"/>
    </mets:div>
    <mets:div ID="bk2" TYPE="book">
      <mets:mptr LOCTYPE="URL" xlink:href="http://path/bk2-mets.xml"/>
    </mets:div>
    <mets:div ID="bk3" TYPE="book">
      <mets:mptr LOCTYPE="URL" xlink:href="http://path/bk3-mets.xml"/>
    </mets:div>
  </mets:div>
</mets:structMap>
```

the BEGIN and END values correspond to the ID values for these sections (in this case, page numbers) in the XML document. (In addition to IDREF, other enumerated values for the BETYPE attribute include: BYTE, SMIL, MIDI, SMPTE-25, SMPTE-24, SMPTE-DF30, SMPTE-NDF30, SMPTE-DF29.97, SMPTE-NDF29.97, and TIME. With the exception of BYTE, the other values can be used to point to a specific location in an audio or video file.) The <seq> element links a division to a group of content files which should be displayed sequentially. For example, as illustrated in Figure 8, the <seq> element wraps a group of <area> elements corresponding to the book's page image files, and through the BEGIN and END attribute values, indicates the page ordering of the images. The <par> element wraps two or more content files that should be displayed in unison (the text and images of a web page, for example). It too uses the <area> sub-element to point to the corresponding files or sections of files.

Structural Map Linking Section

The optional Structural Map Linking Section (<structLink>) facilitates documentation of hyperlinks between any two divisions in the <structMap> and was designed primarily to preserve hyperlinks in ar-

FIGURE 8. Logical Structural Map of Chapter One

```
<mets:structMap TYPE="LOGICAL">
 <mets:div ID="beelos00b" TYPE="book" LABEL="The Loss of the S.S. Titanic"
   DMDID="beelos00d">
 <mets:div TYPE="front" LABEL="frontmatter"/>
 <mets:div TYPE="body" LABEL="body of text">
  <mets:div TYPE="chapter" ORDER="7" ORDERLABEL="I" LABEL="CHAPTER I:
    CONSTRUCTION AND PREPARATIONS FOR THE FIRST VOYAGE">
   <mets:fptr>
    <mets:area FILEID="beelos00x" BEGIN="p.1" END="p.13" BETYPE="IDREF"/>
   </mets:fptr>
   <mets:fptr>
    <mets:seq>
     <mets:area FILEID="t9_0013" BEGIN="p.1" END="p.1" BETYPE="IDREF"/>
     <mets:area FILEID="t9_0014" BEGIN="p.2" END="p.2" BETYPE="IDREF"/>
     <mets:area FILEID="t9_0015" BEGIN="p.3" END="p.3" BETYPE="IDREF"/>
     <mets:area FILEID="t9_0016" BEGIN="p.4" END="p.4" BETYPE="IDREF"/>
     <mets:area FILEID="t9_0017" BEGIN="p.5" END="p.5" BETYPE="IDREF"/>
     <mets:area FILEID="t9_0018" BEGIN="p.6" END="p.6" BETYPE="IDREF"/>
     <mets:area FILEID="t9_0019" BEGIN="p.7" END="p.7" BETYPE="IDREF"/>
     <mets:area FILEID="t9_0020" BEGIN="p.8" END="p.8" BETYPE="IDREF"/>
     <mets:area FILEID="t9_0021" BEGIN="p.9" END="p.9" BETYPE="IDREF"/>
     <mets:area FILEID="t9_0022" BEGIN="p.10" END="p.10" BETYPE="IDREF"/>
     <mets:area FILEID="t9_0023" BEGIN="p.11" END="p.11" BETYPE="IDREF"/>
     <mets:area FILEID="t9_0024" BEGIN="p.12" END="p.12" BETYPE="IDREF"/>
     <mets:area FILEID="t9_0025" BEGIN="p.13" END="p.13" BETYPE="IDREF"/>
    </mets:seq>
   </mets:fptr>
    </mets:div>
 </mets:div>
 </mets:div>
</mets:structMap>
```

chived Web sites. It uses the single sub-element <smLink> (Structural Map Link) to express the links between two divisions, using the attributes from and to which reference the ID values of the corresponding divisions in the <structMap> section. The <smLink> element may also include one or more xlink attributes, including xlink:title, the value of which is a text string documenting the relationship between the two referenced divisions.

Behavior Section

The optional Behavior Section (<behaviorSec>) provides information about executable code associated with the content of the digital library object and may include attributes ID, CREATED, and LABEL. Examples include an XSLT stylesheet for transforming an XML file to HTML, a page-turning program for displaying digital images of a book, a java applet required to interact with a complex digital object, or a software program such as QuickTime or Windows Media Player needed to listen to an audio file or view a video file. The <behaviorSec> element groups and wraps these behaviors in a hierarchical structure by means of the sub-element <behavior> and its sub-elements <interfaceDef> and <mechanism>. Attributes for the <behavior> element include ID, STRUCTID (references to <structMap> sections or divisions), BTYPE (behavior type identifier), CREATED, LABEL, GROUPID (an identifier that establishes correspondence between two or more behaviors), and ADMID (reference to one or more administrative metadata sections applicable to the behavior). The <interfaceDef> element points to an interface definition object which could be another METS object or some other entity such as a Web Services Definition Language (WSDL) file, while the <mechanism> element contains a pointer to the executable code that implements the set of behaviors defined by the interface definition. Attributes for both the <interfaceDef> and <mechanism> elements include LOCTYPE, LABEL, and xlink attributes, particularly xlink:href.

The <behaviorSec> in Figure 9 references the XSLT transformation of the XML file of the book to HTML for online display.

METS PROFILES, IMPLEMENTATIONS, AND TOOLS

To facilitate interoperability and sharing of data, the METS Editorial Board has defined the components of a METS Profile and has designed an XML Schema for encoding one (McDonough 2003a, 2003c):

> METS Profiles are intended to describe a class of METS documents in sufficient detail to provide both document authors and programmers the guidance they require to create and process METS documents conforming to a particular profile.

FIGURE 9. Behavior Section

```
<mets:behaviorSec ID="beelos00l" LABEL="XSLT for Transformation from XML to
  HTML">
 <mets:behavior ID="beelos00t" BTYPE="xslt" STRUCTID="beelos00b"
       ADMID="beelos00a3">
   <mets:interfaceDef LABEL="XMLSpy XSLT Engine" LOCTYPE="OTHER"
     OTHERLOCTYPE="local"/>
   <mets:mechanism LOCTYPE="URL" LABEL="XSLT Stylesheet"
     xlink:href="http://path/brittlebks.xsl"/>
 </mets:behavior>
</mets:behaviorSec>
```

A METS Profile may prescribe the use of particular extension schemas and controlled vocabularies, specify the arrangement and use of elements and attributes for a particular class of documents, and recommend tools for creating and processing METS documents that comply with the profile (see McDonough 2003b). A registry developed by the METS Editorial Board in cooperation with the Library of Congress Network Development and MARC Standards Office will provide open access to registered METS Profiles through the METS web site.

Meanwhile, an increasing number of libraries and archives are implementing METS for a vast variety of digital library projects. See the METS Implementation Registry at <http://sunsite.berkeley.edu/mets/registry/> for more information.

Software for creating XML documents is available both commercially and through open source. However, although it is possible to create a METS document by hand, the complexity of the standard suggests this is not an efficient way to do so. Fortunately, some tools specific to METS are already available while others are currently under development. Links to tool-providers are published on the METS web page.

CONCLUSION

As the number of digital libraries of image, text, audio, and video collections continues to proliferate, a metadata framework for encapsulating descriptive, administrative, and structural metadata along with the digital content it describes is imperative to support interoperability, scalability, and long-term preservation. The Metadata Encoding and Transmission Standard (METS) is such a framework. METS provides a highly flexible means of wrapping multiple metadata sets into a single document (or set of documents), and while some have raised concerns that this flexibility may be more a deficit than an asset since it has the potential to obstruct rather than promote interoperability (see for example Gartner 2002, 10), the definition of METS Profiles and of standardized extension schemas as well as the participation of international digital library professionals in the development, maintenance, and implementation of METS virtually assures the success of the standard. Although only the Structural Map Section is mandatory, implementers of the METS standard should seriously consider including as many of the optional elements and attributes as are applicable to their projects and affordable in terms of budget, personnel, and time. The long-term benefits of doing so will far outweigh the immediate costs, ensuring that the digital library collections we are building today can be migrated to the technological environments of the future.

ADDITIONAL READING

Cundiff, Morgan V. 2004. An introduction to the Metadata Encoding and Transmission Standard (METS). *Library hi tech* 22n1: 52-64.

Guenther, Rebecca and Sally McCallum. 2003. New metadata standards for digital resources: MODS and METS. *Journal of the American Society for Information Science and Technology* 29: 12-15.

McDonough, Jerome. 2002. Encoding digital objects with METS. In *XML in libraries*, Roy Tennant, ed. New York: Neal-Schuman, pp. 167-180.

Tennant, Roy. 2004. It's opening day for METS. *Library journal* 129n9: 28.

WORKS CITED

Consultative Committee for Space Data Systems. 2002. *Reference model for an open archival information system* (OAIS), Blue Book, ISO 14721:2003 (January 2002), http://ssdoo.gsfc.nasa/gov/nost/wwwclassic/documents/pdf/CCSDS-650,0-b-1.pdf.

Encoded Archival Description (EAD), <http://www.loc.gov/ead/>.

Gartner, Richard. 2002. METS: Metadata Encoding and Transmission Standard, TSW 02-05, Joint Information Systems Committee (JISC), <http://www.jisc.ac.uk/uploaded_documents/tsw_02-05.pdf>.

ISO Archiving Standards–Reference Model Papers. http://ssdoo.gsfc.nasa.gov/nost/isoas/ref_model.html.

Learning Technology Standards Committee of the IEEE. 2002. *Draft Standard for Learning Object Metadata*, IEEE 1484.12.1-2002 (15 July 2002) <http://ltsc.ieee.org/wg12/files/LOM_1484_12_1_v1_Final_Draft.pdf>.

The Making of America II white paper, version 2.0 (15 September 1998), http://sunsite.berkeley.edu/moa2/wp-v2.html.

The Making of America II home page <http://sunsite.berkeley.edu/MOA2> (last updated 10 October 2001).

MARC 21 XML Schema (MARCXML), http://www.loc.gov/standards/marcxml/.

McDonough, Jerome. 2003a. Candidate Profiles for UCB METS Objects <http://sunsite3.berkeley.edu/mets/ucbprofiles/>.

McDonough, Jerome. 2003b. METS: A status report. Coalition for Networked Information (CNI) Spring 2003 Task Force Meeting (28-29 April 2003), <http://www.cni.org/tfms/2003a.spring/powerpoints/PB-METS-MCDonough.ppt>.

McDonough, Jerome. 2003c. METS profile 1.0 requirements. (13 June 2003), <http://www.oc.gov/standards/mets/profiles_doc/METS.profile.requirements.rtf>.

McDonough, Jerome, Leslie Myrick and Eric Stedfeld. 2001. Report on The Making of America II DTD, Digital Library Federation Workshop (February 2001), <http://www.diglib.org/standards/metssum.pdf>.

Metadata Object Description Schema (MODS), http://www.loc.gov/standards/mods/.

METS Home Page, http://www.loc.gov/standards/mets/.

NISO Metadata for Images in XML Schema (MIX), <http://www.loc.gov/standards/mix/>; Schema for Rights Declaration (METSRights) http://www.loc.gov/standards/rights/METSRights.xsd.

The open digital rights language (ODRL) initiative, <http://odrl.net/>.

Sawyer et al. 2002. The Open Archival Information System (OAIS) reference model and its usage. Consultative Committee for Space Data Systems (2002), <http://www.ccsds.org/documents/SO2002/SPACEOPS02_P_T5_39.PDF>.

Simple Dublin Core XML Schema, http://www.dublincore.org/schemas/xmls/.

Structural, technical, and administrative metadata standards: a discussion document. (December 2000), http://www.diglib.org/standards/stamdframe.htm.

TEI Consortium. 2002. Chapter 5: The TEI header. *Text Encoding Initiative: The XML Version of the TEI Guidelines* <http://www.tei-c.org/P4X/HD.html>.

Text Encoding Initiative (TEI) Consortium Web Page. 1999. <http://www.tei-c.org>; *XSL Transformations (XSLT)*, Version 1.0, W3C Recommendation (16 November 1999) http://www.w3.org/TR/xslt.

Text Metadata Schema, Version 2.2, <http://dlib.nyu.edu/METS/textmd.xsd>; Library of Congress, *Extension Schemas for the Metadata Encoding and Transmission Standard*, <http://lcweb.loc.gov/rr/mopic/avprot/metsmenu2.html> (revised February 2003).

W3C Cascading Style Sheets Home Page. 2004. <http://www.w3.org/Style/CSS> (last updated 26 July 2004).

W3C XML Schema Web Site, <http://www.w3.org/XML/Schema>.

Planning and Implementing a Metadata-Driven Digital Repository

Michael A. Chopey

SUMMARY. Metadata are used to organize and control a wide range of different types of information object collections, most of which are accessed via the World Wide Web. This chapter presents a brief introduction to the purpose of metadata and how it has developed, and an overview of the steps to be taken and the functional expertise required in planning for and implementing the creation, storage, and use of metadata for resource discovery in a local repository of information objects.

KEYWORDS. Information objects, collections, metadata, resource discovery

METADATA AND RESOURCE DISCOVERY ON THE WORLD WIDE WEB

When metadata emerged as a possible solution for resource discovery in a World Wide Web environment in the mid-1990s, many thought that

---

Michael A. Chopey is Catalog Librarian, University of Hawaii at Manoa Libraries, Hamilton Library, Honolulu, HI 96822 (E-mail: chopey@hawaii.edu).

[Haworth co-indexing entry note]: "Planning and Implementing a Metadata-Driven Digital Repository." Chopey, Michael A. Co-published simultaneously in *Cataloging & Classification Quarterly* (The Haworth Information Press, an imprint of The Haworth Press, Inc.) Vol. 40, No. 3/4, 2005, pp. 255-287; and: *Metadata: A Cataloger's Primer* (ed: Richard P. Smiraglia) The Haworth Information Press, an imprint of The Haworth Press, Inc., 2005, pp. 255-287. Single or multiple copies of this article are available for a fee from The Haworth Document Delivery Service [1-800-HAWORTH, 9:00 a.m. - 5:00 p.m. (EST). E-mail address: docdelivery@haworthpress.com].

Available online at http://www.haworthpress.com/web/CCQ

doi:10.1300/J104v40n03_12

an advantage of metadata, as compared to traditional bibliographic data for library catalogs, was that metadata could be created and maintained by individuals with little or no training or experience in cataloging or indexing. (For a concise history of the term and concept "metadata," see Caplan 2003, 1-3.) Indeed the vision behind many of the earliest metadata schemes or initiatives, for example, PICS (Platform for Internet Content Selection (W3C 1997)), or even the use of "META" tags within the HTML standard itself (Weibel 1996), was that resource description could be accomplished by the authors of web documents at the time the documents were created or published on the World Wide Web.

Clearly, this vision has not been realized. In fact, to a large extent, these well meaning early plans for large-scale Internet resource discovery have backfired, in the sense that most commercial Internet search engines will not index the contents of an HTML <META> field in a World Wide Web document because in the universe of documents indexed by commercial search engines, the <META> field is perceived as more likely to contain deliberate misinformation for marketing or promotion purposes than legitimate, useful metadata input by authors to aid in the discovery of their documents' content.

Metadata schemes that were developed with library input similarly began with a focus on simplicity and ease of application. In the development of the Dublin Core Metadata Element Set (DCMES) (DCMI 2003), one of the primary goals has been to make the standard as uncomplicated as possible, without the complex rules for content that are found in the International Standard Bibliographic Description (ISBD) family of cataloging codes (IFLA 2004) and the *Anglo-American Cataloguing Rules, 2nd edition* (*AACR2* 2004), for example, and without the strict rules for required data and data structure that are found in the MARC (MAchine Readable Cataloging) Format for Bibliographic Data (MARC21 2003). In their 1995 report on the OCLC/NCSA Metadata Workshop, which resulted in the establishment of the Dublin Core Metadata Initiative, Weibel et al. (1995) summarized the consensus of the workshop in these words:

> Since the Internet will contain more information than professional abstractors, indexers and catalogers can manage using existing methods and systems, it was agreed that a reasonable alternative way to obtain usable metadata for electronic resources is to give the authors and information providers a means to describe the resources themselves, without having to undergo the extensive training required to create records conforming to established standards.

> As one step toward realizing this goal, the major task of the Metadata Workshop was to identify a simple set of elements for describing networked electronic resources. To make this task manageable, it was limited in two ways. First, only those elements necessary for the discovery of the resource were considered. It was believed that resource discovery is the most pressing need that metadata can satisfy, and one that would have to be satisfied regardless of the subject matter or internal complexity of the object.

The assumptions that led to the development of "simple" metadata schemes such as the Dublin Core, and to the belief that they would need to be easily understood and implemented by authors or web publishers without a background in information professions were–and still are–valid. Because of the sheer volume of information published on the World Wide Web, it would be impossible to "catalog" any significant amount of this information with anything but the simplest set of description standards. Library cataloging is time-consuming and labor-intensive and requires mastery of a complex set of standards and rules, but library cataloging is largely a shared enterprise conducted in a much smaller and more manageable universe of information than the World Wide Web. A large percentage of the items that most libraries catalog are collected by hundreds or thousands of other libraries that can use the same bibliographic record, stored in the same format, and acted upon by essentially the same software, so that economies of scale can be achieved as any given item can be cataloged once–by one cataloger at one library–and the bibliographic record for that item can be immediately available to as many libraries around the world as might want to use it in their own catalogs.

No such economies of scale are likely to ever be realized in the information universe of the Internet, of course, because most documents and other information objects available on the Internet are single-instance items, published and made available by a single organization that would ideally be responsible for their maintenance and for providing the metadata that would make the items discoverable.

Furthermore, there have been two distinct but often overlapping efforts in metadata development over the past ten years. One effort has been to develop and set standards to help organize the World Wide Web on a large scale. The other has been to develop metadata schemes particularly suited to the needs of a certain resource description community, such as visual art museums, geospatial data providers, or government information distributors, or to the characteristics of a certain type of resource, such as art images, literary texts, or archival finding aids.

Though the best known result of the 1995 OCLC/NCSA Metadata Workshop was the Dublin Core Metadata Element Set, a metadata scheme that has thus far been adopted mostly for the purpose of controlling local collections of objects within their own local domains (rather than for the purpose of making Internet objects discoverable in the larger context of the Internet), the spirit of that workshop's recommendations were further reaching. The workshop aimed to begin to develop solutions to the larger problem of meaningful resource discovery on the Internet by developing a standard for resource description that could easily be applied across applications on the Internet, and whereby the resource descriptions created according to that standard could subsequently be harvested by "automated tools [that] could discover the descriptions and collect them into searchable databases."

Though the adoption of the Dublin Core on a scale wide enough to realize this vision has not yet occurred–and might not ever occur exactly in the way originally hoped for–other initiatives (many led by participants in that very same 1995 workshop) have made great strides in the past ten years toward achieving interoperability of metadata standards on the scale of the entire Internet. Local metadata applications are more and more likely to desire interoperability with other applications, or at least the ability to link outside themselves to other stores of information, such as information about a personal name contained in an authority file, or information about a subject term contained in an external subject thesaurus.

METADATA AND RESOURCE DISCOVERY IN A LOCAL DIGITAL COLLECTION

As libraries have demonstrated over the past century or so, it is possible to develop rules and standards for resource description and access that can be followed by institutions around the world with collections of different sizes and scopes, and which can allow for uniformity in the method of accessing a collection of any size or type. The standards for resource description and access that have been developed by libraries should enable a user who has learned how to access a small specialized collection through its catalog to easily use the catalog of a larger, more general collection, and vice versa. The desire on the part of libraries for uniformity in access methodology across collections and the desire to share bibliographic data for commonly held items have been the two main driving forces behind the development of national and international cataloging standards and formats.

Because metadata for digital collections is not likely to be stored for use by any institution except the one creating and maintaining it, the driving force behind the development of metadata standards for digital collections in the future is most likely to be a desire for uniform access methodology across collections. As a practical matter, much of the cooperation among institutions that has occurred to date and led to current metadata standards has probably been motivated more by a sense of trepidation about venturing into this entirely new venture alone, and by the tradition of open information sharing among the communities developing metadata standards, than anything else. Planners and implementers of new projects with a metadata component are still considered pioneers, as standards and documentation for many metadata schemes and types of metadata implementations are often still very sketchy as to the specifics of element definitions, data values, and best practices for technical details on such things as storing metadata and designing effective access mechanisms to retrieve it. Fortunately, guidance from metadata pioneers is becoming more available to new planners and implementers. (An example of this, and one that is highly recommended as a source of guidance on the planning and implementing metadata for various types of collections is: Diane I. Hillmann and Elaine L. Westbrooks, eds., *Metadata in Practice* (Chicago: American Library Association, 2004).)

NATURE AND TYPES OF METADATA FOR LOCAL DIGITAL COLLECTIONS

Generally speaking, metadata for discovery of digital information objects within a collection are designed to retrieve a more granular level of resource than that which bibliographic data in a library catalog are designed to retrieve. For example, if a botanical organization published on the World Wide Web a collection of several thousand digital photographs of individual flowers, a library would not likely want to expend the time and effort required to create several thousands of bibliographic records for those individual photographs, nor would library catalog users be well served by having the catalog's subject and title and name indexes cluttered with subject, name, and title entries for thousands of such micro-level resources. The ideal resource discovery scenario from a general-use library standpoint would be to have one full bibliographic record in the library catalog describing the digital collection, with a URL link from the online catalog to the online botanical collection. The online botanical collection would be organized by metadata that would allow the searcher to conduct searches that are meaningful in that collection, perhaps using subject terminology different or more specialized than would be appropriate in a general-use library catalog.

This has in fact emerged as a common resource discovery scenario, and it is one that seems to work well for information seekers. The challenge in this scenario is that the burden of describing several thousand information objects, newly available for discovery in a manner in which they never had been available before, has fallen not to the expert information organizers in the library, but instead to the botanical organization, which most likely has never attempted to build any kind of an online database of records like the type they now need in order to provide effective online access to the collection. Librarians and information specialists approach this uncharted territory with a firm knowledge of the fundamentals of information organization. They know the access points through which information seekers are likely to approach an information retrieval system, and know how to effectively designate and assign such access points for a collection of a given size and scope. Organizations that wish to provide metadata for the digital objects they produce and collect are likely to have a specialized knowledge of the characteristics and subject content of the objects themselves and the needs of the clientele that seek them, even if their staff does not include experienced information specialists per se.

The most effective and best developed and maintained metadata schemes that have emerged to date are those that combine the expertise of information specialists with the expertise of the producers or curators of the digital information objects and datasets that are sought by Internet researchers in a given discipline or "community." I will discuss the process of metadata creation for digital-object-based collections in which the digital objects themselves, and the metadata that describe and organize them, can be delivered via the World Wide Web to users with standard web browsers, and in which metadata records are created as separate entities from the objects they describe. This model discussed here is a common one for the management of digital image collections, textual document collections, and other collections in which no specialized software (beyond a web browser and accessories typically found in a personal computer) is required to process or display the data that comprise the collection, and in which the Metadata are not an integral part of the content of the collection for markup and display purposes (as is the case, for example, with Encoded Archival Description (EAD), a metadata scheme used for the markup of archival finding aids). First, a summary of the general considerations for planning and implementing the metadata component for any type of collection, and then on to some more specific considerations for different types of collections.

PLANNING AND IMPLEMENTING: FUNCTIONAL EXPERTISE REQUIRED

The successful implementation of a metadata-driven digital repository requires the collaboration of staff with expertise in several different areas, including web design and programming, database or retrieval system design, and what can be called "cataloging" for lack of a better term, even though the cataloging function in a metadata context often encompasses more than it would in traditional library or cultural heritage collection cataloging.

In addition to all of this required expertise, in many projects the most important guidance in planning for the creation and use of the metadata will come from the curator(s) or compiler(s) of the collection, whose knowledge of the characteristics of the resources in the collection, and knowledge of how users seek to discover, identify, and select resources from the collection, should inform all of the most important decisions related to the design of the search and browse mechanisms and navigational aids, and the selection of data elements to be included in the metadata records. The cataloging function, at least in the planning stage, cannot be carried out without close consultation with the curators or compilers of the collection, whose guidance is essential in setting the rules for describing the characteristics of a resource and the rules for transcribing data found on, or associated with, the resource. Finally, because many digital collections are described and controlled by metadata on two levels–those that describe the collection's original items in their original formats, and those that describe the digital manifestations of the original items–the expertise of a digital object formatting or digitization specialist is often required to provide the details of the latter. For example, the curator will provide the details of the original item (e.g., art print: sugar lift aquatint; 8 × 10 inches), while the digital object formatting specialist (perhaps the staff member overseeing the scanning of the original) will provide the details of the digital surrogate (e.g., file format, file size, resolution).

Web Design and Programming Function

The web design and programming component is of immediate importance in the planning of any project that uses metadata to facilitate access to an online collection of information objects. Ideally, the curators or compilers of an online collection have already conceptualized the design of the opening or "welcome" screen, the search interface, and navigational aids within the site–and have consulted with the web designer or programmer to ensure that the vision can be realized–even before a metadata scheme has been selected or defined. If the curators or compilers of the collection know that users will want to "enter" the collection by selecting from the opening screen a category of resources to search or browse in, such as "images, 1920-1939," an exhaustive list of such potential categories should be drawn up by the curator and cataloger as a controlled vocabulary list to be included in one of the metadata scheme's defined data elements. Some types of online collections are better accessed by browsing in pre-coordinated indexes or categories, in which case the formulation of controlled vocabularies is a crucial part of the planning and design of the metadata scheme. Other collections are most effectively accessed by post-coordinated searches executed through a search form, in which case a crucial factor in the selection or design of a metadata scheme is the inclusion of all possible data elements a user might wish to search on. As the size of a collection grows, additional data elements–and more specific values within data elements–might become useful for limiting the results of a search or enabling a more specific search, so this fact should be anticipated in defining the data elements to be included in the metadata scheme and the data values to be contained therein. This aspect of the planning is necessarily a collaborative process involving the curators or compilers, whose knowledge of the collection and its users is necessary for anticipating what data elements will need to be defined in the metadata scheme; the cataloger, whose knowledge of metadata schemes and data structuring informs the selection and design of the metadata scheme and the form in which data should be entered to be most effectively retrieved and displayed; and the web designer or programmer, who will design the searching, browsing, and navigational mechanisms according to the curator's and cataloger's specifications.

The web design-programming function is also called upon for the design of the metadata record creation tool that indexers will use to input data and generate metadata records for that project. Though remote-access metadata creation tools are sometimes available via the World

Wide Web for this purpose, many metadata implementations rely on locally defined data elements and data values in their metadata records that cannot be designated in a general-use metadata creation tool. (See for example, the freely available "Dublin Core Metadata Template" provided by the Nordic Metadata Project (available at http://www.lub.lu.se/cgi-bin/nmdc.pl), or the *Connexion®* cataloging tool available to OCLC subscribers at http://connexion.oclc.org/.)

A metadata creation tool is generally set up as a "web form," which might be installed on an indexer's workstation or might be available to indexers via a local or wide area network or the Internet. The indexer uses the form to enter data values appropriate to the object being described in defined fields, and then saves the record, whereupon the record is automatically encoded in the format in which it will be stored, or at least transported to, the online collection's database. The encoding of the metadata might affect how the metadata are retrieved and displayed by the project's search and display mechanisms and how the record is parsed for storage in the collection database. Encoding metadata records in a standard syntax allows a project to exchange records with other metadata applications outside of the project for which the metadata are created. If the indexer is creating a record in Dublin Core, he or she might enter data values into the web form as follows:

Element	Qualifier	Scheme	Value
Title			St. Francis and the leper: detail of mural by Jose Clemente Orozco in National Preparatory School, Mexico City.
Identifier		URI	http://128.171.57.100/speccoll/tina%5Fmodotti/jcctm17.gif
Type		Local	black-and-white photographs
Contributor	namePersonal		Modotti, Tina, • 1896-1942.
Date	created		1923
Description			RecordType=Work
Description			Measurements.dimensions=22 x 18 cm.
Description			Creator.role= Photographer

when the record is saved, it might automatically be encoded as follows:

```
<?xml version="1.0"?>
<rdf:RDF xmlns:rdf="http://www.w3.org/1999/02/22-rdf-syntax-ns#"
xmlns:dc="http://purl.org/dc/elements/1.0/"
xmlns:dcq="http://purl.org/dc/qualifiers/1.0/">
<rdf:Description about="http://128.171.57.100/speccoll/tina%5Fmodotti/jcctm17.gif">
<dc:title>St. Francis and the leper: detail of mural by Jose Clemente Orozco in National
Preparatory School, Mexico City.</dc:title>
<dc:creator>Modotti, Tina, 1896-1942.</dc:creator>
<dc:date>1923?</dc:date>
<dc:description>recordType=Work</dc:description>
<dc:description>Measurements.dimensions=22 x 18 cm.</dc:description>
<dc:description>Creator.role=Photographer</dc:description>
<dc:description>Location.currentRepository=Charlot Collection, Hamilton Library, University
of Hawaii at Manoa</dc:description>
<dc:description>IDNumber.currentAccession=JCCTM17</dc:description>
<dc:description>Photographer identified by Jean Charlot on verso: Tina
Modotti</dc:description>
<dc:identifier>http://128.171.57.100/speccoll/tina%5Fmodotti/jcctm17.gif</dc:identifier>
<dc:language>und</dc:language>
<dc:subject> <rdf:Description> <dcq:subjectQualifier>namePersonal</dcq:subjectQualifier>
<rdf:value>Orozco, Jose Clemente,1883-1949</rdf:value> </rdf:Description> </dc:subject>
<dc:type>Image</dc:type>
<dc:type>black-and-white photographs</dc:type>
</rdf:Description>
</rdf:RDF>
```

In this illustration, the record is encoded in XML (eXtensible Markup Language) to facilitate parsing of the stored data by the project's storage and retrieval mechanisms, to facilitate display of its elements in a World Wide Web environment if necessary, and to allow for transmission of this metadata to another metadata application if desired. It is also wrapped in RDF (W3C Resource Description Framework) to facilitate the sharing of the metadata record with other RDF-compliant applications and to make the record meaningful within the context of the emerging *Semantic Web* (W3C 2001). The semantics of the metadata in this illustration, e.g., the choice of the word "title" as an element in the metadata scheme, is governed by the Dublin Core Metadata Element Set and also by local rules. The rules governing the form that data values take (e.g., the omission of an initial article in the transcription of the title data, or the use of the controlled vocabulary term "black-and-white photographs" as a data value in the "type.Local" element) are dictated by the project's own local rules for content and transcription, the formulation and documentation of which are part of the cataloging function. The metadata standard might or might not recommend specific vocabulary as the content for any given data element.

The web form used by an indexer to create metadata records might also be programmed to contain pull-down menus from which the indexer selects terms from a controlled vocabulary when inputting content for a given data element. It might also be programmed to contain URL links to an online authority file or thesaurus maintained by an agency outside of the project itself from which the indexer might select authority-controlled names or subject terms to use as data values in certain data element fields.

Database or Retrieval System Design Function

A system that stores metadata and uses it to retrieve information objects associated with the metadata can be designed in many different ways. The design is usually dependent on the nature of the objects being controlled by the metadata, the structure of the metadata itself, and the retrieval and display needs of the system. After XML-encoded metadata are created, its storage in and indexing by the local system might be accomplished in a number of different ways.

As noted, a metadata record can be created by a metadata generation tool that automatically converts indexer-input data into an XML metadata record that can be parsed, stored, and indexed in the local database system, separate from the information object that the record describes. This is one common approach to metadata creation and storage. Another common approach is for the XML-encoded metadata to be embedded in the digital information object itself, usually at the time the digital information object is created.

The former approach allows for more flexibility in the design of a database to store and retrieve the metadata elements. In this approach, what generally happens is that a metadata record is created by a metadata generation tool, and then the record is imported into a local database system. Though the metadata record is most likely encoded in XML for transmission and parsing, in fact when it is imported into a local database system, it is deconstructed and its data elements loaded into the table or tables of a relationship database. The database design and web design-programming functions make certain the data elements stored in these relational database tables are usable for front-end browsing, searching, and navigational tools envisioned by the curators or compilers of the collection.

The latter approach, in which the Metadata are integrated with the digital information object itself, is employed, for example, by systems designed to make use of Encoded Archival Description (EAD

2002) or the Text Encoding Initiative's TEI P4 metadata standard (Sperberg-McQueen and Burnard 2002), two widely known and well documented metadata schemes that use XML not only to encode metadata, but also to encode the text of the document itself. In the case of these "document-centric" systems, as Caplan (2003, 23) calls them, the local system for metadata storage and use can be seen as a "content management system," which integrates all functions pertaining to "authoring, storage and maintenance, query, and presentation." The database or retrieval system design function in this case faces a very different challenge from that faced by the designer of the more free-standing database used to store and retrieve detached metadata. On the other hand, designers of document-centric content management systems are probably more likely to closely follow a pattern established by the metadata standard itself and by other implementers of the standard, and are therefore less likely to have to invent local solutions specific to their own projects and collections.

Cataloging Function

In many ways, the cataloging function is the function most crucial to the success of any metadata application, and there are numerous benefits to having an experienced professional cataloger involved in all stages of the planning and implementation of a local metadata application. While most library catalogers today have probably not studied or been trained in any metadata scheme other than *AACR*2/MARC cataloging, the leap from that expertise to mastering the documentation of any given descriptive metadata scheme should be relatively easy for a cataloger, provided he or she is given sufficient information about the objects being described and the research needs of the collection's users. An experienced cataloger will be able to understand the data element definitions of an existing metadata standard, and, if necessary, define new elements to serve the specific needs of a collection and its users. He or she will be able to determine which characteristics of the objects in the collection need to be described, which data fields should be used to contain the descriptive data and access data for the objects in the collection, and how the data should be input for optimal retrieval, indexing, and display. Working with the curator or compiler of the collection and the web designer, the cataloger can make recommendations for the search, browse, and navigational mechanisms to be made available to users of the online collection, based on what data is available for retrieval in the metadata records and how the data is structured. A cataloger can identify an existing subject thesaurus or list of subject terms that is appropriate for the collection, or help build and define a project-specific one. The cataloger should also have a central role in creating any list of controlled-vocabulary terms that might be needed for any given data element in the collection's metadata records, and for defining the terms. Finally, if the collection's metadata will include personal names, corporate body names, place names, or other proper nouns, the cataloger should be involved in designing the reference structure in those indexes when appropriate.

CHECKLIST FOR PLANNING AND IMPLEMENTING A LOCAL METADATA APPLICATION

Table 1 identifies steps in the planning and implementation of a digital repository managed and organized with metadata. Check marks identify the functional expertise required at each stage of the planning and implementation. The areas of functional expertise identified here are: curatorial, digital object formatting, web design and programming, database and retrieval system design, cataloging and indexing, and administrative/managerial. Depending on the size and scope of the collection and the organization sponsoring the collection and retrieval system, some roles might overlap and some might be further subdivided into more specific functions. A committee with representation by at least one staff member from each functional area should be convened at the outset to execute this plan. Decisions made at every stage should be thoroughly documented.

Envision the Final Product

This stage entails planning what the user of the collection will see upon accessing the home page or welcome screen of the collection on the World Wide Web; what search, browse, and navigational options will be available from that screen and others; and, what the user will be directed to upon clicking any given hypertext link (including a hypertext link embodied by a thumbnail image or other graphic, which is a popular means of providing navigation between pages in the WWW environment) on any given page. Although it is best to plan as much as possible of the final product before the construction of the site begins, most esthetic and navigational functions can be adjusted relatively easily at any point later in the development of the repository, so it is not as

TABLE 1

	Curatorial	Digital object formatting	Web design and Programming	Database/ Retrieval system design	Cataloging and Indexing	Administrative/ Managerial
Envision the final product	✓		✓	✓	✓	
Plan appearance and technical characteristics of digital objects	✓	✓				
Estimate disk storage requirements			✓	✓		✓
Determine staffing requirements						✓
Determine equipment/technical infrastructure required						✓
Project costs						✓
Secure funding						✓
Procure equipment/technical infrastructure						✓
Hire or select staff						✓
Designate metadata scheme and element set	✓	✓			✓	
Define parameters and input standards for data values	✓	✓			✓	
Designate exchange syntax for metadata			✓	✓		
Design and construct metadata creation tool				✓	✓	
Design database for metadata storage and retrieval			✓	✓	✓	
Assemble rights and credit information	✓	✓				
Train digital object formatting/digitization technicians		✓				
Scan/digitize objects; gather already-digitized objects		✓				
Design and construct user interface	✓		✓	✓		
Program search, browse, and navigational functions	✓		✓	✓		
Inspect site for Web Content Accessibility Guidelines (WCAG) compliance		✓	✓			
Test final product	✓					✓
Design channels for ongoing feedback from users			✓			✓
Publicize and release project	✓					✓
Secure continuing funding						✓

crucial to get these exactly right in the planning stages as it is to identify all of the possible access points that users of the repository will desire. Ideally, the person doing the web design under the curator's direction will be the same person who acts as webmaster when the repository is released to the public.

Esthetics

Designing what the user will see upon accessing the home page requires a collaboration between the vision of the curator and the skills of the web designer for making that vision a reality. Decisions to be made at this stage include all esthetic considerations from the color of the background, to the size, color, and style of the fonts, to the selection of images, graphics, and special effects to be displayed on the various pages of the online collection. The choices have an impact on the amount of storage space required, and possibly on response time. Most repositories will want to apply at least some level of standard design template to each page the user accesses in the course of navigating and viewing a collection. The standard template might include copyright information, an e-mail link for contacting the webmaster for information or to provide feedback, the name and logo or graphic associated with the repository and/or institution sponsoring it, etc.

Navigation Functions

In some digital repositories, the user accesses the entire collection from search and browse functions on the repository's home page. In others, the user first selects from among subject or other categories, and thereby enters a sub-collection to search or browse in. (The "sub-collection" referred to here and elsewhere in this chapter is not necessarily (and for practical purposes, probably rarely is) a "collection" in any real sense. The objects in the sub-collection do not necessarily reside together in any defined space, nor does their metadata. The sub-collection is created dynamically or "on-the-fly" when the user clicks on a hypertext link.) Determining the optimal categories for sub-collections is important mostly for enabling effective browsing, not for enabling effective searching–enabling a *search* of the entire repository should be no more or less difficult to program than a search of some subset of it, even if the metadata for the subsets resides in separate database tables. Furthermore, most repositories will want to offer an option to search the entire collection at any point in a user's journey through it, even when sub-collections have been defined and the user has entered one.

Another important consideration in providing navigational capabilities in a digital repository is to allow a user to move to any part of the collection, or any search screen or index, with a minimal number of mouse clicks from any other part of the collection or from any stage in the retrieval of data. Allowing a user to cache as much of his or her session as possible can also prevent frustration when a user wants to backtrack. Some collections allow users to retrieve the "search history" of a session at any point and either re-execute a search or refine one. Useful feedback from users can be obtained during the pre-release testing period and in an ongoing fashion during the life of the project, but care should be taken during the planning and design stage to anticipate potential navigation problems.

Browsing Functionality

In the context of a digital repository, the term "browsing" can refer to the act of viewing the objects in the collection (or surrogates of them, such as thumbnail images of digital photographs, or citations to textual documents) in either a serendipitous fashion or in a manner that is more or less pre-coordinated by the designers of the repository, or, it can refer to the act of browsing an index of access points that is organized in alphabetical or some other order.

Facilitating the former type of browsing is a process that involves the curatorial, web design, and cataloging functions of the project. The curator might map out on paper all of the categories through which a pre-coordinated browse of the collection might proceed. The web designer would enable the hypertext linking between screens and would write the scripts to gather all of the objects in the collection that should be accessible at that level of the browse. These scripts would use terms or phrases contained in the metadata of the target objects to gather all of the relevant objects for a given category. For example, if the curator determined that a useful browse of a collection of objects related to Japanese civilization would begin on the home page with the user selecting a period or era in Japanese history to browse or search within, the curator might define the categories on the home page as: Jōmon culture, Yayoi culture, Tomb Period, Late Yamato, Nara Period, etc. The user would "enter" one of these categories for further browsing or searching by clicking on a text link or icon. That link would contain a script written by the web designer that would execute a search of the metadata in collection database and retrieve every object that pertained to that category. So for example, if the user clicked on the "Yayoi culture" link or icon, a search would be executed that gathered every object in the collection whose associated metadata contained the word "Yayoi" in some predefined data element or elements. The cataloging function would need to know every category that might be defined anywhere in the site, so that the metadata will contain the appropriate terms to gather every object that belongs to that category.

Enabling browsing of indexes, such as name, title, or subject indexes, likewise requires the collaboration of the curatorial, web design, and cataloging functions. The curator should determine the types of indexes to be made available for browsing, and the places within the site where the indexes will be available. The web designer designs the appearance and linking functionality of the indexes, and the cataloger ensures that there are defined data elements in the metadata records that correspond to the indexes selected by the curator.

For example, the curator might determine that useful indexes for a particular textual document collection would be: author name, document title, and subject. The web designer would place these indexes (perhaps in the form of "pull-down menus," for one popular design example) in the pages within the site where the curator has determined that browsing a particular index might be useful, and would write the scripts to populate that index with the appropriate data from a defined field within the metadata, and to execute the gathering of relevant documents when an access point within an index is selected. The access points contained within this type of index come from a defined data element within the metadata records for the collection. For example, an author index might access a data field defined as "Author" or "Creator." The index is dynamic in that every time a new object and its associated metadata are added to the collection, the index expands to include that new access point. It might also be desirable for the index to count the occurrences of a given access point within the index, e.g., the number of documents in the collection written by a given author. An index must also be designed to sort the data that populates it–usually alphabetically, but sometimes chronologically or according to some other order.

The cataloging role is crucial in constructing useful indexes. The cataloger must ensure that the metadata scheme chosen or designed for the collection defines the data element needed for any given index, and that the data element is defined in such a way as to enable browsing (and also other kinds of searching) at the appropriate level of specificity. For example, if the curator determines that indexes and other retrieval mechanisms should allow a user to search for or browse all names associated with objects in the collection, but also to search for or browse names of persons or corporate bodies performing a particular role, the cataloger needs to define that particular data element accordingly. In the Dublin Core metadata scheme, this might be accomplished by assigning the data element "Creator" with a locally-specified data element refinement, which might be anything from "photographer" to "course architect" to "funding agency." It would then be the responsibility of the web design and database programming functions to ensure that the data is parsed correctly upon import to the collection database, and that search mechanisms and indexes are able to retrieve the data correctly from the database.

In order for an index to be useful, the data that populates it also must be constructed in a consistent manner and one that is logical for sorting. Data consistency is the responsibility of the cataloging function, and is accomplished by creating documentation with clear and thorough rules for data entry, and by effective training of indexers (who actually create the metadata records).

The creation of a subject index can be simple or complex, depending on how large and detailed the list or thesaurus of subject terms defined for the collection is. The most fundamental principle in constructing a subject index is to use a controlled vocabulary. That is, there should only be one authorized subject term or phrase for a given topic or concept. Most controlled vocabulary lists can be made more useful by providing a reference structure to direct users from unauthorized synonyms to authorized forms.

Many general and discipline-specific subject thesauri exist and can be adopted or adapted for use in a metadata-driven digital repository. Examples of general subject thesauri are *Library of Congress Subject Headings* or the *Sears List of Subject Headings*. Discipline-specific thesauri include lists such as the *Art & Architecture Thesaurus* (*AAT* 2000) or the *Thesaurus of Psychological Index Terms* (Gallagher 2004). Adopting an existing thesaurus makes planning easier, but some thesauri are very complicated, and can be applied correctly and effectively only by highly trained and experienced indexers. If the decision is made to construct a local list or thesaurus, the work should be done under the direction of, or in close consultation with, a professional cataloger experienced in the principles of subject analysis and document indexing. There is an international (ISO 1986) standard for the construction of thesauri, but its documentation might be hard to understand and apply by anyone who is not already very familiar with subject cataloging and document indexing principles.

Once a subject list has been selected or devised, there are still decisions to be made about how subject browsing and searching will be implemented in the collection. A browsable subject index can be constructed in the same manner as a name or title or other index, but since subject terms in a list are likely to have hierarchical and horizontal relationships with other subject terms in the list, the display of results of a subject browse or search is an additional consideration for the curatorial, cataloging, web design, and database/retrieval system design functions. For example, a hypothetical thesaurus for use with a collection of botanical literature might include among its authorized subject vocabulary the term *lichens*. The reference structure for that hypothetical thesaurus might indicate that *lichens* has broader term *Cryptogams* and narrower terms *Ascolichens*, *Epiphytic lichens*, *lichen-forming fungi*, and *rare lichens*, and that *Ascolichens* in turn has narrower terms *Caliciales*, *Graphidales*, *Lecanorales*, *Lichinales*, *Peltigerales*, *Pertusariales*, and *Verrucariales*. If a user elected to browse on the term *lichens*, an effective display of results might be something like the following:

Broader term: Cryptogams

Lichens [22]

Narrower terms:

Ascolichens
Epiphytic lichens
Lichen-forming fungi
Rare lichens

indicating that the collection contains 22 items on the term selected, and pointing the user to related terms that might also be of interest. If the user clicked on one of the other links, a similarly displayed result would appear, placing the selected term within the context of *its* related subject terms. Library catalog software is designed to display subject term relationships in a fashion somewhat similar to this, but the means of accomplishing this with library catalog software involves loading into the library catalog database an entire file of records wherein each term in the thesaurus has its own record containing all of its broader and related terms. This would be a highly inefficient method for any metadata-driven repository to try to replicate. A more efficient solution for a metadata-driven repository would be to encode the thesaurus in XML and program the display of subject search or browse results to reference the XML document simultaneously as the search or browse queries the database of object-associated metadata.

Search Functionality

If good metadata records with well-formed, precisely defined data are created for the objects in a digital collection, and if the metadata records are parsed and stored correctly when they are loaded into a collection database, enabling effective searching of the collection metadata should be a relatively simple matter from a web design standpoint. Inexpensive products are available to web developers for the implementation of web-based search engines that query the contents of a web-based relational database, and the format of these search engines is familiar to most WWW users. So the most important factors in enabling effective and fruitful searching of a metadata-driven digital repository are to identify the attributes of the objects in the collection by which the objects will be sought by users (curatorial function), to define and label each of these attributes precisely as a separate data element in the metadata scheme (cataloging function), and to ensure that the data in each searchable data element field is entered in a manner that ensures effective retrieval (cataloging function). The means of achieving these objectives are discussed further under "Define metadata scheme and element set" below.

Plan the Appearance and Technical Characteristics of the Digital Objects in the Collection

This step, which requires the collaboration of the curatorial function and the digital object formatting function, entails setting standards for the quality of digital objects in a collection, the technical specifications to which they will be created, and the file formats in which they will be stored. The digital objects in a collection might exist already in digital form before the repository is created, or might be created after the repository has been established. They can be objects that are "born digital" or objects that existed in a different form and were scanned or otherwise converted to digital form for inclusion in the repository. In setting standards for the technical characteristics of the digital objects in a collection, the curator should consider the following factors, in consultation with the digital object formatting specialist.

Quality vs. Size

The quality (e.g., image resolution in a visual object, or sound clarity in an audio file) of a digital object is often positively correlated with its size. In some types of collections, therefore, the curator must sometimes balance the benefits of creating high quality digital objects with the benefits of creating smaller objects of lesser quality. In setting standards for the size of digital objects in the collection, the curator also takes into account the extra time that it might take a larger item to load on a user's machine, and disk storage requirements on the collection's own servers.

Object Renderability

Ideally, the objects in a digital collection are renderable by a standard web browser without plug-ins or specialized software or accessories. For some types of objects, the need for plug-ins or specialized software or accessories is, of course, unavoidable. In such cases, the curator and digital formatting expert should endeavor to make the objects renderable by the most standard and widely available plug-ins or software possible, and preferably non-proprietary. When other considerations, such as cost and storage, allow, it might be beneficial to users of the collection to offer objects in more than one format.

Format Longevity

An effort should be made to ensure that the format in which objects are encoded or stored are likely to endure. In long-term cost projections, the possibility that the digital objects in the collection might need to be reformatted in the future should be taken into account.

Usability of Objects by Users with Disabilities

Whenever possible, objects should be available in alternative formats so as to be usable by people with disabilities. Information about the requirements of users with different kinds of disabilities can be obtained from the World Wide Web Consortium's Web Accessibility Initiative. Grant funding of digital projects is sometimes contingent upon compliance with government policies for accessibility, such as the ADA (Americans with Disabilities Act) guidelines in the United States.

Estimate Disk Storage Requirements

Projections of storage requirements should take into account the space required to store the digital objects themselves, the metadata associated with the objects, and the infrastructure of the repository, including search engines, databases, documentation, graphics, etc. They should also allow for data backup.

Determine Staffing Requirements

The managerial leader of the project should coordinate this activity in consultation with committee members representing each area of functional expertise. Each functional area in the project should be responsible for determining its staffing needs and for writing job descriptions. The creation of a metadata-driven repository can be accomplished in a finite amount of time, or it can be ongoing. Many projects begin with a backlog of existing not-yet-digitized or digitized but not-yet-cataloged materials, and will need more staff for certain functions at startup than in the ongoing phase. In other projects, the size and scope of a collection might grow after it has been implemented, and therefore staffing needs might be greater later.

In web design and database programming, more staff time is likely to be needed in the planning and startup stages than later. In the area of cataloging, the expertise of a professional cataloger will be needed mostly in the planning stages. The cataloger will write documentation and train indexers. In the actual metadata creation stage, however, most of the work in the area of cataloging can be done by indexers. Ideally, all members of the original planning committee will be available after implementation for consultation on maintenance issues.

Determine Equipment/Technical Infrastructure Needed

For most metadata-driven digital repositories the following equipment and technical infrastructure will be needed:

- Servers, and possibly backup servers, on which to store the digital objects in the collection and the metadata for the objects.

- Computer workstations for indexers, digitization technicians, web design and programming personnel, and database management personnel. These might be workstations dedicated to the work of the project, or workstations they already use for other work they do for the sponsoring institution. Staff using existing workstations might need extra software installed to perform their project functions.
- Network hardware and software to connect workstations to the project's servers.
- Server and database software.
- Digitization hardware such as scanners, digital cameras, analog-to-digital sound recorders, etc.
- Digitization software or other digital object creation software.
- Internet domain name and IP addresses.
- Reference materials, possibly including subscriptions to established thesauri if these are used by indexers.

Estimate Costs

Cost projections should include staff time, hardware costs, software and licensing costs, telecommunications costs, and the cost of the physical plant where staff will perform their project functions. Each functional area should supply cost estimates for that to the administrative/managerial function.

Secure Funding

Many digital repositories are funded by grants. The manager should seek the services of an experienced grant writer who is well informed about the mission of the repository and the needs of its users, whether that person is part of the planning team or outside of it. The process of seeking grant funding can refine or even alter the mission or goals of the online collection.

Procure Equipment/Technical Infrastructure

This stage should be carried out by the manager after funding has been secured. Documentation compiled during the "determine equipment/technical infrastructure needed" should be used.

Hire or Select Staff

Staff can be selected from within the ranks of the sponsoring institution or from outside of the organization. In either case, a project that secures grant funding can usually apply part of the grant funding toward the salaries of these staff members. Each functional area in the project should have documented its projected staffing needs and written job descriptions in the earlier stage "identify staffing needs." If possible, representatives from each functional area should also be involved in the hiring process. In areas in which extensive training of staff might be required, such as indexing, an effort should be made to hire staff who can accept a long-term commitment to the project, so that re-training can be avoided and optimal efficiency can be achieved from project staff.

Designate Metadata Scheme and Element Set

Well before this stage is reached (probably during the "envision the final project stage"), the cataloging function of the project will most likely have determined what established metadata scheme will be employed, or, if a locally invented metadata scheme is to be used, the general parameters of that local scheme.

There are many benefits to selecting an established metadata standard, especially if there is any chance that the repository institution might later wish to integrate its collection with other collections, or make its collections searchable through outside applications' search mechanisms. By adopting an established metadata standard, a project may gain access to users' manuals, documentation on recommended best practices for data values and encoding, and possibly tools for data input. A project can also benefit from the experience of other projects using that scheme, as other implementers will often publish usage guidelines and best practices for their own projects in addition to those promulgated by the scheme's maintenance agency. Methods of encoding metadata are often designed with established metadata schemes in mind, so a project might find documentation on methods of encoding metadata more useful and applicable when using an established metadata scheme. The project's web and database programmers are likely to be able to find in electronic discussion forums shareable scripts and other techniques for making use of the project's metadata if an established metadata scheme is employed.

Metadata schemes are sometimes extensible, meaning that a project can adopt the structure and syntax of a metadata scheme, and use some or all of its defined data elements at their broadest definitions, while still allowing for local description needs. In Dublin Core, this is accomplished by means of data element qualifiers (DCMI 2004), which refine the meaning of a data element while still allowing the element itself to be understood by other applications in its broader, unqualified meaning. For example, the Colorado Digitization Program (CDP), sponsor of the *Heritage Colorado* digital objects repository, has defined in its local metadata scheme (which is an extension of Dublin Core), the qualified element "Format: creation" to express such attributes as file size, compression, or creation software (Bischoff and Meagher 2004). "Format" is a Dublin Core element; "creation" is a CDP-defined local qualifier. In the context of *Heritage Colorado*, the data contained in this field has a meaning that is defined specifically by the element-qualifier combination. If the data were sent to another Dublin Core application outside of *Heritage Colorado*, that application might not be able to "understand" the more specific qualified meaning, but it *would* understand that the data in this field has to do with the associated object's format, and would render it and make it searchable as such. Most digital object repositories will identify some attributes of objects in the collection that should be expressed in the objects' metadata and must be expressed using locally defined metadata extensions.

I have discussed in some detail the functions carried out by *descriptive* metadata–namely, enabling searching, browsing, and navigation within the collection, and expressing information about the attributes and characteristics of an object that a user of the object might need to know–but not discussed were administrative metadata, another important class of metadata for the management of a collection. Administrative metadata express information that is usually of more interest to the repository's staff than to its users, and which might only by viewable or searchable by staff. For example, administrative metadata might include information about the formatting of an object in terms that are more specific and technical than would need to be expressed in the descriptive metadata for the user's purposes, but which would be useful for staff that might need to reformat the object at some point in the future. Other examples of information that might be carried in the administrative metadata for an object are the price the sponsoring institution paid to acquire the object, information about the donor of an object, the name of the indexer who created the metadata record for an object, an accession number for inventory control, etc. The elements to be included in the administrative metadata should be determined by the cataloger in consultation with the curatorial, digital object formatting, and managerial functions.

In this important stage of the planning of a metadata-driven repository, it is crucial that the cataloging function document all decisions made about the metadata scheme to be used in the project, and write them up in the form of a local metadata standard. This will become the basis for informing much of the database programming and web design of the online repository, and, when expanded with instructions for inputting and encoding the metadata (see below), will become the project's usage guide for metadata creation and manipulation, and probably the most important piece of documentation produced by the project.

Define Parameters and Input Standards for Data Values

After the metadata scheme and its data elements have been designated and documented, the cataloger should carefully define each element as to the nature of data that should occupy the field labeled with that data element. These definitions should be documented in the usage guide in terms and language that can be understood by the indexers (and possibly digital formatting technicians) who will be creating the project's metadata. The cataloger should also provide detailed instructions for inputting data, specifying the exact form that the data should take (including punctuation, spacing, and capitalization), and guidelines for transcribing data found on the object for which the metadata are being created. For some elements, the cataloger might stipulate that the data value for that element conform to a standard (such as ISO . . . standard for the expression of a "Date" element like "Date.Created") or that the data value be selected from a list, such as a standard list of subject terms or a thesaurus. Some data elements might reference an online registry of some sort, like the "virtual international authority file" envisioned by Barbara Tillett (2001).

Designate Exchange Syntax for Metadata

The representation of metadata in a syntax that will make the metadata record readily machine-processable is mostly of concern to projects that share metadata with other applications. For these purposes, XML is probably the most widely used exchange syntax, so it is recommended that the metadata creation tool for the type of project discussed here be designed to output metadata records in XML format. Even for a project that does not intend to exchange metadata records with another metadata application, XML can be recommended as a syntax in which to format the project's metadata records because XML is easily parsed by the database programs that will deconstruct the metadata record to store its elements in the repository's database tables.

Construct Metadata Creation Tool

As shown in the example on p. 263, the project's metadata creation tool will most likely be a web-form based application in which the indexer selects a data element label for each field of data input, and inputs the data for that field in the form specified.

Assemble Rights and Credit Information

In some types of repositories, it is important that this information be available at the time the digital objects are created, because usage or legal restrictions on some items may require that a watermark about copyright or creator be embedded in the object, or that the downloadability of an item be disabled. Also, in some metadata creation work flows, it might be more efficient to have the administrative metadata input by digital formatting technicians at the time the object is digitized, and rights management and credit information might be a component of the administrative metadata in a project's metadata scheme.

Train Digital Object Formatting/Digitization Technicians; Scan/Digitize Objects; Gather Already-Digitized Objects

In this stage, technicians will be trained to perform digitization or digital reformatting to the specifications documented digital formatting function in the stage "Plan the appearance and technical characteristics of the digital objects in the collection." Detailed instructions for operating the scanning or other digital formatting hardware should be created at this stage, and used in the training of technicians. Digital formatting technicians might also be trained in the creation of administrative metadata, using documentation created by the cataloging function.

Train Indexers; Create Metadata

At this stage all of the documentation needed for the training of indexers should have been written by the cataloging function. Documentation can be revised as necessary if it is not easily understood by the indexers, who will most likely not be professional catalogers. The goal should be to allow indexers to create metadata with minimal supervision. In the early stages of metadata creation, all records created by indexers should be stored in a "review file" for inspection by a professional cataloger, who will file the reviewed record to the live database. As indexers become more experienced, they may be allowed to store records directly to the live database, but the review file should be available throughout the life of the project so that indexers can file records to it when they are uncertain about the data for any given field. Some repositories will use authority-controlled headings (name and/or subject) in their records. In such cases, the indexer should probably be authorized to select already-established headings from the repository's authority file, but not to enter new, unestablished headings. Records requiring headings that have not yet been established should be stored in the review file, from which a professional cataloger will periodically retrieve them and establish the headings in question (and add them to the authority file).

As noted above, metadata record creation can be accomplished efficiently with a web-based form designed by the repository. Indexers should be encouraged to report problems with the form and the record filing process (such as slow response time or bugs), and suggest improvements to make their work easier and the overall metadata creation workflow more efficient. Indexers will be responsible for transcribing data found on the digital objects (or surrogates of them) and also for analyzing the objects in order to record other characteristics and attributes. The workflow should be designed to make it as easy as possible for indexers to ascertain the information they need at the metadata creation stage. For example, if file size is recorded in the metadata for objects in the collection, the file size should be readily ascertainable by the indexer, perhaps provided by the digital formatting function. Many repositories will wish to have the curatorial function provide suggested name headings and subjects and other controlled vocabulary data so that the indexer is not responsible for determining them. Transcription can be problematic in some types of digital collections because, in textual document indexing for example, a data element such as "title" might be ambiguous or difficult to determine. In newspaper indexing, a given article might have several different titles, including a generic or recurring column title, a more specific title, a subtitle, and a running title that changes when the article continues on a different page. A digital book or report might likewise have a title that differs between the title page, the cover, and the running title appearing at the top or bottom of each page in the item. In library cataloging, one title is always chosen as the main title, and the problem of choosing this main title is addressed by a separate set of rules in the cataloging code for every class of material that might be cataloged by a library, and an ordered list within each class for choosing the "source of information" for the title and other data that might need to be transcribed. A digital repository might adopt this approach in creating its rules for transcription, or the repository might determine that all titles should be transcribed with appropriate refinement of the "title" element, but without any one title chosen as the main title. In any case, the documentation used by the indexers should give clear and unambiguous instructions for identifying every data element that needs to be transcribed (including title, publisher, place of publication or origin, publisher or distributor, date, standard number appearing on the item, etc.), in addition to the instructions for how that data should be transcribed. Some types of digital objects, such as art images or sound files, might have no transcribable data at all. In such cases, the curatorial function will be responsible for supplying much of the data that an indexer will enter in the metadata record. The curatorial function might need guidance from the cataloging function (in the form of documentation created by the cataloging function) on how to determine and supply this data.

Import/Attach Metadata

In some types of collections, the metadata for the digital objects in the collection will be embedded in the objects themselves. In others, the metadata will exist in separately stored metadata records. The model presented in this chapter assumes that metadata will be created in a separate step from the creation or formatting of the digital object, but this does not necessarily mean that the metadata will not be attached to the digital objects after they are created. In either case–whether the metadata are attached to the digital objects or stored separately from them–the workflow shifts from the cataloging function to the database/retrieval system design function at the point at which a completed metadata record is filed to the database. At that point, the database/retrieval system design function might determine (possibly in consultation with the web design function) that it is more efficient to store the metadata records with the objects themselves, or to store them separately. The database/retrieval system design function will also determine how the record is stored in the repository database to ensure efficient retrieval of the data in the records for browsing, searching, and navigational functions of the repository's user interface. Metadata creation will be an ongoing process in many repositories, but a mass of metadata of some size must be created before any of the retrieval functions of the system can be tested.

Design and Construct User Interface; Program Search, Browse, and Navigational Functions

This stage is executed by the web design function according to the vision laid out by the team at the "envision the final product" stage. As the user interface is being constructed, the curatorial function should be monitoring its progress to ensure that the curatorial vision of the final product is being realized. The web design function might present alternative layouts at each stage of the construction for the curatorial function, or perhaps the entire planning and implementation team, to examine and select the best alternative. Many of the search and browse features of the user interface will be designed using web design and database software. This is an advantage not only because it makes the web designer's task easier, but also because it is likely to result in interfaces that are familiar to World Wide Web users, making the repository easier to use and navigate by users. The web designer should be familiar with relevant guidelines and standards for accessibility for people with disabilities, and should program into the user interface alternative means of access wherever they are required.

Inspect Site for Web Content Accessibility Guidelines (WCAG) Compliance

Documentation on the requirements of users with disabilities can be obtained from the World Wide Web Consortium's Web Accessibility Initiative, which maintains links to governmental policies, implementation plans for web accessibility, information on developing organizational policies on web accessibility, information on selecting and using authoring tools for web accessibility, and links to additional resources on web accessibility including resources outside of W3C. Although this documentation will have been consulted by the web design function during the construction of the user interface, a separate step of inspecting the final pre-release product for compliance with Web Content Accessibility Guidelines (WCAG) standards should be undertaken under the direction of the administrative/managerial function. Findings and design changes made at this stage should be documented, and subsequent reviews should be conducted every time a change is made to the user interface that might affect access by users with disabilities.

Test Final Product

The final pre-release product should be thoroughly tested by the entire planning and implementation team. The curator or manager might also wish to assemble a focus group of target users to test and provide feedback on the product so that changes can be made to the user interface before the product is made available to the public.

Design Channels for Ongoing Feedback from Users

This stage can be completed at any stage during the planning. It might entail simply attaching a "contact webmaster" link on every page of the site, in which case a member of the post-release repository management team will receive these messages and channel them to the appropriate functional area. Alternatively, a project can decide to allow for more specific feedback at certain places in the user interface, such as a link for reporting data errors, for example, which would be directed to the cataloging function.

Publicize and Release Project; Secure Continuing Funding

Increasing the visibility of a project among its target user community, and in some cases among the general public, can greatly increase the chances of receiving continuing funding to keep the repository operational and possibly to expand the collection and add affiliate collections to the repository. It can also help the sponsoring institution receive funding for other similar projects it might wish to pursue. Because the design and maintenance of metadata-driven repositories of digital objects is an endeavor that interests many kinds of institutions who do not have any experience in undertaking such a venture, there is usually great interest in presentations by implementers of successful projects at professional organization conferences and workshops. Presenting at such conferences and workshops is one way of increasing the visibility of a project. Another is to publish articles about project planning and implementation in relevant journals and other media.

WORKS CITED

Anglo-American Cataloguing Rules, 2nd ed. (AACR2). 2002 revision, 2004 update. Chicago: American Library Association.

Bishoff, Liz and Elizabeth S. Meagher. 2004. Building Heritage Colorado: The Colorado digitization experience. In Diane I. Hillmann and Elaine L. Westbrooks, eds., *Metadata in practice*. Chicago: American Library Association, pp. 22-25.

Caplan, Priscilla. 2003. *Metadata fundamentals for all librarians*. Chicago: American Library Association.

Colorado Digitization Program, *Heritage Colorado*. Available at: http://www.cdpheritage.org/heritage/.

Dublin Core Metadata Initiative (DCMI). 2003. Dublin Core metadata element set, version 1.1: reference description, available at: http://dublincore.org/documents/dces/.

Dublin Core Metadata Initiative (DCMI). 2004. DCMI metadata terms, available at: http://dublincore.org/documents/dcmi-terms/Qualifiers.

Gallagher, Lisa A. ed. 2004. *Thesaurus of psychological index terms*, 10th ed. Washington, DC: American Psychological Association.

Getty Vocabulary Program. 2000. *Art & architecture thesaurus* Los Angeles, Calif.: J. Paul Getty Trust.

Hillmann, Diane I. and Elaine L. Westbrooks, eds. 2004. *Metadata in practice*. Chicago: American Library Association.

International Federation of Library Associations and Institutions (IFLA). 2004. Family of ISBDs, available at: http://www.ifla.org/VI/3/nd1/isbdlist.htm.

International Standards Organization (ISO). 1986. *Documentation: Guidelines for the establishment and development of monolingual thesauri*, 2nd ed., ISO 2788. Geneva: ISO.

Library of Congress. Cataloging Distribution Service. 2004. *Library of Congress subject headings*, 27th ed. Washington, DC: Library of Congress.

Library of Congress. Network Development and MARC Standards Office. 2003. *MARC 21 concise format for bibliographic data*, 2003 concise ed. available at: http://purl.access.gpo.gov/GPO/LPS35317.

Library of Congress. Network Development and MARC Standards Office and Society of American Archivists. 2002. *Encoded archival description (EAD): Official EAD version 2002 website*. Washington, DC: Library of Congress, available at: http://www.loc.gov/ead/.

Sears List of Subject Headings. 2004. 18th ed. Bronx, N.Y.: H. W. Wilson.

Sperberg-McQueen, C.M. and Lou Burnard eds. 2002. *Guidelines for text encoding and interchange*. Oxford: Published for the TEI Consortium by the Humanities Computing Unit, University of Oxford.

Tillett, Barbara. 2001. Authority control on the Web. In *Proceedings of the bicentennial conference on bibliographic control for the new millennium: Confronting the challenges of networked resources and the Web, Washington, D.C., November 15-17, 2000*, ed. Ann M. Sandberg-Fox, Washington, DC: Library of Congress, Cataloging Distribution Service, p. 207-220.

United States. Department of Justice. Americans with Disability Act, *ADA homepage*, available at: http://www.usdoj.gov/crt/ada/adahom1.htm.

Weibel, Stuart. 1996. A proposed convention for embedding metadata in HTML. In *W3C workshop on distributed indexing and searching*, May 1996, available at: http://www.w3.org/Search/9605-Indexing-Workshop/reportOutcomes/S6Group2.html.

Weibel, Stuart et al. 1995. OCLC/NCSA metadata workshop report, available at: http://www.oclc.org:5047/oclc/research/conferences/metadata/dublin_core_report.html.

World Wide Web Consortium (W3C). 1997. Platform for Internet content selection (PICS), available at: http://www.w3.org/PICS/.

World Wide Web Consortium (W3C). Resource Description Framework, available at: http://www.w3.org/RDF/.

World Wide Web Consortium (W3C). 2001. Technology and Society Domain. Semantic Web, available at: http://www.w3.org/2001/sw/.

World Wide Web Consortium (W3C). Web Accessibility Initiative homepage, available at: http://www.w3.org/WAI/Resources/.

Index

Numbers followed by "f" indicate a figure.

AACR2. See Anglo-American Cataloging Rules-2 (AACR2)
AAT. *See Art & Architecture Thesaurus (ATT)*
ACH. *See* Association for Computers and the Humanities (ACH)
ACL. *See* Association for Computational Linguistics (ACL)
ADA. *See* Americans with Disabilities Act (ADA)
Administrative Metadata Section, of METS document, 243-244
Agnew, G., 2
Ahronheim, J.R., 13
AIP. *See* Archival Information Package (AIP)
ALA. *See* American Library Association (ALA)
Albrechtsen, H., 80,148
ALCTS. *See* Association for Library Collections & Technical Services (ALCTS)
All data model, in XML, 223
ALLC. *See* Association for Literary and Linguistic Computing (ALLC)
American Heritage Virtual Archive Project, 199
American Library Association (ALA), 2,39
Americans with Disabilities Act (ADA), 276
Andrew W. Mellon Foundation, 11
Anglo-American Cataloging Rules, 13,39,44,46,49-50,63
Anglo-American Cataloging Rules-2 (AACR2), 13,45,105,106, 108-110,112,115,119, 122-125,129-130,154,155, 158,256
Ann Arbor Accords, 28
APPM. *See Archives, Personal Papers, and Manuscripts (APPM)*
Archival control
  described, 184-186
  metadata standards for, 183-212
Archival Information Package (AIP), 49
Archives, Personal Papers, and Manuscripts (APPM), 185, 186
Aristotle, 62
Art & Architecture Thesaurus (ATT), 272
Artifact(s), Etruscan, 135-151. *See also* Etruscan artifacts
Association for Computational Linguistics (ACL), 11,123
Association for Computers and the Humanities (ACH), 11,123
Association for Library Collections & Technical Services (ALCTS), 2
Association for Literary and Linguistic Computing (ALLC), 11,123
Association of American Publishers, 121

Attribute(s), in XML, 223-226
Audio Technical Metadata Extension Schema (AUDIOMD), of Library of Congress, 244
AUDIOMD. *See* Audio Technical Metadata Extension Schema (AUDIOMD)
Authorship, in creation of metadata schemas, 110-112

Baca, M., 2,130,131
Baker, T., 42
Barks, C., 109
Barthes, R., 62,110-111,131
Basham Kelly Papers (1936-1988), guide to, 202-204
Beckett, 112
Beghtol, C., 81
Behavior Section, in METS document, 250
Berners-Lee, T., 71
Bible, 137
Bibliographic control
  described, 38-39
  metadata and, 37-56
    background of, 38-42
    convergence of, 47-49
    future directions in, 49-51
    introduction to, 38
    operational definitions, 38-42
Bibliographic description, conventional, metadata configuration for, 68,69f
Bicentennial Conference on Bibliographic Control for the New Millenium, 50
Blair, D.C., 98
British Library, 10
British Museum, 39
Burnett, K., 38,41,42

Campbell, D.G., 14,57
Cantara, L., 15,237
Caplan, P., 2,4,20,42,48-49,60,114, 115,266
Carpenter, M., 109
Cataloging
  descriptive, 13-14
  to metadata, 153-181. *See also* Dublin Core, records of, for Library Catalog
Cataloging in Publication (CIP), 10-11
CC:DA. *See* Committee on Cataloging: Description and Access (CC:DA)
CCSDS. *See* Consultative Committee for Space Data Systems (CCSDS)
CDATA attribute, in XML, 224
CDISC. *See* Clinical Data Interchange Standards Consortium (CDISC)
CDP. *See* Colorado Digitization Program (CDP)
CEN. *See* Comité Européen de Normalisation (CEN)
CEN Workshop Agreement (CWA), 18
Chadwyck-Healy, 186
Chan, L.M., 38-39
Chopey, M.A., 15,255
CIMI. *See* Consortium for the Computer Interchange of Museum Information (CIMI)
CIP. *See* Cataloging in Publication (CIP)
Clinical Data Interchange Standards Consortium (CDISC), 42
Coleman, A.S., 15,153
Collection, defined, 184
Colorado Digitization Program (CDP), 279
Commission of the European Communities (CEC/DG-XIII), 11

Comité Européen de Normalisation (CEN), 18
Committee on Cataloging: Description and Access (CC:DA), 2
Consortium for the Computer Interchange of Museum Information (CIMI), 29,46
Consultative Committee for Space Data Systems (CCSDS), 238
Content designation, 5-7
Content genealogy model, 139f
Contextualizing, 80
"Core Categories for Visual Resources," of Visual Resources Association, 46
Cornell University, 238
Crawford, J., 13
Creating and Documenting Electronic Texts, 107
Critique of Pure Reason, 22
CSDGM. *See* Content Standard for Digital Geospatial Metadata (CSDGM)
CUSTARD project, 185
Cutter, C.A., 25-27,39,42-43,50,58,59
CWA. *See* CEN Workshop Agreement (CWA)
Cwiok, J., 14-15,103

DACS. *See Describing Archives: A Content Standard (DACS)*
Data Documentation Initiative (DDI), 29
DCMES. *See* Dublin Core Metadata Element Set (DCMES)
DCMI. *See* Dublin Core Metadata Initiative (DCMI)
DDC system. *See Dewey Decimal Classification (DDC)* system
DDI. *See* Data Documentation Initiative (DDI)
de Saussure, F., 63
Death of a Salesman, 62
Dekkers, M., 47
Describing Archives: A Content Standard (DACS), 186
Descriptive cataloging, 13-14
Descriptive Metadata Section (dmdSec), in METS document, 241-243, 242f,243f
Dewey Decimal Classification, 39, 157-158
Dewey Decimal Classification (DDC) system, 22
DIG35 Specification: Metadata for Digital Images, 32
DIGIPROVMD. *See* Digital Production and Provenance Metadata Extension Schema (DIGIPROVMD)
Digital collection, local
  metadata for, nature and types of, 259-261
  resource discovery in, metadata and, 258-259
Digital Library Federation (DLF), 49, 237,238
Digital like object (DLOs), 30,45
Digital Production and Provenance Metadata Extension Schema (DIGIPROVMD), 244
Digital repository, metadata-driven, planning and implementing of, 255-287. *See also* Metadata-driven digital repository, planning and implementing of
DIP. *See* Dissemination Information Package (DIP)
Dissemination Information Package (DIP), 49
DLF. *See* Digital Library Federation (DLF)
DLOs. *See* Digital like object (DLOs)

Document type definition (DTD), of EAD, 12,66,120-121,187, 220-221,238,243
"Documents from the Women's Liberation Movement," 115, 116,125
Dorner, D.G., 1
DOS machine, 214
DTD. *See* Document type definition (DTD)
Dublin Core, 18,28-32,38,44,45,50-51, 57,58,60,65,67-69,106,108, 112,113,115,117-119, 127-129,257,258,263-264, 278,279
  described, 154-156
  metadata creation form, 173-174
  metadata of, creation of, 158-170
  records of, for Library Catalog, 153-181
    introduction to, 154
    sample resource descriptions, 175-181
Dublin Core Metadata Element Set (DCMES), 87,114-115,256, 258,264
  Version 1.1, 18
Dublin Core Metadata Initiative (DCMI), 23,27,114,118,256
Dublin Core Metadata Schema, 272
  creator element in, 114-117
Dublin Core Metadata Set, 11-12
"Dublin Core Metadata Template," 263
Duke University, 115
Duke's Special Collection Library, 115
Dunbar, R., 116,125,126
Dvorak, 61

EAC. *See* Encoded Archival Context (EAC)
EAC record
  encoded, sample, 211-212
  sample, 209-210
EAC Tag Library, 183,187,189,196
EAD. *See* Encoded Archival Description (EAD)
"EAD Help Pages," 199
EAD record, encoded, sample, 204-209
EAD Round Table, 199
EAD Tag Library, 120-121
EAD/EAC implementation, 198-200
Eagleton, T., 71
EDItEUR, EPICS Data Dictionary of, 121
Eggert, P., 112,149
Electronic resources, metadata in, 70f
Element(s), in XML, 221-223
Element data models, in XML, 222-223
Empty content model, in XML, 222
Encoded Archival Context (EAC), 105,184
  background of, 194-196
  introduction to, 183-212
  structure of, 196-198,197f,198f
Encoded Archival Description (EAD), 12,28,33,42,45-46,59,63,66, 105,214,243,261,265-266
  background of, 186-187
  introduction to, 183-212
  structure of, 187-194,189f-191f
Encoded Archival Description Application Guidelines, 187
Encoded Archival Description (EAD) schema, 120
  author element in, 120-121
Encoded Archival Description Tag Library, 187
Encoded Archival Description (EAD) Version 1.0, 184
Eno, 215
Environmental domain, of metadata schemes, 29
EPICS Data Dictionary, of EDItEUR, 121
ERIC Clearinghouse on Information and Technology, at Syracuse University, 118

Ethic(s), in exploratory study of metadata creation in health care agency, 85
Etruscan artifacts, in museum of archeology
analysis of, 135-151
introduction to, 136-137
case study of, 139-148,140t
described, 143-148,145t
metadata forms and information ecologies of, 147-148
representation taxonomy in, 141-142
EU-NSF Working Group on Metadata, 51
Extensible Markup Language Schema (XSD), 238
Extensible Stylesheet Language for Transformation (XSLT), 233-234,239

Faulkner, W., 195
Federal Geographic Documentation Committee (FGDC) Content Standard for Digital Geospatial Metadata (CSDGM), 24
Ferraioli, L., 75
FGDC/CSDGM, 32
File Allocation Table, 40
File Section, in METS document, 244-246,245f,246f
FINDAID DTD, 187
Finding aid, defined, 185
Fitzgerald, E., 64
Fonds, defined, 184
Foskett, A.C., 61
Foucault, M., 110-111,112
FRBR. *See Functional Requirements for Bibliographic Records (FRBR)*
Fripp, 215
Frye, N., 62,65-67,71
Functional Requirements for Bibliographic Records (FRBR), 27,43,50

Gateway to Educational Materials (GEM), 113,118-119
Gateway to Educational Materials (GEM) Element Set, 30,31,46
GEM. *See* Gateway to Educational Materials (GEM)
GEM Element Set. *See* Gateway to Educational Material (GEM) Element Set
General International Standard for Archival Description (ISAD(G)), 185,194
Generalized Markup Language (GML), 214,220
Getting Mileage Out of Metadata: Applications for the Library, 2
Gill, T., 40,48
Gillaspy, M.L., 88,89
Gilliland-Swetland, A.J., 20,40
GILS Core Element Set, 126
GILS schema. *See* Government Information Locator Services (GILS) schema
Global Information Exchange, 120,128
Global Information Locator Services (GILS) schema, originator element in, 126-127,128
Global Reach, 38
GML. *See* Generalized Markup Language (GML)
Gone with the Wind, 137
Google, 67
Gorman, G.E., 1
Government Information Locator Services (GILS), 29,59
Graham, I.S., 8
Greenberg, J., 14,17,20

GROUPID, 244,246f
Guidelines for Online Information Exchange, 121
Guidelines for the Creation of Content for Resource Discovery Metadata, of National Library of Australia, 87

Harter, S.P., 88,89
Health care agency, metadata creation in, exploratory study of, 75-102
  analysis of, 94,96-98
  case study approach in, 82-83
  data analysis procedures in, 85-86
  data collection in, 83-85
  discussion of, 94,96-98
  document attributes in, 90-92,90f
  domain analysis in, 80-82
  ethical considerations in, 85
  introduction to, 76-79
  metadata in, 86-87
  method in, 82-86
  non-document attributes in, 92-94, 95f
  philosophy-epistemology link in, 79-80
  qualitative design in, assumptions and rationale for, 82
  relevance of, 88-89
  researcher's role in, 83
  results of, 89-94,90f
  subject determination in, 87-88
Health Insurance Portability and Accountability Act (HIPAA) regulation, 92
Heritage Colorado, 279
Hert, C.A., 96-97
Hillman, D.I., 1,12,259
HIPAA regulation. *See* Health Insurance Portability and Accountability Act (HIPAA) regulation
Historicism, 80
Hjorland, B., 79,80,88,89,99
Howarth, L.C., 14,37,42
HTML (HyperText Markup Language), 8-10,64,186,187,214-217
  described, 214-217
  XML *vs.*, 214-217
HTML meta tags, 60
Huber, J.T., 88,89
Hudgins, J., 2
Huthwaite, A., 38,46
HyperText Markup Language (HMLT). *See* HTML (HyperText Markup Language)

IATH. *See* Institute of Advanced Studies in the Humanities (IATH)
IBM, 214
IDREF data type, 225
IEEE, LOM of, 243
IFLA, 137,138. *See* International Federation of Library Associations and Institutions (IFLA)
IFLA DIGITAL LIBRARIES: Metadata Resources Web page, 19
Image Technical Metadata Extension Schema (IMAGEMD), 244
IMAGEMD. *See* Image Technical Metadata Extension Schema (IMAGEMD)
Instantiations, 138
Institute of Advanced Studies in the Humanities (IATH), of University of Virginia, 198
Intellectual Property Rights (IPR), 169
InterCat, of OCLC, 44
International Conference on Cataloging, 27
International Federation of Library Associations and Institutions (IFLA), model for bibliographic control, 27

International Organization for Standardization (ISO), 154-155,238
International Standard Archival Authority Record for Corporate Bodies, Persons, and Families (ISAAR(CPF)), 195
International Standard Bibliographic Description (ISBD). *See* ISBD (International Standard Bibliographic Description)
International Standard Bibliographic Description for Electronic Resources (ISBD[ER]), 44
International Standards for Bibliographic Description: Punctuation as Markup, 5-6
International Standards Organization (ISO), 18,214
Internet, 27,38,44,51,132,258,263
Internet Explorer, 9
Internet World Conference, 44
Introduction to Metadata: Pathways to Digital Information, 2
IPR. *See* Intellectual Property Rights (IPR)
ISAAR(CPF). *See International Standard Archival Authority Record for Corporate Bodies, Persons, and Families (ISAAR(CPF))*
ISAD(G). *See General International Standard for Archival Description (ISAD(G))*
ISBD(ER). *See* International Standard Bibliographic Description for Electronic Resources (ISBD[ER])
ISBD (International Standard Bibliographic Description), 5,13,39,44,50,63,64,66,124, 256
ISBD revision, 71
ISO. *See* International Standards Organization (ISO)
ISO 15836-2003, 18
ISO/IEC (International Standards Organization/International Electrotechnical Commission) 11179, Metadata Registries Standard, 23,24
ISO/IEC 18038, Identification and Mapping of Various Categories of Jurisdictional Domains, 24
ISO/IEC 20943, Procedures for Archiving Metadata Registry Content Consistency, 24
ISO/IEC 20944, Metadata Registry Interoperability and Bindings, 24
ISO/IEC JTC1 SC32 WG2 Development/Maintenance, 23

Jakobson, R., 62,64
Jones, W., 13

Kant, I., 22,23
King Lear, 62
King Magnus, 65
Kwasnik, B.H., 89

Lagoze, C., 20,21,45,46
Language(s)
  markup. *See* Markup languages
  synchronic and diachronic views of, 63-64
LCSH. *See Library of Congress Subject Headings (LCSH)*
LEADERS project. *See* Linking EAD to Electronically Retrievable Project Sources (LEADERS) project

Learning Object Metadata (LOM), of IEEE, 243
Library and Information Science, 58
Library of Congress, 10,39,50,195
 AUDIOMD of, 244
 MARC Standards Office of, 238
 Network Development and MARC Standards Office of, 12,237,251
Library of Congress Classification, 39
Library of Congress Subject Headings (LCSH), 22,24,157,160,272
Linking EAD to Electronically Retrievable Project Sources (LEADERS) project, 199-200
LOM. *See* Learning Object Metadata (LOM)
Long Island University Institutional Review Board, 83
Lubetzky, 59
Lynch, C., 46,51

MAchine Readable Cataloging (MARC), as markup, 6-7
MAchine Readable Cataloging (MARC) formats. *See* MARC formats
Mackenzie, M., 94,96
Making of America II (MOA2) Project, 238
Malone, T.W., 97
MALVINE (Manuscripts and Letters Via Integrated Networks in Europe 2003) project, 199
Mangiafico, P., 116
Manuscripts and Letters Via Integrated Networks in Europe 2003 (MALVINE) project, 199
MARC. *See* MAchine-Readable Cataloging (MARC)
MARC 21 XML Schema (MARCXML), 243
MARC AMC. *See* USMARC Archival and Manuscripts Control (MARC AMC)
MARC coding, 60,64,66
MARC Format for Bibliographic Data (MARC21), 256
MARC formats, 30,105,121,130, 154-156,158
MARC records, collection-level, 185
MARC Standards Office, of Library of Congress, 238
MARC21. *See* MARC Format for Bibliographic Data (MARC21)
Marco, F.J.G., 76
MARCXML. *See* MARC 21 XML Schema (MARCXML)
Markup languages, 5-7
 history of, 213-214
 mathematical, 24
 in publishing, 7
Mathematical Markup Language (MathML), 34
MathML. *See* Mathematical Markup Language (MathML)
Meissner, D., 199
METADATA, 19-20
Metadata, 57-73
 AACR2 as, 13
 background of, 59-61
 bibliographic control of, 37-56. *See also* Bibliographic control, metadata and
 bibliographic description of, 68,69f
 from cataloging to, 153-181. *See also* Dublin Core, records of, for Library Catalog
 concepts of, 4
 content, 135-151. *See also* Etruscan artifacts, in museum of archeology, analysis of
 content designation in, 5-7
 creation of, in health care agency, 86-87
 exploratory study of, 75-102. *See also* Health care agency, metadata creation in, exploratory study of

defined, 2,19-20,40-42,104-106
described, 40-42,58
in electronic resource, 70f
functions of, 20-22,21t
implications of, 70-72
introduction to, 1-15,58
language and representation of, 61-68,67t
limitations of, 70-72
for local digital collections, nature and types of, 259-261
MARC 21 as, 13,14
markup languages in, 5-7
metaphoric, 68-69
metonymic and, 68-69,70f
for resource description, 10-14
resource discovery on local digital collection and, 258-259
resource discovery on WWW and, 255-258. *See also* Metadata-driven digital repository, planning and implementing of
standards for archival control, 183-212
typologies and functionalities of, 20,21t
understanding of, 17-36
Metadata Applications and Management, 1
Metadata Encoding and Transmission Standard (METS), 237-253
described, 238
implementation of, 250-251,251f
Metadata Encoding and Transmission Standard (METS) PROFILE, 250-251,251f
Metadata Encoding and Transmission Standard (METS) schema, 49
Metadata Encoding and Transmission Standard (METS) tools, 250-251,251f
Metadata for Images in XML Schema (MIX), 244
Metadata Fundamentals for All Librarians, 2
Metadata in Practice, 1,259
Metadata Object Description Schema (MODS), 31,243
Metadata Objectives and Principles, Domains, and Architectural Layout (MODAL), 17-19,25,26f,33-34
Metadata Object Description Schema (MODS), 240
Metadata schemas, 17-36
analysis of, 25-33,26f
architectural layout of, 31-33
conceptualization of, 22-25
context for, 22-24
creator element within, 103-133
background of, 104-112
conception of authorship in, 110-112
described, 106-108
discussion of, 113-120
elements equivalent to, 120-127
future directions in, 130-132
introduction to, 104-112
meta-analysis of, 128-130,129t
representation and functionality of, 112-127
domains of, 29-31
environmental, 29
object class, 29-30
object format, 30-31
objectives and principles of, 25-29
Metadata supported functions, 19-22,21t
Metadata systems, cataloging and, displacement in, 67t
Metadata-driven digital repository, planning and implementing of, 255-287
assemble rights and credit information in, 268t,281
browsing functionality in, 270-274
cataloging function in, 266-267
checklist for, 267-285,268t

construct metadata creation tool in, 268t,281
create metadata in, 268t,281-283
database or retrieval system design function in, 265-266
define parameters and input standards for data values in, 268t,280
design and construct user interface in, 268t,284
design channels for ongoing feedback from users in, 268t,285
designate exchange syntax for metadata in, 268t,280
designate metadata scheme and element set in, 268t,278-280
determine equipment/technical infrastructure needed in, 268t,276-277
determine staffing requirements in, 268t,276
envision final production in, 267-274,268t
esthetics in, 269
estimate costs in, 268t,277
estimate disk storage requirements in, 268t,276
format longevity in, 275
functional expertise required in, 261-267,268t
gather already digitized objects in, 268t,281
hire or select staff in, 268t,277-278
import/attach metadata in, 268t,283
inspect site for WCAG compliance in, 268t,284
navigation functions in, 269-270
object renderability in, 275
plan appearance and technical characteristics of digital objects in collection in, 268t, 274-276
procure equipment/technical infrastructure in, 268t,277
program search, browse, and navigational functions in, 268t,284
publicize and release projects in, 268t,285
quality *vs.* size in, 275
scan/digitize objects in, 268t,281
search functionality in, 274
secure continuing funding in, 268t, 285
secure funding in, 268t,277
test final product in, 268t,285
train digital object formatting/ digitalization technicians in, 268t,281
train indexers in, 268t,281-283
usability of objects by users with disabilities in, 275-276
web design and programming function in, 262-265
MetaModel, 19
Metaphor
displacement in, 65-68,67t
metonymy and, 64-65
"works," 137-139,139f
Metonymy
defined, 62
metaphor and, 64-65
METS. *See* Metadata Encoding and Transmission Standard (METS)
METS document, building of, 239-250, 240f-243f,245f,246f,248f,249f
Administrative Metadata Section of, 243-244
Behavior Section of, 250
Descriptive Metadata Section of, 241-243,242f,243f
File Section, 244-246,245f,246f
METS header of, 240-241,241f
root element of, 239-240,240f
Structural Map Linking Section of, 248-249
Structural Map of, 246-248,248f, 249f

METS header, 240-241,241f
METS schema. *See* Metadata Encoding and Transmission Standard (METS) schema
METSRights. *See* Schema for Rights Declaration (METSRights)
Microsoft, 226-227
Miller, P., 104-105
MIX. *See* Metadata for Images in XML Schema (MIX)
Mixed content data model, in XML, 223
MOA2 Project. *See* Making of America II (MOA2) Project
MODAL (Metadata Objectives and Principles, Domains, and Architectural Layout), 17-19, 25,26f,33-34
MODS. *See* Metadata Object Description Schema (MODS)
Myers, J.E., 19,20

NAF. *See* National Authority File (NAF)
NASA. *See* National Aeronautics and Space Administration (NASA)
Nash, G.B., 149-150
National Aeronautics and Space Administration (NASA), 238
National Authority File (NAF), 195
National Information Standards Organization (NISO), 18,154
National Inventory of Documentary Sources in the United States, 186
National Library of Australia, Guidelines for the Creation of Content for Resource Discovery Metadata of, 87
National Library of Canada, 10
National Union Catalog of Manuscript Collections (NUCMC), 186
Navarro, M.A.E., 76
NEH. *See* U.S. National Endowment for the Humanities (NEH)
Nesting tags, in XML, 218
Netscape, 9
Network Development and MARC Standards Office, of Library of Congress, 12,237,251
New York Public Library, 238
1996 International Conference on the Principles and Future Development of *AACR*, 27
NISO. *See* National Information Standards Organization (NISO)
NISO Z39.85-2001, 18
No More Fun and Games: A Journal of Female Liberation, 116
Nordic Metadata Project, 263
Notepad, 9
NUCMC. *See National Union Catalog of Manuscript Collections (NUCMC)*

OAC. *See* Online Archive of California (OAC)
OAIMHP. *See* Open Archives Initiative Metadata Harvesting Protocol (OAIMHP)
OAIS Reference Model. *See* Open Archival Information System (OAIS) Reference Model
OAL-PMH. *See* Open Archives Initiative Protocol for Metadata Harvesting (OAL-PMH)
Object class domain, of metadata schemes, 29-30
Object format domain, of metadata schemes, 30-31
OCLC, InterCat of, 44
OCLC/NCSA Metadata Workshop, 256,258

ODRL. *See* Open Digital Rights Language (ODRL)
Oedipus the King, 62
Oliver Twist, 67
ONIX. *See* Online Information Exchange (ONIX) schema
Online Archive of California (OAC), 199
Online Information Exchange (ONIX) schema, 120,121-123,128
Online Public Access Cataloging (OPAC), 154
OPAC. *See* Online Public Access Cataloging (OPAC)
Open Archival Information System (OAIS) Reference Model, 49, 237
Open Archives Initiative Metadata Harvesting Protocol (OAIMHP), 65
Open Archives Initiative Protocol for Metadata Harvesting (OAL-PMH), 49
Open Digital Rights Language (ODRL), 244
Opening and closing tags, in XML, 217

Panizzi, A., Sir, 39,59
Paris Conference, 5
Paris Principles, 5,27,39,50
Park, S., 38,41,42
PCDATA content models, in XML, 222
Pennsylvania State University, 238
PICS (Platform for Internet Content Selection), 256
Pitti, D.V., 105,108,186-187,194
Platform for Internet Content Selection (PICS), 256
Poughkeepsie Principles, 28
Prologue, in XML document, creation of, 229
Publishing, markup languages in, 7

RAD. *See Rules for Archival Description (RAD)*
RDF. *See* Resource Description Framework (RDF)
Reference Model for an Open Archival Information System (OAIS), 238
Resource description, metadata for, 10-14
Resource Description Framework (RDF), 47
Resource discovery, on WWW, metadata and, 255-287. *See also* Metadata-driven digital repository, planning and implementing of
Rich Site Summary (RSS), 29,33
Rights Metadata Extension Schema (RIGHTSMD), 244
RIGHTSMD. *See* Rights Metadata Extension Schema (RIGHTSMD)
RLG, Working Group on Preservation Issues of Metadata of, 27
Root element
  in METS document, 239-240,240f
  in XML document, creation of, 229-233
RSS. *See* Rich Site Summary (RSS)
Rules for a Dictionary Catalog, 25,27
Rules for Archival Description (RAD), 185
Rumi, 109
Russian Formalists, 61,71

Schema for Rights Declaration (METSRights), 244
Scheme(s), defined, 22
SDM. *See* Submissions Data Modeling (SDM)
Sears List of Subject Headings, 272
Semantic Web, 264

SGML (Standard Generalized Markup Language), 7-8,12,41-42,44, 186,187,214,220
Shaw, G.B., 65
SIP. *See* Submission Information Package (SIP)
Smiraglia, R.P., 1,15,63,106,109-112, 135,137
Social Science and Humanities Research Council of Canada, 11
Society of American Archivists, 12, 199
Standard Generalized Markup Language (SGML). *See* SGML (Standard Generalized Markup Language)
Stanford University, 238
"Statement of Principles," 27
Structural Map, in METS document, 246-248,248f,249f
Structural Map Linking Section, in METS document, 248-249
Submission Information Package (SIP), 49
Submissions Data Modeling (SDM), 42
Svenonius, E., 61
Svenonius theory, 61
Synechdoche, 62
Syracuse University, ERIC Clearinghouse on Information and Technology at, 118

Taylor, A., 59
TEI. *See* Text Encoding Initiative (TEI)
Text Data Schema, 244
Text Encoding Initiative (TEI), 11,42, 45-46,59,63,65,66,67,214, 239,266
  guidelines for, 28
Text Encoding Initiative (TEI) Header, 240
  author element in, 123-126
Text Encoding Initiative (TEI) schema, 120,128
The Metadata Company, 20
The Rubaiyat of Omar Khayyam, 64
The Spanish Tragedy, 62
The Vatican Code, 39
Thesaurus of Geographic Names, 168
Thesaurus of Psychological Index Terms, 272
Thurman, A.C., 15,183
Tillett, B.B., 13,38,45,137,280
"Toronto Tenets Principles and Criteria for a Model for Archival Context Information," 196
Tunnicliffe, 214

UKOLN Metadata Web site, 19
University College London, LEADERS of, 199-200
University of California–Berkeley, 186-187,238
University of California–Berkeley Library, 12
University of Pennsylvania Museum of Archaeology and Anthropology, Etruscan artifacts from, 135-151. *See also* Etruscan artifacts, in museum of archeology
University of Toronto, 196
University of Virginia, 196
  IATH of, 198
U.S. Department of Education, 118
U.S. National Endowment for the Humanities (NEH), 11
USMARC Archival and Manuscripts Control (MARC AMC), 186

Vassar Planning Conference, 28
Vellucci, S.L., 137
Video Technical Metadata Extension Schema (VIDEOMD), 244

VIDEOMD. *See* Video Technical Metadata Extension Schema (VIDEOMD)
Visual Document Description Categories, 42
Visual Resources Association (VRA), 42,113
  "Core Categories for Visual Resources" of, 46
  Core Categories of, 31-32
Visual Resources Association (VRA) core, 117
  creator element within, 117-118
VRA. *See* Visual Resources Association (VRA)
VRA Core. *See* Visual Resource Association's Core Categories (VRA Core)

W3C Cascading, 239
Wall, J., 112
WCAG compliance. *See* Web Content Accessibility Guidelines (WCAG) compliance
Web Accessibility Initiative, WWW Consortium's, 275,284
Web Content Accessibility Guidelines (WCAG) compliance, inspect site for, 268t,284
Web Services Definition Language (WSDL) file, 250
Weibel, S., 44,47,256-257
Wenger, E., 86
Westbrooks, E.L., 1,259
"Who Is the Enemy?" 116,125,126
Williams, V., 61
Wilson, P., 131
WordPerfect, 214
Working Group on Preservation Issues of Metadata, of RLG, 27
"Works" metaphor, 137-139,139f

World Wide Web (WWW), 3,8,18,26, 38,40,43,44,58,59,71,153,186, 214,215,255-257,259, 260,262-264,267,284
  Consortium's Web Accessibility Initiative of, 275,284
  Consortium's XML Schema language of, 237,238
  resource discovery on, metadata and, 255-287. *See also* Metadata-driven digital repository, planning and implementing of
World-Wide Commons, 47
WSDL file. *See* Web Services Definition Language (WSDL) file
Wuthering Heights, 68
WWW. *See* World Wide Web (WWW)

XML, 239,264
  all data model in, 223
  attributes of, 218
    declaring of, 223-226
  CDATA attribute in, 224
  described, 214-217
  document modeling in, 219-226
  document validity in, 219-226
    testing for, 226-227,227f,228f
  element data models in, 222-223
  element in, declaring of, 221-223
  empty content model in, 222
  enumerated list in, 224-225
  HTML *vs.*, 214-217
  implied attribute in, 226
  introduction to, 213-235
  mixed content data model in, 223
  nesting tags in, 218
  opening and closing tags in, 217
  parsed character data in, 222
  required attribute in, 226
  root element of, 218

tokenized attributes in, 225
values of, 218
well-formedness in
rules for, 217-218
testing for, 218-219,219f,220f
XML document, 64,66
creation of, 229-233
encode Prologue in, 229
root element in, 229-233
XML Schema, 66
XML Schema Language, of WWW Consortium, 237,238
XSD. *See* Extensible Markup Language Schema (XSD)
XSLT (Extensible Stylesheet Language for Transformation), 233-234

Yee, M.M., 137
Yott, P., 15,213

BOOK ORDER FORM!

Order a copy of this book with this form or online at:
http://www.HaworthPress.com/store/product.asp?sku=5660

Metadata

A Cataloger's Primer

___ in softbound at $39.95 ISBN-13: 978-0-7890-2801-3 / ISBN-10: 0-7890-2801-8.
___ in hardbound at $59.95 ISBN-13: 978-0-7890-2800-6 / ISBN-10: 0-7890-2800-X.

COST OF BOOKS ________

POSTAGE & HANDLING ________
US: $4.00 for first book & $1.50 for each additional book
Outside US: $5.00 for first book & $2.00 for each additional book.

SUBTOTAL ________

In Canada: add 7% GST. ________

STATE TAX ________
CA, IL, IN, MN, NJ, NY, OH, PA & SD residents please add appropriate local sales tax.

FINAL TOTAL ________
If paying in Canadian funds, convert using the current exchange rate, UNESCO coupons welcome.

❑ **BILL ME LATER:**
Bill-me option is good on US/Canada/Mexico orders only; not good to jobbers, wholesalers, or subscription agencies.

❑ **Signature** ________________

❑ **Payment Enclosed: $** ________________

❑ **PLEASE CHARGE TO MY CREDIT CARD:**
❑ Visa ❑ MasterCard ❑ AmEx ❑ Discover
❑ Diner's Club ❑ Eurocard ❑ JCB

Account # ________________

Exp Date ________________

Signature ________________

(Prices in US dollars and subject to change without notice.)

PLEASE PRINT ALL INFORMATION OR ATTACH YOUR BUSINESS CARD

Name

Address

City State/Province Zip/Postal Code

Country

Tel Fax

E-Mail

May we use your e-mail address for confirmations and other types of information? ❑ Yes ❑ No We appreciate receiving your e-mail address. Haworth would like to e-mail special discount offers to you, as a preferred customer. **We will never share, rent, or exchange your e-mail address.** We regard such actions as an invasion of your privacy.

Order from your **local bookstore** or directly from
The Haworth Press, Inc. 10 Alice Street, Binghamton, New York 13904-1580 • USA
Call our toll-free number (1-800-429-6784) / Outside US/Canada: (607) 722-5857
Fax: 1-800-895-0582 / Outside US/Canada: (607) 771-0012
E-mail your order to us: orders@HaworthPress.com

For orders outside US and Canada, you may wish to order through your local sales representative, distributor, or bookseller.
For information, see http://HaworthPress.com/distributors

(Discounts are available for individual orders in US and Canada only, not booksellers/distributors.)

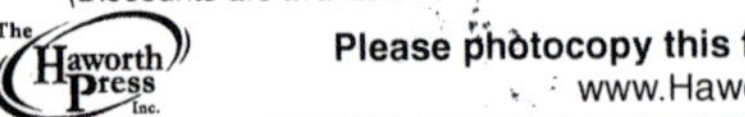

Please photocopy this form for your personal use.
www.HaworthPress.com

BOF05